TALES OF JAPAN

TALES OF JAPAN

Scrolls and Prints from
The New York Public Library

MIYEKO MURASE

New York · Oxford
OXFORD UNIVERSITY PRESS
1986

Oxford University Press

Oxford New York Toronto
Delhi Bombay Calcutta Madras Karachi
Petaling Jaya Singapore Hong Kong Tokyo
Nairobi Dar es Salaam Cape Town
Melbourne Auckland

and associated companies in
Beirut Berlin Ibadan Nicosia

Published by Oxford University Press, Inc.,
200 Madison Avenue, New York, New York 10016

Oxford is the registered trademark of Oxford University Press

Library of Congress Cataloging-in-Publication Data
Murase, Miyeko.
Tales of Japan.
Exhibition catalog. Includes index.
1. Scrolls, Japanese—Exhibitions. 2. Color prints,
Japanese—Exhibitions. 3. Tales in art—Exhibitions.
I. New York Public Library. I. Title.
ND1052.M885 1986 760'.0952'07401471 85-28497
ISBN 0-19-504020-1
ISBN 0-19-504021-X (pbk.)

Exhibition Dates:

The New York Public Library, New York, February 1 to March 25, 1986
Portland Art Museum, Portland, Oregon, September to October, 1986
Suntory Museum of Art, Tokyo, February 10 to March 22, 1987
Kobe City Museum, Kobe, April to May, 1987
Kimbell Art Museum, Fort Worth, Texas, July 11 to September 20, 1987

The New York Public Library is especially grateful to
Continental Insurance, and to the National Endowment for the Arts,
the Mary Livingston Griggs and Mary Griggs Burke Foundation, and the New York State
Council on the Arts for their generous support of the exhibition.
The Library also wishes to express its appreciation to
the Japan–United States Arts Program of the Asian Cultural Council
for their additional support of this publication.

Printing (last digit): 9 8 7 6 5 4 3 2 1

Printed in the United States of America
on acid free paper

Preface

The New York Public Library is delighted at the opportunity to share with a larger audience some of our extraordinary holdings of Japanese art. This catalogue, and the exhibition it documents, is the first in a series drawn exclusively from the Library's Special Collections. While much of this material is known to scholars and researchers, our intent, as part of the Library's mission, is to make it available to a wider public.

In this connection, the exhibition is scheduled to travel to sites beyond New York: the Kimbell Art Museum in Fort Worth, Texas, and the Portland Museum of Art in Portland, Oregon. The Library's national role as a collecting and exhibiting institution is further re-affirmed through this national tour.

An exhibition and its catalogue are always the result of the dedicated collaborative work of many people. *Tales of Japan* is no exception. Our greatest appreciation is to Professor Miyeko Murase of Columbia University whose exceptional scholarship, artistic judgment, and keen mind have been indispensable in mounting the exhibition. It is an added pleasure that her participation, and that of her graduate students, marks yet another chapter in continuing cooperation between The New York Public Library and our sister institution Columbia University.

We are indebted to Continental Insurance, the National Endowment for the Arts, the Mary Livingston Griggs and Mary Griggs Burke Foundation, the New York State Council on the Arts, and the Asian Cultural Council for their support. Many dedicated Library staff have worked on the project. I wish to thank in particular Robert Rainwater, Assistant Director for Art, Prints and Photographs, and Diantha D. Schull, Manager of the Library's Exhibition Program.

I believe *Tales of Japan* is a significant contribution to our knowledge of Japan and Japanese culture through the universal language of art. It is with pride that the Library shares its resources.

VARTAN GREGORIAN
President, The New York Public Library

Foreword

The origins of The New York Public Library's collections of Japanese art date from the beginning of the century when New York City's first public print room was established at the Library. In 1901, a year after Samuel P. Avery's magnanimous gift of nearly 20,000 nineteenth-century etchings and lithographs founded the department, Charles Stewart Smith presented the Library with his collection of 1,763 Japanese prints of the *ukiyo-e* school contained within thirty-five albums. A civic leader and friend of Mr. Avery's, Smith had had great financial success in textile merchandising and in the course of extensive travel for his business had formed important collections of European painting and Japanese painting, ceramics, and prints. In 1892, Smith met the English military man, journalist, and author, Captain Frank Brinkley, in Japan and purchased from him his entire collection of woodblock prints.

With Brinkley's apparent great predilection for *bijin-ga*, or pictures of beautiful women, the Smith Collection at the Library became especially renowned for its large group of figure prints by Kitagawa Utamaro and Hosada Eishi, as well as for noteworthy examples by Kiyonobu, Kiyomasu, Harunobu, Kiyomitsu, Shunman, Bunchō, Koryūsai, Shunsho, Sharaku, and Hokusai. Occasional outstanding acquisitions have joined the Smith Collection in the Print Room. These include seven superb Utamaro prints, one Chōki, one Shunei, and a Hokusai, offered to the Library and purchased from the esteemed Louis V. Ledoux collection at the time of its dispersal in 1949. In 1955, a complete set of Hiroshige's *Fifty-three Stations of the Tōkaidō*, in a first edition of 1834, was purchased for the collection.

Other than ukiyo-e, types of the Japanese print found in the Print Room include an exceedingly important album of thirty Buddhist prints of the late Heian and Kamakura periods (twelfth to fourteenth century), small groups of Nagasaki-e and Yokohama-e prints, and prints of the Russo-Japanese War (1904–1905). In 1985, a sizeable, fine collection of prints of the Sino-Japanese War (1894–1895) was presented to the Library by Donald Keene.

The second principal repository for the Library's Japanese art holdings is the Spencer Collection, which was established in 1912 with the bequest of William August Spencer's personal collection of 232 contemporary French illustrated books and a generous endowment fund. Following Mr. Spencer's direction to acquire the finest "illustrated books and manuscripts that can be procured of any country and in any language and of any period," the Library's trustees, acting on the recommendations of senior staff, added the great monuments of Western printed books, such as the Aldine *Hypnerotomachia Poliphili* of 1499 by Francesco Colonna, the 1481 copperplate edition of Dante's *Divina Commedia*, and Dürer's three great woodcut albums, among others, and landmarks of Western manuscript illumination, notably *The Tickhill Psalter* of the early fourteenth century and the Petworth Manuscript of *Grace Dieu* of the fifteenth century.

Karl Kup, Advisor to the Spencer Collection from 1934 until his retirement in 1968, and for much of the period Keeper of Prints as well, vigorously expanded the range of the Spencer holdings to encompass the book of the Orient. Collecting in areas previously unrepresented by original works in the Library's collections, Mr. Kup began in his earliest years of curatorship to acquire illustrated and illuminated books and scrolls from China, Japan, India, Indonesia, Malaysia, and Thailand for the Spencer Collection. Among all of these, the Japanese holdings occupy, perhaps, the most prominent place, both in number and in breadth of representation. Beginning at a time of international distrust and animosity, Mr. Kup established with a few acquisitions in 1939 a relationship of more than thirty years' duration with the Tokyo antiquarian dealer Shigeo Sorimachi. In 1940, on the first of five round-the-world trips to purchase items for Spencer, Mr. Kup visited Sorimachi's home, selected desirable books and scrolls, and despite mounting difficulties, arranged with Sorimachi for shipment to New York. Aware that Sorimachi as a rich source of supply was in danger of being cut off from contact with the Library, Kup wrote to him in March, 1941: "The main thing is that we do not lose sight of each other, even though I shan't be able to come back to Tokyo so soon. The books from your collection, now here, have pleased the director of The New York Public Library very much—and we are all eager to remain in connection with you."

The connection, broken by the war, was renewed soon after. Through sympathetic understanding on both sides, the shared taste of connoisseurs, and a determination to form a great collection in the West, the relationship flourished in such a way that the Spencer Collection numbered almost 300 Japanese manuscripts in handscroll and book format and over 400 printed books from the twelfth century to the twentieth in the privately printed catalogue completed and published by Sorimachi in 1967 and in a revised edition in 1978. The great majority of the works listed had passed from Sorimachi's hands by way of Kup's discerning judgment into the collection.

As curator from 1972 to 1984, Joseph T. Rankin astutely acquired for Spencer in 1975 Charles H. Mitchell's great collection of approximately 750 Japanese printed books and albums, the largest group of works to enter the collection en bloc. Catalogued in Mitchell's landmark publication, *The Illustrated Books of the Nanga, Maruyama, Shijo and Other Related Schools of Japan; a Biobibliography* (Los Angeles, 1972), the collection added immeasurably to the Library's holdings in a field only marginally represented in Spencer and long neglected in a serious way in the West.

For their great foresight and devotion in forming the Library's Japanese holdings, the past curators of the Spencer Collection are due the gratitude of all present scholars, students, collectors, and connoisseurs of Japanese art and culture, and of the Library's public who may be appreciating now through the exhibition which this catalogue accompanies the unique collaboration of art and literature created by Japanese painters and printmakers. To the memory of Karl Kup's unwavering vision especially, this exhibition and its catalogue are dedicated.

ROBERT RAINWATER
Assistant Director for Art,
Prints and Photographs and
Curator of the Spencer Collection

Acknowledgment

Because of my special interest in narrative painting, I have been aware of the existence of a rich collection of Japanese manuscripts in the Spencer Collection of The New York Public Library, and have made use of them for certain specific research projects in the past. However, as few of these works have been exhibited outside of the library building, they have remained tantalizing objects of curiosity to students of Japanese painting here and in Japan. I was very pleased, therefore, when the Library approached me with the project of organizing an exhibition of these materials for their magnificent new gallery. I hope that this exhibition, and many others like it in the future, will not only arouse the interest of the general public, but also spur scholarly inquiry among students of Japanese culture, both here and abroad.

As is true in other exhibitions of this nature, the successful realization of a project depends on the devotion and hard work of many, many people. My special gratitude goes first to Mrs. Jackson Burke, who continues to give support, moral and otherwise, to various undertakings in the cause of promoting the arts of Japan.

I owe a great deal to the willing cooperation in this project of a large number of Library personnel. Especially crucial to me was the personal enthusiasm of Joseph Rankin, while he held the position of curator of the Spencer Collection. Robert Rainwater, who succeeded Mr. Rankin, could not have done more to smooth the progress of my work. I must also express my heartfelt thanks to Jonathan Seliger of the Print Room, who has been understanding and helpful throughout the preparations for this exhibition. I am also grateful for the support and cooperation of Diantha Schull and Richard Newman of the Exhibition Department.

For the research and writing of this catalogue, I am deeply indebted to friends and colleagues here and in Japan. Yanagisawa Taka, of the Art History Research Institute in Tokyo, and Shimbo Tōru, of Tsukuba University, spent some time with me at the Library, offering me their expertise on Buddhist and other early manuscripts. Two well-known specialists on ukiyo-e woodblock prints, Sadao Kikuchi, former Curator of Painting at the Tokyo National Museum, and Masanobu Matsushita of New York, a friend of long standing, opened doors to what has been a completely new field of study for me.

I want to express my sincere thanks to the group of eight graduate students specializing in Far Eastern Art History at Columbia University. They unstintingly offered their precious time and youthful energy to facilitate the progress of the initial stages of this work. These students were: Min Kim, Ying-Ying Lai, Elizabeth Lillihoj, Noëlle O'Connor, Stephanie Wada, Elizabeth Weiland, Sandy Williams, and Cynthia Woronowicz. They spent long hours gathering basic data, including the measurements of each object, and making the research photographs which were imperative for study purposes in a project of this nature. My special thanks are also due to those of them who provided me with the basic information incorporated into my entries on some of the items included here. They are Min Kim (who helped me with catalogue nos. 38, 39, 41, and 44), Elizabeth Lillihoj (nos. 12–16), Noëlle O'Connor (no. 49), Stephanie Wada (nos. 17–22 and 34), Elizabeth Weiland (nos. 11, 30, 31, 45, 47, and 48), and Cynthia Woronowicz (who worked on woodblock prints). I hope that the final version of this text will not disappoint them. Stephanie Wada deserves special mention and my deepest gratitude. With an unflagging sense of commitment and devotion she went over the entire manuscript of this catalogue, polishing and improving my writing.

Finally, I wish to express my special thanks to Otto and Marguerite Nelson, the incomparable team of photographers who provided us with excellent photographs of all the objects included in this catalogue.

MIYEKO MURASE
Columbia University

Introduction

Offered in this exhibition are a small group of Japanese manuscripts from the Spencer Collection, and woodblock prints from the Print Room of The New York Public Library. The Library's collection of Japanese woodcuts may be rivaled only by those of large museums famous for their holdings of Japanese art, such as the Museum of Fine Arts in Boston, and the Metropolitan Museum of Art in New York. The Library is noted for its superb collection of prints by the nineteenth-century artists Utamaro and Hiroshige, but these prints have been on public exhibition only on a few occasions. The illustrated manuscripts from the Spencer Collection have been viewed by a handful of scholars and specialists here and abroad, and have rarely been exhibited to the public.

The Spencer Collection also includes a large number of printed books and handscrolls. Some of these were selected for the present exhibition (nos. 19, 35, 42, 43-1). Most of the works, however, were chosen from the group of hand-illustrated books and scrolls which so distinguishes this collection. For size and variety the Spencer Collection—the largest of its type outside of Japan—is truly unique and can be matched only by large museum collections in Japan. The Spencer Collection was acquired with foresight and reflects clear vision and a philosophy of acquisition which are appropriate to the collection of a major library.

The steadfast focus on the value of illustrated literary texts is an aspect of Japanese art which is little known in the West. Westerners' relative lack of appreciation of this tradition was perhaps inevitable, for most of the literary texts are unfamiliar and untranslated. Yet pictorial representation of literary material is one of the most important aspects of Japanese art, for in Japan, pictorial images have always been viewed as an indispensable means of communication. *Emaki*, the art of narrative painting in handscrolls, reached its peak from the twelfth to the fourteenth century, yet the large number of exciting and beautiful examples from later periods are ample testimony that this art never lost its creative energy, or patronage. The love of the Japanese for stories told with pictures endured even after the country opened its doors to the West and Western culture in the mid-nineteenth century, a time when many painters traveled to Europe to study Impressionist painting (essentially a non-narrative art). Today, major newspapers carry serialized novels with illustrations, by established authors and painters, in both morning and evening editions. It is often said that the aesthetic principles which were first fostered by narrative painting have affected many aspects of modern Japanese life, influencing comic strips, television shows, and films.

The scrolls and books in this exhibition were selected for both their literary content and pictorial merit. Most of the works are handscrolls. In the Far East, both books and scrolls were used for writing and painting, but the handscroll, with its virtually unlimited extension of horizontal space, was the favored vehicle for illustration of dramatic tales in Japan.

Writing in the Far East traditionally moves from top to bottom of the page, beginning at the upper right and moving to the left. This tradition is the basis of the cardinal premise of emaki, in which text and picture outline the narrative together; the scrolls are opened and viewed from right to left, and the development of episodes proceeds in that direction. The Japanese recognized the enormous artistic potential inherent in this horizontal format. The best among extant narrative paintings, produced between the twelfth and fourteenth century, were all executed in scroll form, as opposed to the codex, or book format.

An amazing array of subject matter can be found in emaki, and in those "lost" scrolls which are recorded in documents. There seem to have been no limits set on the subjects that emaki illustrated—scenes from romantic literature, historical tales, battle stories, biographies, temple histories, mythical tales and legends of non-human creatures were all depicted in handscroll paintings.

After the fourteenth century, however, the popularity of emaki was superseded, first by Zen-inspired ink monochrome painting, and later by the broad appeal of resplendent folding screens and wall panels. Famous artists of different schools occasionally produced emaki on commission; however, from the sixteenth century on, most illustrated handscrolls were by anonymous artists who functioned outside of the keen and often fierce competition for such important commissions as the decorating of castles and palaces. They produced books and scrolls for painting shops which sold "ready-made" items in addition to painted fans, painted shells, and folding screens.

Although ignored until recently by collectors and scholars, these late emaki are now beginning to attract serious attention. The works not only reflect the spirit of a new age and a new clientele which demanded new styles and new subjects, they are also an important development in the continuing history of narrative painting in Japan.

This selection of scrolls also includes manuscripts from different periods, which reflect the changing fashions of different eras and classes of society. The earliest materials shown here are Buddhist in nature; they inform us of the major concerns and preoccupations of the ancient Japanese, from the twelfth to about the fourteenth century. The exhibition also contains a manuscript in which its artist proudly declares her faithful adherence to an ancient model (see no. 20), one of the many works in the collection which bear witness to the survival of traditional forces in literature and painting. Other scrolls and books vividly illustrate the taste of a new audience and social force in the seventeenth and eighteenth century, one which favored amusing and fantastic tales. Equally revealing are manuscripts which were created as records, among them manuals of veterinary medicine (no. 45), records of stage performances of Nō drama (no. 33), instructions on the art of flower arranging (no. 46), and painters' accounts of their own artistic studies and their efforts to preserve artistic traditions (nos. 47–49). All together, these manuscripts mirror and record rich slices of the lives of the ancient Japanese.

Contents

Chronology

Asuka period	538–710
Nara period	710–794
Early Heian period	794–894
Late Heian (Fujiwara) period	894–1185
Kamakura period	1185–1333
Nambokuchō period	1333–1392
Muromachi (Ashikaga) period	1392–1573
Momoyama period	1573–1615
Edo (Tokugawa) period	1615–1868
Modern era	1868–

EDITORIAL NOTE

With the exception of authors who publish in Western languages, all Japanese personal names are given in the traditional East Asian manner with the family name first.

TALES OF JAPAN

I
Praise of the Buddha in Words and Images

Few modern Japanese profess an interest in Buddhism and its teachings, save on the occasion of services offered to the spirits of deceased relatives, or at significant rites of passage. Buddhist dogma and practice definitely are not a part of the everyday life in Japan, yet most Japanese still remain Buddhist in affiliation and the principal teachings of this faith still mold their basic outlook on life and influence the unconscious level of their thinking and behavior.

Buddhism, which originated in India and claimed a large following in China and Korea before reaching Japan in the sixth century, found its most enduring success among the Japanese. It was accepted first by the ruling family of Japan, chiefly as a means of protecting the welfare of the nation. The court's attempt to adopt Buddhism as a state religion, however, was thwarted in the late eighth century; the Buddhist church then turned its attention to the salvation of individuals—in particular, members of the aristocracy. By the thirteenth century, a grass roots proselytizing movement had begun; the lives and activities—recorded in paintings—of such militant advocates of the faith as Ippen (1239–1289) and his disciple Taa (died 1319) reflect this phase of Japanese Buddhism (see no. 10).

None of the Buddhist materials included here were meant as icons for worship; rather, most were destined for sutra (scripture) repositories—"treasure houses" kept by temples—where they were stored away and brought out only on special occasions. The ancient Japanese treated these works with great respect, and thanks to their care, many still exist today. The works preserve not only the traditions of Japanese Buddhism, but also much information pertaining to Chinese Buddhist practices. Sources for Japanese Buddhist rituals and iconography are invariably traced to China, but there fewer documents have survived.

The manuscripts in this section are divided into two groups reflecting two different phases in the history of Japanese Buddhism—sutras with painted frontispieces, made by and for the aristocracy (nos. 1–4), and *zuzō* drawings made by the monks of the Mikkyō (Esoteric Buddhist) sects (nos. 5–9).

Influenced by Chinese practice, Japanese Buddhists placed enormous importance on the act of copying out sutras, regarding it as a work of spiritual merit. Since it was believed that the quantity of sutras copied affected one's chances for salvation, they were also reproduced in large numbers—often as many as 5000 scrolls per group. Artists also paid a great deal of attention to the visual appeal of their work and used expensive materials—dark, indigo-dyed paper, and gold or silver ink for the text and frontispiece decorations. Such scrolls were intended not only as offerings to various buddhas, but as petitions for the happiness and well-being of the donors and their relatives. Sutra-copying reached its peak during the eleventh and twelfth centuries.

Ink drawings belonging to the second group (zuzō) express the more scholarly concerns of Mikkyō monks, who produced them for study and to preserve the correct iconography. They, too, considered the act of copying older zuzō meritorious.

The final item in this section, the *Ten Oxherding Pictures* (no. 11), is an example of the art inspired by Zen, one of the last of the Buddhist sects to take root in Japan. A doctrine of self-discipline and self-reliance, it was introduced from China at the end of the twelfth century. Zen did not actively advocate iconoclasm, yet Zen Buddhists saw little importance in the study of scriptures, and they abhorred the idea of seeking salvation through the worship of icons. Wisdom and enlightenment were sought in the teachings of the great Zen masters, who often composed illuminating essays and verses. Zen monks also considered such "artistic" activities as composing poems and drawing pictures helpful in attaining religious goals. The *Ten Oxherding Pictures* are a reflection of this belief. Far from being confined to prayer halls, Zen dogma had a wide-ranging effect upon the lives and aesthetic standards of the Japanese. The sect's insistence on utter simplicity and spontaneity was assiduously observed, for example, in the rituals of the tea ceremony; in turn it particularly influenced the appearance of art objects such as tea furnishings and utensils.

1
Chapter 544 of the *Dai Hannya Haramittakyō* (*The Greater Sutra of the Perfection of Wisdom*)

Ca. 1125, Late Heian period
Frontispiece attached to a handscroll, gold and silver ink on dark blue paper
H: 25.4 cm, W: 20.9 cm
Spencer no. 3

PUBLISHED: John M. Rosenfield and Elizabeth ten Grotenhuis, *Journey of the Three Jewels: Japanese Buddhist Paintings from Western Collections* (New York, 1979), no. 9; Akiyama Terukazu (ed.), *Emakimono*, vol. 2 of *Zaigai Nihon no Shihō*, ed. Shimada Shūjirō *et al.* (Tokyo, 1980), no. 112.

The group of four Buddhist scriptures (sutras) included here (nos. 1–4) may be viewed as a manifestation of the Buddhist belief that the laborious practice of copying sutras was an act of devotion, and accumulated spiritual merit. The more tedious the work, the more merit to be gained. Donating funds so that someone else might do the actual transcribing was considered just as meritorious. Rich and powerful Buddhists were known to commission literally thousands of sutra scrolls, which were subsequently dedicated to temples. Unlike the sacred books of medieval Europe, these scrolls were rarely used by the faithful; rather, once the sutras were transcribed and ceremonially dedicated to the appropriate Buddhist deities, they were stored in sutra repositories. Many carefully preserved sutra scrolls still exist, but the most beautiful and treasured examples date from the twelfth century, when the practice enjoyed the greatest popularity.

Like the sutras in nos. 1–3, many twelfth century scrolls conform to a standard type. The paper was repeatedly soaked in a dark blue dye which created a depth of color suggestive of precious lapis lazuli. Texts were copied in gold ink, or, on rare occasions, in alternating lines of gold and silver, with seventeen characters generally assigned to each line. Covers were decorated with large floral arabesques executed in gold and silver ink. Frontispiece decorations were also drawn in gold and silver, often following a standard pattern, like that of no. 3. This type of frontispiece usually depicts a distant hill or mountain shaped like a bird's head (intended to represent Vulture Peak near Rajagriha in India)—background for the delivery of a sermon by the historical Buddha, Śākyamuni (Shaka in Japanese). The Buddha is seated on a tall lotus pedestal in the center, flanked by bodhisattvas and monks. A tall offering table with an incense burner is commonly depicted in the foreground.

The first sutra reproduced here is Chapter 544 of the *Dai Hannya Haramittakyō (The Greater Sutra of the Perfection of Wisdom*, Sanskrit: Mahā-prajñā-pāramitā-sutra);[1] it follows the standard format for sutra transcription and illumination. But the scroll is quite unusual, since the text was written in alternating lines of gold and silver ink. The complete text, also known by the abbreviated name of *Dai Hannyakyō*, is the opening sutra of the Chinese *Tripitaka*, the compendium of Buddhist scriptures known in Japan as the *Issaikyō*. One of the most important canonical sources for Mahāyāna Buddhists, the *Dai Hannyakyō* contains metaphysical discourses given by the Buddha Śākyamuni at sixteen meetings. Throughout the lengthy sermon, absolute truth is equated with the void, or emptiness, and wisdom is praised as the best means of reaching enlightenment. From the time the *Dai Hannyakyō* first appeared in Japan around 712 (the date of the earliest known Japanese copy), it was often transcribed—particularly because it was used as part of the liturgy that appealed for divine protection of the state.

Chapter 544 consists of Śākyamuni's sermon from the fourth of his sixteen meetings. The frontispiece decoration is cursorily drawn, with little attention to refinement of detail. However, supple lines capture the essential qualities of pictorial forms and the spirit of the scene. The Buddha is flanked by two bodhisattvas; his audience consists of four laymen dressed as Chinese officials. In front of him stands an offering table; baskets of flowers are visible in the background; in the distance are hills and mountains partially hidden by clouds and mist. Flower petals fill the sky as symbols of the occasion.

The care with which the text was copied in gold and silver ink, and the simple composition, with its few, relatively large pictorial elements executed in supple brush lines, are characteristic of the scrolls commissioned by Fujiwara no Kiyohira (died 1128) for the Chūsonji temple at Hiraizumi in northern Japan. The temple complex at Hiraizumi, with its famous gold-leaf covered Konjikidō (literally, "gold-colored hall"), was built as the tutelary temple of the local Fujiwara family, distant relatives of the ruling clan in Kyoto. Worship of Amida (Buddha of the Western Paradise, Sanskrit: Amitābha), who was considered the most compassionate of the buddhas, had become enormously popular among the nobility of Kyoto, and temples dedicated to him had sprung up throughout the countryside, and as far north as Chūsonji. Hiraizumi lies on a fertile plain along the River Kitagawa, which is known for its alluvial gold, and it had long been a military and political center. Here, Kiyohira, the first of four generations, labored to reproduce the cultured ambiance of Kyoto, hundreds of miles away. By the equally devoted efforts of his son Motohira (died 1157) and grandson Hidehira (died 1187), Chūsonji was expanded to more than 400 buildings. But after 1186, when the shōgun Yoritomo stripped the family of its power, the temple complex and its patronage steadily declined.

Kiyohira's ambitious projects included commissioning a copy of the *Issaikyō* in a set of about 5300 scrolls. Some include colophons which suggest that the project was begun shortly before 1117 and completed eight years later. Unfortunately, for unknown reasons, most of the scrolls were removed from the temple in the late sixteenth century and taken to Mt. Kōya. Today only seventeen scrolls remain in the Chūsonji repository; 4296 of the scrolls are at the Kongōbuji of Mt. Kōya, and 166 are owned by Kanshinji in the Osaka Prefecture.[2]

NOTES

1. Takakusu Junjirō and Watanabe Kaigyoku (eds.), *Taishō Shinshū Daizōkyō* (Tokyo, 1924), vol. 5, no. 220.
2. Ishida Mosaku, *Chūsonji* (Tokyo, 1959), p. 57.

2
Chapter 338 of the *Dai Hannya Haramittakyō* (*The Greater Sutra of the Perfection of Wisdom*)

Ca. 1175, Late Heian period
Frontispiece attached to a handscroll, gold and silver ink on dark blue paper
H: 25.6 cm, W: 20.6 cm
Spencer no. 6

PUBLISHED: John M. Rosenfield and Elizabeth ten Grotenhuis, *Journey of the Three Jewels: Japanese Buddhist Paintings from Western Collections* (New York, 1979), no. 11; John M. Rosenfield, *Japanese Arts of the Heian Period* (New York, 1967), no. 34a.

The two successors of Fujiwara no Kiyohira (died 1128) enjoyed his legacy and continued to expand the temple of Chūsonji in Hiraizumi (see no. 1). One of their projects was the commissioning of a transcription of the entire Buddhist canon, the *Tripitaka* (*Issaikyō* in Japanese). The scroll of the 338th chapter of the *Dai Hannya Haramittakyō* belongs to a section of the *Issaikyō* transcription thought to have been commissioned by Kiyohira's grandson, Hidehira (died 1187). These scrolls, known collectively as the *Hidehira Sutras*, were apparently dedicated in 1176 to commemorate the twentieth anniversary of the death of Hidehira's father, Motohira. The original transcription must have included more than 5000 scrolls, but only 2724 scrolls remain at the temple. Fewer than 200 of them retain frontispiece decorations, and of these several have found their way into American collections.[1]

The text of the Spencer scroll is written in gold ink and records the sermon believed to have been given by Śākyamuni at the first meeting on Vulture Peak. The frontispiece decoration, like many others from this group, is rather crowded, and includes more detail than the example from the *Kiyohira Sutras*. The Buddha group is now in the background; Vulture Peak has a clearly discernible bird's-head shape; and angels, ribbons, and flower petals adorn the sky. Monks listen to the Buddha and witness the scenes being enacted before him.

The narrative scenes in the foreground are not related to the abstruse content of this sutra. A bodhisattva stands in the midst of the foreground, holding a helmet-like object in his hand. He has just delivered three men, dressed in Chinese garb, from four armed attackers who now pay obeisance to him. This scene may depict an episode from the Kannon Chapter of the *Lotus Sutra* (see no. 4), in which the Buddha promises that a prayer to Kannon will deliver the devotee from dangerous situations. Frontispieces from the Hidehira scrolls and many other late twelfth-century sutras include scenes from the famed *Lotus Sutra*—even though the textual content of the scrolls may be totally unrelated to it. The *Lotus Sutra* was the most popular Buddhist scripture of the Late Heian period, with many rich, dramatic stories that were easy to portray in paintings.

The Hidehira scrolls were decorated by many different artists. Their individual painting styles differ slightly, but they adhere for the most part to a single workshop tradition. Figures of buddhas, bodhisattvas, monks, and devotees alike have the appearance of charming, innocent children. The tightly compressed and crowded composition, and concern for minute detail have resulted in the loss of serenity that marks the earlier *Kiyohira Sutras*. Energy and movement fill the composition and lend the small paintings excitement and drama. The emphasis on the narrative scene reflects an artistic trend of the second half of the twelfth century, when secular narrative painting enjoyed a tremendous vogue.

NOTE

1. These are Chapters 282 (Harvard University Art Museum), 454 (Honolulu Academy of Art), and 582 (Kimiko and John Powers Collection), published in Akiyama Terukazu (ed.), *Emakimono*, vol. 2 of *Zaigai Nihon no Shihō*, ed. Shimada Shūjirō *et al.* (Tokyo, 1980), nos. 111, 110, and 113 respectively; and Chapter 400 (the Hyde Collection), published in John M. Rosenfield *et al.*, *The Courtly Tradition in Japanese Art and Literature: Selections from the Hofer and Hyde Collections* (Cambridge Mass., 1973), no. 22.

3

Sarakokukyō (Sutra for the Nation of Sala)

Ca. 1185, Late Heian period
Frontispiece attached to a handscroll, gold and silver ink on dark blue paper
H: 25.8 cm, W: 22.0 cm
Spencer no. 7

The Sarakokukyō (*Sutra for the Nation of Sala*, Sanskrit: Buddhabhāshita-kosala-desa Sutra), transcribed in this scroll, describes how the Buddha Śākyamuni converted the people of a nation known as Sala.[1] According to this sutra, Sala was vast and fertile, and its inhabitants devoted their lives to hedonistic pleasure. The Buddha, dismayed at the futility of their existence, convinced them to pursue, instead, the life of four virtues: Charity, Temperance, Faith in the Buddha, and Honoring knowledge.

The frontispiece of this sutra depicts a scene of the Buddha preaching to his followers. The composition is simple and hieratic. The abbreviated landscape setting, the placement of figures and other pictorial elements, the sharp, rather mechanical drawing, and the large floral arabesques are reminiscent of the covers and frontispieces that adorn many of the scrolls known collectively as the *Jingoji Sutras*, in the collection of Jingoji, a mountain temple outside Kyoto. Many scrolls from this group bear a large rectangular "Jingoji" seal (H: 4 cm, W: 2 cm) in dark red ink, placed between the frontispiece and the first line of text. A close inspection of the Spencer scroll suggests that a similar seal was impressed below the line following the title but was subsequently erased. This scroll, then, was probably separated from the compendium of the Buddhist canon known as the *Issaikyō* (*Tripitaka* in Chinese) (see also nos. 1 and 2) belonging to Jingoji. According to the *Jingoji Ryakki*,[2] a history of the temple, this transcription of the *Issaikyō* was begun by the retired emperor Toba (reigned 1108–1123) just before his death in 1156, and was completed in 1185 by his son Goshirakawa, who lived at the temple after abdicating in 1158. The original set must have included about 5000 scrolls, since a temple inventory of 1794 reports that some 4722 were still in situ.[3] During the nineteenth century, however, some were stolen, and still more were sold to finance repairs of temple buildings. Only 2273 of the scrolls remain at Jingoji today.

NOTES

1. Takakusu Junjirō and Watanabe Kaigyoku (eds.), *Taishō Shinshū Daizōkyō* (Tokyo, 1925), vol. 14, no. 520.
2. Bussho Kankōkai (ed.), *Dai Nihon Bukkyō Zensho: Jishi Sōsho*, vol. 3 (Tokyo, 1915), p. 115.
3. Tanaka Kaidō, *Ko Shakyō Sōkan* (Nara, 1942), p. 355.

4
Myōhō Rengekyō (*Lotus Sutra*)

Late fourteenth century, Nambokuchō period
Frontispiece attached to a handscroll, gold and silver ink on dark blue paper
H: 27.6 cm, W: 79.6 cm
Spencer no. 19

PUBLISHED: John M. Rosenfield and Elizabeth ten Grotenhuis, *Journey of the Three Jewels: Japanese Buddhist Paintings from Western Collections* (New York, 1979), no. 13.

The *Myōhō Rengekyō* (*Lotus Sutra*, Sanskrit: Saddharma Puṇḍarīka), known in Japan by its abbreviated title *Hokekyō*, was by far the most popular and influential work from the vast body of Buddhist scriptural writing preserved in the Far East.[1] While the abstract thought and metaphysical profundity that characterize most Buddhist scriptures escaped many believers, the *Lotus's* dramatic content, which couched religious teachings in literary tales, appealed to a much broader audience. Scenes from the lucid narratives that distinguish this sutra from other scriptural works were also considered attractive subjects

for painting; the Buddhists of pre-T'ang dynasty China illustrated tales from the *Lotus Sutra* in paintings on temple walls, hanging scrolls, and handscrolls.[2]

The *Lotus Sutra*, which is believed to contain the final sermon of Buddha Śākyamuni at Vulture Peak, was probably written and promulgated in India during the first century A.D. The text, which is organized into twenty-eight chapters,[3] consists of a rich variety of stories used by the Buddha to encourage his followers to seek salvation. All sentient beings who believe in this sutra will be saved, and the mere invocation of the names of buddhas and bodhisattvas can also lead to salvation. Believers regard the *Lotus* as Śākyamuni's final bequest to this world, the supreme and most sublime of sutras.

Worship of the *Lotus* is mentioned in Japan as early as the late sixth century. Not only did it lay the foundation for the later development of Japanese Buddhism, it also shaped Japanese culture. The *Lotus* attained its religious pre-eminence when the influential Tendai sect adopted it as their basic text, and it was often used for birthday celebrations, or memorial services intended to insure a happy fate for the souls of those who had died. Thus, the *Lotus* became the most frequently copied scripture of the Heian period. In fact, some ninety percent of all the Heian sutras in existence are said to be copies of the *Lotus*.[4] It was usually transcribed in sets of seven or eight scrolls, with frontispieces depicting stories from the text. These tales became so well known that they were even represented on the frontispieces of totally unrelated sutras (see no. 3).

The *Lotus* remained popular after the Heian period; the Spencer scroll is an example of a transcription from a later time. The frontispiece, which is about four times wider than that of an average sutra scroll, depicts many episodes, selected from the twenty-eight chapters of the work. In this crowded composition, narrative scenes are spread out in front of the preaching Buddha, as if to bear witness to his words. The Buddha and his audience are seated on an elaborately decorated platform, which separates them from the narrative scenes. Two bands of light-rays issuing from the Buddha's forehead illuminate the six worlds of reincarnation *(Rokudō)* into which all sentient beings are destined to be reborn. This detail is a reference to the introductory chapter of the sutra, which relates how the Buddha, before explaining the great dharma, reveals to his followers the nature of the various kinds of sentient existence, from the lowest to the highest level. In the lower band of light-rays retribution is dealt out to wrong-doers, some of whom are doomed to torment in Hell. In the upper ray, the succession of existences that lead to buddhahood, and finally to nirvana, is illustrated. The narrative scenes which are spread out before the Buddha group are roughly divided into two groups by a river. About eighteen separate scenes, each representing a different chapter, can be clearly identified.

Dominating the composition are a large burning house and a sumptuous *stupa* (pagoda) housing two buddhas seated side by side. The house in flames is a reference to one of the best-known parables in the sutra, an episode from Chapter 3, "Hiyubon" ("Parable"), in which the Buddha reveals the most expedient methods of leading the foolish to the truth. The house, in which foolish people reside, is filled with dangerous or foul objects, among them scorpions and corpses. The people, who are likened to children, are led to safety, willy nilly, through a single gate, but only after they have been enticed by three carts presented to them as playthings: a goat-cart, a deer-cart, and a bullock-cart. The carts symbolize the three traditional vehicles that lead to buddhahood: the goat-cart symbolizes the monks who achieve enlightenment with the help of others; the deer-cart, those who attain enlightenment through their own efforts; and the bullock-cart is a symbol of the bodhisattvas, who achieve enlightenment for the sake of other beings.

The elaborate stupa enveloped in golden rays is an image drawn from a story from Chapter 11, "Kenhōtōbon" ("Apparition of the Jeweled Stupa"). In this episode, a Buddha of the past, Prabhūtaratna (Tahōbutsu in Japanese), sits in a beautiful stupa Śākyamuni has summoned from underground. Prabhūtaratna has vowed to appear only when the *Lotus* has been expounded. Śākyamuni enters the stupa, sits down next to Prabhūtaratna, and continues his sermon for the large crowd that has gathered to witness this auspicious event.

Stories from other chapters of the sutra are illustrated in a sequence which generally moves from right to left in the composition. For example, the story from Chapter 2, "Hōbenbon" ("Expedient Devices"), is depicted directly below the rays of light emanating from the Buddha's forehead. Here, the Buddha promises that the difficulty of the path to buddhahood will be overcome by anyone who erects a stupa, or carves or paints an image of the Buddha as an act of homage—an assurance that encouraged almost frenetic activity in the arts during the Late Heian period. Stories from Chapters 4, 5,

6, 7, and 12 can be identified in the foreground, near the bank of the river. Scenes depicted on the far side of the river include episodes from Chapters 10, 11, 13, 17, 19, 22, 25, and 28.

The scroll contains the text of only the Introduction and the first two chapters of the *Lotus*. Like many other transcriptions of this sutra, the set to which the Spencer scroll once belonged must have consisted of seven or eight scrolls. As most of the popular and best-known stories from the *Lotus* are depicted in this one frontispiece, it is quite likely other frontispieces from this set were similar in composition. The cover of the Spencer scroll, of purple-colored paper, is a later replacement, although the narrow strip of blue paper pasted on it to identify the work is the original. The colophon is in the same hand as that of the text, and records the name "Ogura Kaga no Kami Nyūdō Zeun" ("a lay monk, Ogura Zeun"), who is also identified as the governor of Kaga province ("Kaga no Kami"), northeast of Kyoto.[5]

This frontispiece shimmers with the golden lustre of the many figures, swirling clouds, and large buildings, which were drawn and painted in gold ink alone, giving a stronger impression of ornateness than do sutra frontispieces of the Heian period. This tendency toward ornate, crowded compositions, which characterizes sutra decorations from the fourteenth century on, probably reflects the influence of Chinese woodcut prints and of Korean sutras that were affected by Chinese style. Many Chinese and Korean sutra frontispieces have extremely dense compositions which closely resemble that of the Spencer scroll.[6] Indeed, the provenance of this particular work has been questioned—in the Cleveland Museum of Art, a scroll identified as a Chinese work of the Sung dynasty bears a frontispiece that is nearly identical to that of the Spencer *Lotus*.[7] The unusual length of the Spencer frontispiece, and the placement of the Buddha group on a platform to the right, with the narrative scenes spread out to the left, are typical of Chinese and Korean works.

Like the frontispieces of many Korean scrolls, whose production reached a peak in the mid-fourteenth century,[8] the Spencer illumination is striking in its many shades of gold. However, the rich effect was created not so much by using gold lines to fill in details and background areas—a technique characteristic of Korean sutras—but by filling in the bodies of buddhas and bodhisattvas with gold ink and leaving channel-like areas blank to create dark, "negative" outlines. This technique was used in other Heian-period sutra decorations, but never to the extent that it was applied in the Spencer piece.

Although many "foreign" features may be detected in this scroll, the work is undoubtedly Japanese. For example, one notable Chinese and Korean element is absent, the word "hensō." The title of a scroll, usually written at the top right of the composition, often included this word, which means "illustration of Buddhist text." The paper is also not so heavy or coarse as the paper used for Korean pieces, and the scroll is smaller in size.[9] The brushstrokes, particularly those used to define secular figures, are closer to those of Japanese sutra decorations than to Chinese or Korean examples. This scroll, therefore, may be identified as a Japanese work from the late fourteenth century.

NOTES

1. For the most recent English translation of this sutra, see Leon Hurvitz (trans.), *Scripture of the Lotus Blossom of the Fine Dharma* (New York, 1976).
2. For a study of artistic representations of this sutra, see LeRoy Davidson, *The Lotus Sutra in Chinese Art: A Study in Buddhist Art to the Year 1000* (New Haven, 1954), and Willa Tanabe, *Paintings of the Lotus Sutra: The Relationship of Ritual, Text and Pictures* (Ph.D. dissertation, Columbia University, 1983). For a good summary of the literary references to the lost wall paintings of this sutra in Japan, see Miya Tsugio, "Danzan Jinja zō Hokke Mandara (The Hokke Mandara Owned by Danzan Jinja), part III," *Bijutsu Kenkyū*, no. 223 (July 1962), pp. 56–57.
3. Sometimes, especially in China, the sutra is divided into 27 chapters.
4. Komatsu Shigemi, *Heike Nōkyō no Kenkyū* (Tokyo, 1976), 2 vols., p. 47.
5. John M. Rosenfield and Elizabeth ten Grotenhuis, *Journey of the Three Jewels: Japanese Buddhist Paintings from Western Collections* (New York, 1979), p. 71. Although no direct connection is found, a certain Mitsuie who also used the title of Kaga no Kami signed his name on a pair of mandalas in 1396 (now in the Nara National Museum). For the inscription, see Tokyo Kokuritsu Bunkazai Kenkyūjo (ed.), *Nihon Kaigashi Nenki Shiryō Shūsei* (Tokyo, 1984), no. 311.

6. For a comparative study of Chinese woodcuts, see Miya Tsugio, "Sō-Gen hampon ni miru Hokekyō-e (Frontispieces in Sung and Yüan Printed Lotus Sutras, part I)," *Bijutsu Kenkyū*, no. 325 (September 1983), pp. 99–110.

7. *Cleveland Museum of Art Bulletin*, no. 154 (February 1971), item no. 70.64, and Wai-kam Ho, *et al.*, *Eight Dynasties of Chinese Painting: The Collections of the Nelson Gallery-Atkins Museum, Kansas City, and the Cleveland Museum of Art* (Cleveland, 1980), no. 49. In the introductory essay to this catalogue, Wai-kam Ho refers to the Spencer scroll as a Sung Chinese work, see *op. cit.*, p. xxxii.

8. Hayashi Susumu, "Kōrai jidai no sōshoku-gyō," in Kikutake Jun'ichi and Yoshida Hiroshi (eds.), *Kōrai Ga* (Tokyo, 1981), p. 36.

9. Hayashi, "Kōrai jidai," p. 31.

5
Icons and Mandalas for Rituals Dedicated to the *Ninnōkyō* (*Sutra of the Benevolent King*)

I. Ca. 1175, Late Heian period
   One handscroll, ink on paper
   H: 29.3 cm, L: 374.5 cm
   Spencer no. 5

II. Late twelfth century, Late Heian period
   One handscroll, ink on paper
   II: 30.7 cm, L: 459.7 cm
   Spencer no. 10

PUBLISHED: Ono Gemmyō (ed.), *Taishō Shinshū Daizōkyō Zuzō*, vol. 12 (Tokyo, 1934), pp. 937–940; Nakano Genzō, "Ninnōkyō-hō to Fudō Myōō Zō," in Sawa Takaaki and Hamada Takashi (eds.), *Mikkyō Bijutsu Taikan*, vol. III (Tokyo, 1984), pp. 193–194; Nishigōri Kyōsuke, "Ninnō kyō mandara no keishiki" ("Style of paintings in the Jen-wang-ching Mandala"), *Bukkyō Geijutsu*, no. 101 (April 1975), pp. 65, 67, 72, 75.

The religious life and art of Japanese Buddhism were profoundly affected by the beliefs of a new sect which was introduced to Japan in the early ninth century by two great masters who had studied in China: Saichō (posthumously known as Dengyō Daishi, 766–822) and Kūkai, or, posthumously, Kōbō Daishi (774–836). The new teaching was known in Japan as Mikkyō (literally, "teachings of deep mysteries"), Esoteric Buddhism, or Vajrayāna (Thunderbolt Vehicle).[1] The teachings of traditional Buddhism, sometimes called Exoteric Buddhism, regard the Law of the historical buddha, Śākyamuni, as the embodiment of buddhahood. In contrast, Vajrayāna, which arose in India during the fifth century A.D., views the entire universe as a manifestation of energy and light emanating from its central divinity, the mythical buddha Mahāvairocana, the Great Illuminator (Dainichi in Japanese). Dainichi is present everywhere, in every thought, deed, and word; all other buddhas and bodhisattvas are part of this supreme god. By extension of this belief, Mikkyō holds that buddhahood is attainable on this earth, and, further, that the world is capable of becoming a true buddha paradise.

The most occult of all the Buddhist sects, Mikkyō holds that the Buddha's truth is expressed in three mysteries—in his body, speech, and thought—revealed only to individuals who are properly initiated. The secret and strictly prescribed liturgy is elaborate, including the incantation of spells and the burning of wood on which magical formulas are inscribed. Initiates enter a trance-like state in which they experience a mystical union with the buddhas. Before this belief reached Japan, traditional Buddhism occupied an important position in the lives of the Japanese, promising benefits in this world and the well-being of the state and communities. The new sect was the first in Japan's religious history to promise individual salvation through such worldly rewards as success in one's career and love affairs.

The master Kūkai introduced the Shingon (True Words) branch of Mikkyō and made the monastery on remote Mt. Kōya (south of Osaka) his headquarters.[2] In 823 the court requested him to complete the temple of Tōji (Eastern Temple) in Kyoto, which had been under construction for 30 years. Renamed Kyōō-gokokuji (King's Counselor–Nation's Protector Temple), its official name today, this temple gave Kūkai the urban foothold he needed to extend his Shingon teachings to the aristocracy of the capital.

The master Saichō went to China initially to study T'ien-t'ai tenets (Tendai, in Japanese), which were based upon the teachings of the *Lotus Sutra* (see no. 4); soon, however, he also became involved with Mikkyō, probably because it was in vogue in China and had strongly influenced the T'ien-t'ai sect. Saichō's group, headquartered at Mt. Hiei (northeast of Kyoto), incorporated many aspects of Mikkyō teaching into its own. In time, however, a deep antagonism and formal schism developed between the followers of Saichō and Kūkai, and the two Mikkyō schools developed: Taimitsu (Tendai Mikkyō) and Tōmitsu (Tōji Mikkyō).

The new liturgy of Mikkyō inspired major innovation in Buddhist art. Its large pantheon of gods contains many exotic deities who reflect strong Hindu influence, particularly the wrathful guardian figures, who are endowed with many heads and limbs and who protect the faithful and subjugate evil forces.[3] The most significant new art form introduced by Mikkyō was a schemata, known as a *mandala* (*mandara* in Japanese), which represents the myriad of gods and their mutual relationships within a secret world.[4] The word "mandala" originally meant "that which possesses (*la*) the essence and totality (*manda*)." Later, it signified the place where this state of perfection is realized, and where the rituals prescribed for attaining that goal are held. In its final definition, mandala referred to any visual representation of Mikkyō gods.

Strict rules govern Mikkyō's complex rituals and iconography. As Kūkai's Chinese mentor, Hui-kuo (746–805), explained, the complexities of the sect's iconography—minute details of the physical attributes of deities, their *mudrā* (hand gestures), and objects symbolically associated with them—could be better expressed in visual terms.[5] Special ink drawings, some touched up with light colors, were made in Mikkyō circles as records of the temples' intricate icons. Such drawings were known as *zuzō* (image-painting).[6] Certain zuzō, or iconographic drawings (as they are known in the West), were produced as underdrawings for versions of the actual icons. Most of the zuzō, however, were made to serve as tools of instruction and thus often served as manuals of Mikkyō iconography. Zuzō usually included careful notes on the identities of deities, necessary attributes to be represented, and other critical aspects.

These commentaries were essential, since many rival groups arose within the Mikkyō sect, each using zuzō to proclaim the legitimacy of its own iconographic tradition. The notes were also invaluable sources for different interpretations of scriptures, which often contained ambiguous and contradictory descriptions of deities. Some copyists made willful changes, so that their own school's iconographic traditions would be distinct from those of other Mikkyō groups.

Collecting or copying zuzō became tradition within Mikkyō circles, enjoying a particular vogue during the late twelfth and early thirteenth centuries. Scholarly monks examined the variations and conflicting characteristics of the different pictorial representations of deities. Some collections of zuzō were closely associated with particular masters or schools. The transmission of Truth from master to pupil was often accompanied by the bestowal of such "secret drawings" upon the initiate and, eventually, artistic talent became an indispensable qualification for Mikkyō monks, who often signed their drawings.

In contrast to zuzō, finished Mikkyō Buddhist icons in color—only a few of which have survived from the Heian period—were usually cooperative works by artists attached to workshops, and were therefore devoid of strong individual qualities. Zuzō are thus invaluable to the study of the iconography and aesthetic modes of different periods. Drawings of strange deities are being collected increasingly today for their aesthetic value. They may be appreciated for the pure beauty of line, "unfettered" by color.

Although iconographic drawing and the models for many zuzō themselves can be traced to China (and ultimately to India), only a small number of early examples are known in China.[7] A few Chinese drawings of the T'ang (618–906) and Sung (906–1279) periods have been preserved in Japanese collections, where they were deposited by Japanese monks returning from the continent. The first such drawings were brought home by Kūkai, who presented a catalogued list of the works he had collected to the court in 806.[8] Inspiration for many later works may ultimately be traced to these Chinese models.

The two drawings included here depict the deities and mandalas associated with the ritual dedication for the sutra *Ninnō Hannya Paramittakyō*.[9] The work is known by its abbreviated title, *Ninnōkyō (Sutra of the Benevolent King)*, and is traditionally believed to have been translated by the great Central Asian monk, Kumāragiva (died ca. 400). However, since no Sanskrit original has been found, many scholars regard it as a Chinese work.[10] Because it is chiefly concerned with the protection of a nation, this sutra was considered particularly efficacious for invoking national safety and insuring a good harvest. During the Nara period, when Buddhist teachings provided a moral foundation for government conduct, the *Ninnōkyō* occupied an important place in Japanese public life. Ninnō-e, rituals dedicated to this sutra, were held regularly as early as 660 at the imperial palace and in important temples in Nara, under royal patronage.[11]

Kūkai also brought to Japan the mandalas and icons used in the Ninnōkyō rites.[12] We now know, however, that the sutra he brought back was not Kumāragiva's translation but a version known as the "new translation," made in 765 by Amoghavajra (Fukū, in Japanese) (705–774), under the title *Jen-wang hu-kuo pan-jo po-lo-mi-to-ching (Ninnō-Gokokū Hannya Paramittakyō)*.[13] This version emphasizes the role played by twenty deities, many of whom were "new" iconographic types, as guardians of the sutra: There are five bodhisattvas from the Esoteric teachings and five from the Exoteric, five guardian kings (Myōō), and five directional guardians (for the four cardinal points and their center).

A short commentary, *Jen-wang hu-kuo pan-jo po-lo-mi-to-ching T'o-lo-ni nien-sung i-kuei (Ninnō Gokoku Hannya Paramittakyō Darani Nenju Giki*, in Japanese),[14] edited by a Chinese monk, Liang-pen (716–777), was indispensable to the production of drawings and statues for the Ninnōkyō rites, as it gives specific instructions on the proper execution of the rituals themselves. Particularly important for the monk-artists were the first two chapters, which specify the appropriate physical properties of the deities to be represented, giving their names, the colors of their bodies, and their attributes, and the rules for drawing mandalas.

The two scrolls pertaining to the Ninnōkyō rites which are included here are closely connected with the Kyoto temple of Tōji, the center of Ninnōkyō ritual and zuzō studies. Both scrolls were executed in the quick and supple style that was typical of ink drawing in the late twelfth century. A postscript on Spencer scroll no. 5 states that a mandala included in this scroll was made in the spring of the fifth year of the Jōan era (1175), to be used in the ceremony at Tōji. The other scroll, Spencer no. 10, was in the collection of the Kanchi-in, a sub-temple of Tōji, in 1934, when it was first published in the compendium of zuzō called the *Taishō Daizōkyō Zuzō*.[15]

Although the same deities are represented in these scrolls, the copyists' interests, knowledge, and the variant models they used led to some differences. Scroll no. 5 may be aesthetically more pleasing because of its vigorous brush work, which captures the essential qualities of the deities in a quick and lively manner. Scroll no. 10, on the other hand, is unique because it assembles various types of icons and mandalas used in Ninnōkyō rites. The different types of imagery in the scroll and the brief written comments that accompany them shed light on how this ritual changed through time.

According to a postscript on scroll no. 10, this "secret" work was repaired in 1748 by the monk Kenga, thirteenth abbot of the Kanchi-in (1684–1769), in commemoration of the seventeenth anniversary of the death of Kōrin Chisei of Enju-in. Kenga also wrote, on the new cover of the scroll, the title *Ninnōkyō-hō-Mandara* (*Rules of the Ninnōkyō Mandala*), and *Shinkaku Bon* (*Shinkaku Scroll*). This tells us that the scroll was once in the possession of the monk Shinkaku (1117–1180) of Mt. Kōya, a noted scholar and collector of zuzō, himself the editor of one of the major collections of zuzō, the *Besson Zakki*.[16]

Departing from usual practice, the artists pasted together nine sheets of paper at their short ends to produce a rather short handscroll. In the first drawing, Yakushi, the Healing Buddha (Bhaiṣajyaguru), is depicted as the central deity, attended by a bodhisattva and a monk: It reflects elements drawn from the old Nara period version of the Ninnōkyō rituals, which were dedicated to this buddha. Yet this triad is guarded by four fierce Myōō—with Fudō (Acala in Sanskrit), one of the most important Mikkyō deities in their midst—showing that a profound change had taken place in the theological underpinnings of the Ninnō-e. The guardian Myōō, with their angry countenances and weapons, had replaced the benign bodhisattvas worshipped in the earlier Ninnōkyō rituals.

Below this group are four rows, each with five bodhisattvas, the guardians of the five directions. Their inclusion suggests that Shinkaku must have examined a record of Ninnōkyō-related deities. The different appearance of the deities and the notes in the margins clearly indicate how Ninnōkyō iconography evolved. The first row of figures, standing deities who appear to be traditional, benign bodhisattvas, are identified as belonging to the Nara temple of Akishinodera. They represent therefore, the sutra's iconography before the influence of Mikkyō. The second group are the Myōō, four of whom are portrayed in lively poses with arms flying and legs kicking and are identified as "popular types." The third group, which consists of Fudō-like deities, each in a seated position, exemplifies figures from the "Ono Mandara," a type of mandala attributed to the monk Ningai (951–1046) of the Kyoto temple, Ono Mandaradera.[18] The fourth row, a group of "traditional" bodhisattvas, is identified merely as a type developed by a "certain person."

The zuzō section illustrated here follows these four groups and is accompanied by a long note. It is identified as the "Ninnōkyō Mandala According to the Great Master (Kūkai)." Four of the five narrow columns contain the deities (standing) of the north, the east, the "central direction," and the west (from right to left), four deities to a column. The second column from the left, assigned to the deities of the south, is left empty because, according to the note in the margin, "the original scroll that depicted the southern deities was lost." The note also gives a brief historical background: the

23

sixteen deities were based on original drawings made by Kūkai on four hanging scrolls of paper, kept in the temple of Yamadadera at Kimpusen (south of Nara).[19] The set was later acquired, the note continues, by the abbot of Tokudaiji, but was "unexpectedly removed to the storage of the Hōrin-in at Miidera," east of Kyoto.[20] Around the deities are other notes which name the figures and cite their attributes and the colors of their bodies. These notes are based on descriptions give in the *Ninnōkyō Gokoku Hannya Paramittakyō Darani Nenju Giki.*

Two additional groups of bodhisattvas and guardian kings are represented in the two rows below this group. Commentary in the margin tells us that these figures were copied from drawings in the sutra repository at Miidera, the most important center for iconographic studies in the Tendai sect. The Miidera drawings were in turn based on a version brought from China by the monk Enchin (posthumously, Chishō Daishi, 814–891), the founder of that temple, who brought many Chinese iconographic drawings to Japan in 858. Both groups of deities are seated, but beyond that, few elements distinguish them from figures intended for the Shingon sect. It was, however, quite fitting for Shinkaku, an astute scholar of zuzō, to have included Tendai iconography, although the Tendai sect was the arch-enemy of his own Shingon school.[21]

These drawings are followed by a list of the deities' names, both in Chinese and Sanskrit characters, and more detailed descriptions of their attributes.

Another important feature of this scroll is seen in its second group of drawings, which gives pictorial instructions on how to paint mandalas for the Ninnōkyō rituals. Four mandalas are included in this scroll; the drawing for the second one was made by "the late abbot Kakuin," according to the accompanying note. Since Kakuin of Mt. Kōya died in 1164 and Shinkaku, who assembled these drawings, died in 1180, this scroll should be dated to the intervening period.

Spencer scroll no. 5 includes less historical information about individual figures, but is important because it identifies the collections to which some of the source-mandalas belonged and the special occasions for which they were produced.[22] For example, the mandala reproduced here is identified in the accompanying note as the "mandala of the Abbot of Ono." It is also noted that this abbot (Ningai) had a monk-artist named Nyoshō paint the original for the rituals, which were conducted for noblemen as a prayer for increased personal wealth.

The Ninnōkyō rituals, which during the Nara period were intended for the benefit of the nation and the public, were performed increasingly for individuals during the Heian period—to ward off accidents, to increase personal wealth, to ensure the defeat of personal enemies, and to guarantee the success of love affairs[23]—all purposes which would have been regarded as unthinkable during the Nara period. The mandala reproduced here, which was considered particularly effective for increasing personal wealth, depicts Fudō in the center with the deities associated with the easterly direction at the top, so it could be hung on the east wall of the prayer hall.

Following this drawing is a schematic arrangement of the names of the deities represented in it. The note that accompanies the diagram, however, states that its model was a work belonging to Daigoji, which was based on the "Ono Mandala" but was "converted" for use in another Ninnōkyō ritual devoted to prayers for personal safety. It is thought that this change was made at the Daigoji temple by its abbot, Jōkai (1074–1149), who moved the deities of the north to the top of the composition and hung the revised mandala on the north wall.[24]

The final mandala in Spencer scroll no. 5, another diagram of the names of deities, is accompanied by the above-mentioned postscript stating that it is a copy of the mandala used at Tōji in the Ninnōkyō rite conducted in the spring of 1175. This gives us the earliest possible date for the scroll.

NOTES

1. For Mikkyō, see Minoru Kiyota, *Shingon Buddhism: Theory and Practice* (Los Angeles and Tokyo, 1978).
2. For the life and work of Kūkai, see Yoshito S. Hakeda, *Kūkai: Major Works* (New York, 1972).
3. Ishida Hisatoyo, *Mikkyō Ga*, no. 33 of *Nihon no Bijutsu*, ed. staffs of the National Museums of Tokyo, Kyoto, and Nara (Tokyo, 1969); Takaaki Sawa, *Art in Japanese Esoteric Buddhism*, trans. R.L. Gage, *Heibonsha Survey of Japanese Art*, vol. 8 (Tokyo, 1972).
4. Giuseppe Tucci, *The Theory and Practice of the Mandala* (London, 1961); Ryūjun Tajima, *Les deux grands mandalas et la doctrine de l'ésotérisme shingon* (Tokyo, 1959); Sawa Takaaki and Hamada Takashi (eds.), *Mikkyō Bijutsu Taikan*, vol. I (Tokyo, 1983).
5. Quoted by Kūkai in his catalogue of Chinese sutras and drawings that he brought home from China. See Hakeda, *Kukai*, pp. 145–146.
6. Sawa Takaaki, *Hakubyō Zuzō no Kenkyū* (Kyoto, 1982); and Hamada Takashi, *Zuzō*, no. 55 of *Nihon no Bijutsu*, ed. staffs of the National Museums of Tokyo, Kyoto, and Nara (Tokyo, 1970).
7. For examples of Chinese works, see Roderick Whitfield, *The Art of Central Asia: The Stein Collection in the British Museum, I, Paintings from Dunhuang* (Tokyo, 1982).
8. For a summary of this catalogue, see Hakeda, *Kukai*, pp. 140–150, and for a complete list, see Sofū Sen'yōkai (ed.), *Kōbō Daishi Zenshū*, vol. I (Kyoto, 1910), pp. 69–104.
9. Takakusu Junjirō and Watanabe Kaigyoku (eds.), *Taishō Shinshū Daizōkyō*, vol. 8 (Tokyo, 1924), pp. 825–834, hereafter, *Daizokyo*.
10. Mochizuki Shinkō, *Bukkyō Kyōten Seiritsu-shi Ron* (Kyoto, 1978), 2d ed., pp. 425–441.
11. Kameda Tsutomu, "Mafu Bokuga Bosatsu to Ninnō-e to (An Image of Bosatsu in the Shōsō-in and the Ninnōye)" I, *Kokka*, 659 (February 1947), p. 117.
12. Kūkai's catalogue only includes items which were intended for official use, and not those he kept for his own personal use. The *Ninnōkyō Mandara* was apparently one he kept for his own use. See Sawa, *Hakubyō Zuzo*, p. 37.
13. *Daizokyo*, vol. 8, no. 246, pp. 834–44.
14. *Daizokyo*, vol. 19, no. 994, pp. 514–19.
15. This scroll was partially reproduced in Ono Gemmyō (ed.), *Taishō Shinshū Daizōkyō Zuzō*, hereafter referred to as *Zuzo* (Tokyo, 1934), vol. 12, pp. 938–940.
16. The *Besson Zakki* is reproduced in *Zuzo*, vol. 3.
17. Nakano Genzō, "Ninnōkyō-hō to Fudō Myōō," in Sawa and Hamada, *Mikkyo Bijutsu*, vol. 3, p. 193.
18. Ono Mandaradera in Kyoto, founded by Ningai, is officially known as Zuishin-in.
19. The originals of these drawings were supposed to have been painted by Kūkai himself, but are no longer extant. There are, however, two copies of these paintings (both made in 1181), now at Tōji and Daigoji, which include later replacements of the southern deities. In these copies, and in the Spencer scrolls no. 10 and 5, one bodhisattva who is traditional in appearance, Fugen (Samantabhadra in Sanskrit; second column, second from top in Spencer scroll no. 10), is identified as Fugen 'Taisei' (Ta-sheng in Chinese), instead of 'bosatsu', as is more common in Japan, suggesting a Chinese origin of these images.
20. Miidera on Lake Biwa is officially known as Onjōji.
21. In the twelfth century, the 'secrecy' of zuzō seems to have been undermined. Chishō's zuzō, kept at Miidera, seem to have been the frequent target of raids by the Tōmitsu group of monks. See Nakano Genzō, "Sō shōrai zuzō no dempa (Transmission of Buddhist Iconography Imported from Sung China)," *Kokka*, 1026 (1979), p. 35.

22. The drawings in this scroll are very similar to those included in the *Kakuzen Shō*, another large and important collection of zuzō, edited by Kakuzen (1143–?1213). See *Zuzo*, vols. 4 and 5; vol. 4 (pp. 368–371) reproduces the same deities and mandalas as this scroll does. This scroll must have once belonged to the collection of Abbot Kōki of Chishaku-in in Kyoto (1752–1822), who impressed his seal on its frontispiece.

23. Ariga Yoshitaka, "Jinjōji-bon Ninnōkyō Mandara Zu kō (An Interpretation of the Ninnōkyō Mandala of the Jinjōji)," *Bukkyō Geijutsu*, no. 120 (September 1978), p. 28. This mandala is also accompanied by a short note that hesitatingly attributes the drawing to Abbot Genkai (1093–1157), the sixteenth abbot of Daigoji.

24. Nishigōri Kyōsuke, "Ninnōkyō Mandara no keishiki (Style of Paintings in the Jen-wang-ching Mandala)," *Bukkyō Geijutsu*, no. 101 (April 1975), p. 74.

6
Four Guardians of the Cardinal Directions (*Shitennō*), from the *Zuzō Shō* (*Collection of Iconographic Drawings*)

1264, Kamakura period
By the monk Kōei (or Kōin)
One handscroll, ink and light colors on paper
H: 28.7 cm, L: 1,229 cm
Spencer no. 17

Zuzō, drawings of Buddhist deities made for the purpose of clarifying iconography, began to be assembled, studied, and copied in earnest from the eleventh century on in Japan (see no. 5). Originally intended to transmit "secrets" of Buddhist iconography from master to pupil, zuzō were eventually made available to people outside the select group of initiates. This was due in part to an increasing interest in the original models for the drawings, particularly those fashioned after imported Chinese works. Also, many branch schools had formed within the Mikkyō sect, and each made efforts to assemble zuzō to legitimize its own theological contentions. At the same time, the continuing transmission of "secret" iconographic traditions led to corruption of, and deviations from, the original scriptural requirements for such works. This caused grave concern among the learned Mikkyō monks, who began to codify the iconographic properties of deities according to specifications set forth in scriptures.

The oldest extant compendium of zuzō, the *Zuzō Shō*, also known as the *Jikkan Shō* (*Collection in Ten Scrolls*), was edited early in the twelfth century. It was an encyclopedic work containing a representative selection of the deities who were worshipped widely at the time. The circumstances under which this collection was compiled are unknown and no fragments of the original manuscripts have been preserved. The oldest extant copy, owned by the Daigoji temple in Kyoto and dated ca. 1193, includes a statement attributing its original model to the monk Yōgen (1075–1151) of the Mt. Kōya monastery, who compiled it around 1129 at the request of the retired emperor Toba (reigned 1107–1123). It attributes the drawings to the monk Ejū of Daigoji.[1] The apparent involvement of two monks in the production of this work eventually led to controversy later on; scarcely one hundred years after the original set was completed, a colophon in a version owned by the Jōraku-in temple in Kyoto, dated to 1226, stated that although the original work was commonly attributed to Yōgen, its real author was Ejū. The controversy continues even today.[2]

The original format and scope of the *Zuzō Shō* may be reconstructed with the help of later copies, especially the set in the Daigoji collection (ca. 1193).[3] In its original state, the *Zuzō Shō* contained 142 illustrations in ten scrolls; the illustrations were divided into sections according to the categories of deities: buddhas (scrolls 1 and 2); mandalas (scroll 3); bodhisattvas (scrolls 4 and 5); manifestations of Kannon, the most merciful of all bodhisattvas (scrolls 6 and 7); wrathful gods (scroll 8); and devas, the Hindu gods incorporated into the Buddhist pantheon as guardians (scrolls 9 and 10). Each deity is identified both by its Japanese and Sanskrit name; by its symbolic name that captures its essential qualities (in Sanskrit); and by its attributes and mantras (*dharani* in Sanskrit) ("true words" used in incantations). The compendium also includes brief notes on the history of the deities' rituals and a commentary on the divergent iconographic traditions of different schools. Some of the examples cited in this collection may have been modeled after works of painting or sculpture which still exist. Also important are the passages from scriptural sources that specifically describe the iconographic features of each deity or mandala.

The *Zuzō Shō*, which is indeed worthy of its reputation as an encyclopedia of Mikkyō iconography, established a standard formula for later collections of iconographic drawings, and has been copied many times through the ages.

The scroll included here may originally have been a part of a ten-scroll set; it corresponds to the ninth scroll of a complete series. Twenty-five figures of such important Mikkyō guardians as the "Group of Twelve" (*Jūniten*) are included, as are such popular icons of Mikkyō as Kankiten (Nandikeśvara in Sanskrit), who is usually represented with two elephant-headed, human-bodied figures embracing, and deities astride birds, such as Naraenten (Sanskrit, Nārāyaṇa) and Kumaraten (Sanskrit, Kumāra).

The four guardians reproduced here are not exclusive to Mikkyō. They are *Shitennō*, the guardians of the cardinal directions, gods who have occupied an important place in Buddhist iconography from the earliest years of Japanese Buddhism. Dressed in armor, Shitennō are commonly placed at the four corners of the podium used for statues of buddhas, or at the four corners of mandalas. From right to left, Jikokuten, Zōchōten, Kōmokuten, and Tamonten guard the east, south, west and north, respectively.

Each guardian is accompanied by a description written according to a standard format used throughout the scroll (mentioned above), followed by a rather long comparison of

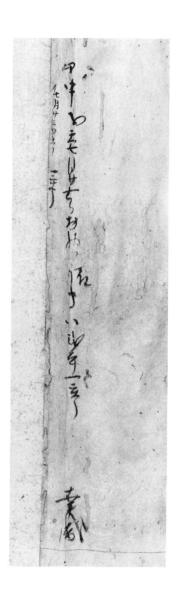

two known sculpted sets of the deities: a mid-eighth-century group in the Great Buddha Hall of Tōdaiji, Nara,[4] and a ninth-century set in the Kōdō of Tōji, Kyoto.

Each of the Shitennō in the Spencer scroll stands on a rock base and wears armor that was popular in Japan at the time—plate armor over a kimono-like garment. Each holds the weapons that symbolize his military role. The deity of the north, Tamonten, is also known in popular religion as Bishamonten. Considered an especially effective guardian of personal wealth, Tamonten is always distinguished from other guardian deities by a miniature pagoda in his right hand.

At the end of the scroll a brief postscript states that the work was made on request and that it was modeled after a certain zuzō collection. It includes the sixty-year cyclical calendar date of the Year of the Monkey (Kōshin), which corresponds to the years 1204, 1264, or 1324 (and dates earlier or later). The signature on the statement may read either "Kōei" or "Kōin."

Although the author of the scroll did not identify his model, it was probably the Daigoji scroll, or one based on it, since his work closely resembles the late twelfth century version in many respects.[5] The drawings in the Spencer scroll are somewhat amateurish and lack such details as decorative designs on the armor. However, the ink lines are vigorous and resilient, a characteristic of many of the zuzō of the thirteenth century. Of the possible dates for the production of this scroll, the year 1264 is therefore the most reasonable.

NOTES

1. For the most detailed study of this scroll, see Tamura Ryūshō, "Zuzō Shō seiritsu to naiyō ni kansuru mondai (Various Problems in the Compilation of *Zuzō Shō*)," *Bukkyō Geijutsu*, no. 70 (March 1969), pp. 42–66.
2. For a summary of this controversy, see Tamura, "Zuzo Sho," p. 43.
3. The last scroll in this set is a much later replacement. Only a few figures from this set have been reproduced; see Tamura, "Zuzo Sho," and Hamada Takashi, *Zuzō*, no. 55 (Tokyo, 1970), of *Nihon no Bijutsu*, ed. staffs of the National Museums of Tokyo, Kyoto, and Nara. A copy in the collection of Entsūji, Mt. Kōya, is almost complete, and reproduced in its entirety. See Ono Gemmyō (ed.), *Taishōshinshū Daizōkyō Zuzō*, vol. 3 (Tokyo, 1932), pp. 1–55.
4. The group of Shitennō at Nara was destroyed in the civil war of 1567. Replacements started in 1799 still exist, the heads of Zōchōten and Jikokuten were made, but only Kōmokuten and Tamonten were completed.
5. See Tamura, "Zuzo Sho," for a partial reproduction of this version.

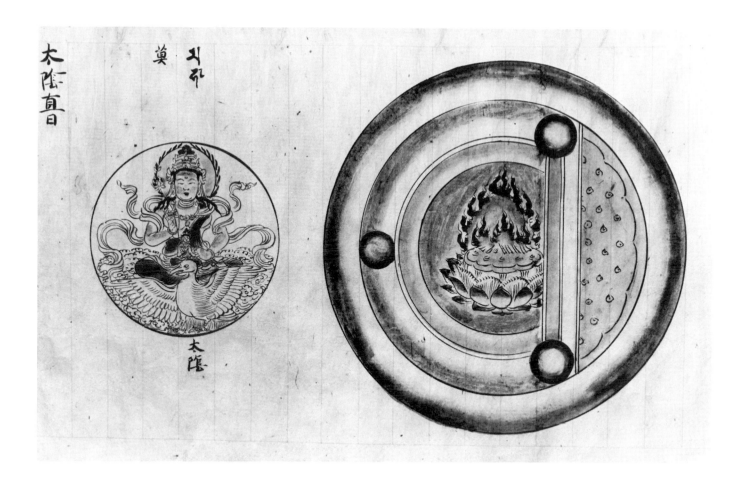

7
The Moon and Five of the Twenty-eight Lunar Mansions from the *Seishuku Gomahō* (*Manual of the Astral Homa Rituals*)

Early to mid-twelfth century, Late Heian period
One handscroll, ink and light color on paper
H: 30.6 cm, L: 1,191.1 cm
Spencer no. 14

In many ancient civilizations, astronomy was not distinguished from astrology, and astrologers were held in particular honor. They had mastered, it was believed, the art of prognostication and had the ability to select auspicious days for conducting business, affairs of love, and seeing to personal matters. The ancient art of star-gazing was shared by many different cultures, and it is often difficult to pinpoint the origin of certain aspects of astral iconography. Anthropomorphic representations of the celestial bodies, for example, endowed them with attributes that remain much the same throughout the various cultures and civilizations of the ancient world.

Ancient Chinese astrologers were connected with the sovereign, who was himself known as the "Son of Heaven." Knowledge of astral phenomena was central to many of the sciences in ancient China, but it was probably modified by elements introduced from the outside world[1]—particularly the beliefs and rituals brought from India with Mikkyō, or Esoteric Buddhism (see no. 6). Once brought to China, Esoteric Buddhism, which viewed the entire universe as a manifestation of its supreme Buddha, Mahā-vairocana (Dainichi in Japanese), incorporated other cult practices, including the cosmology of China's native Taoism, into its tradition. Designed to foretell destiny and to help overcome the influence of unfavorable astral configurations, Esoteric Buddhism's rituals played an indispensable role in the religious life of China.

The art of divination in Japan derives from beliefs and practices that were introduced through the Chinese. Scriptures on the art of determining the course of destiny were a part of the large body of Chinese literature brought home by Japanese monks—most important among them, Kūkai (774–836).[2]

The three manuscripts on stars and planets included here were made for use in Mikkyō circles. The first (no. 7) is a manual for rituals performed on the days determined by the configuration of the stars; the second (no. 8) is a sort of horoscope based on the nine constellations; the third (no. 9) is a listing of the twenty-eight Lunar Mansions.

A notation in small letters at the beginning of this scroll of the Homa Rituals states that the work was dedicated as a prayer for the peaceful afterlives of the parents of the donor and the prosperity of his clan. The frontispiece, the cover, and the text are lost, but a similar work (dated to 1362) in the Kanchi-in, a sub-temple of Tōji, indicates that the Spencer scroll's title must have read "The Homa [burning of offerings for purification] Rituals Dedicated to the Seven Planets and Twenty-Eight Lunar Mansions."[3] The Kanchi-in scroll also helps to determine the nature of the long text that was lost from the Spencer scroll, describing the rituals believed to be effective in invoking divine assistance to achieve prosperity of the clan, the respect and affection of others, the defeat of an enemy, and personal health and longevity. Also included are details pertaining to the rituals—such as utensils to be used, offerings to be made, and preparations for the purification that preceded the actual rituals.

Ink drawings with light touches of red, orange, blue, and green delineate the hearths upon which the offerings were burned in sacred fire. Circular, triangular, and square hearths are depicted, each with some floral embellishment and a *vajra* (thunderbolt), a ritual object used in Mikkyō ceremonies; lotus-shaped burners, such as the one reproduced here are also shown. Alongside the hearths are images of the seven planets, each depicted as a bodhisattva seated within a circle. The sequence begins with Jupiter (on a bull); followed by Venus, Mars (on a lion), Mercury, the Sun (on a horse), the Moon (on a bird, shown here), and Saturn (on an elephant). Above the figures of the planets are Chinese inscriptions in black ink, which give the Sogdian names of the planets, along with their Sanskrit equivalents, written in Siddham characters with red ink.

The hearth reproduced here is intended for rituals which were performed to avert calamities associated with lunar influence. The Moon is depicted within a disk, as a bodhisattva astride a goose. Above the disk is a Chinese character for the Sogdian name of this body ("darkness"), and its Sanskrit equivalent. A long text following the illustration reveals among other things that the Moon assists ministers and nobles at court, and has a favorable influence on activities involving liquids—digging wells, watering gardens and forests, making wine, washing garments, and bathing. Days influenced by

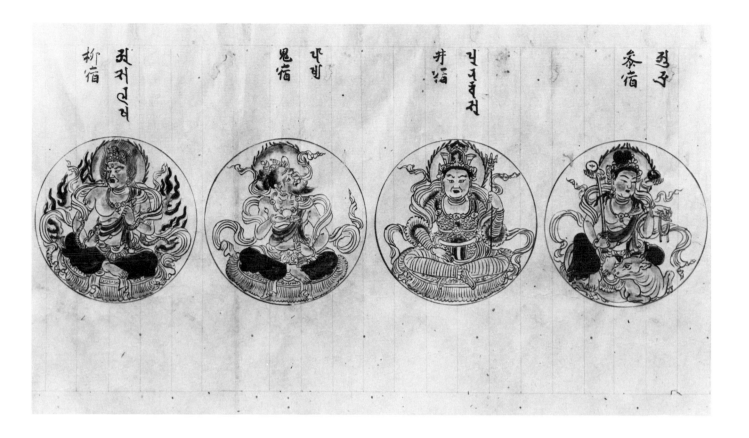

the Moon are also good for taking a wife and building a house. However, one should avoid putting grain in storage, and certainly should not engage an army, perform medical operations, sew garments, or travel on such days. Furthermore, lost objects will not be found, prisoners will not be released, and plans for deception will fail.

Those born under the influence of the Moon are filial and talented, intelligent, yet modest; men will have many wives and women will have no difficulty finding husbands. If surrounded by enemy forces when under lunar influence, generals should wear garments and armor of green and raise banners decorated with green jewels.

Following the picture and description of the planet Saturn are the representations of the Twenty-Eight Lunar Mansions. Known in India as *Naksatras*, the system of Twenty-Eight Lunar Mansions is based on the length of time it takes the Moon to rotate around the earth. Its mythological roots may be found in the belief that this restless satellite has twenty-eight (twenty-seven in India) night "lodgings" and an equal number of consorts. The system seems to have been known in China before Han times (206 B.C. to A.D. 221).[4]

There are only twenty-six figures in the Spencer scroll; the first two were apparently lost. Like the seven planets, each mansion is depicted as a bodhisattva within a disk. Above them their Chinese names are written in black ink, and their mantras ("true words") in red ink. The four mansions reproduced here are (from right to left): Shinshuku, on a bull (in Orion); Seishuku, dressed in armor (in Gemini); Kishuku, an old man (in Cancer); and Ryūshuku, a fierce-looking deity (in Hydra).

The Spencer scroll closely resembles the Kanchi-in scroll, which is complete and aids us in reconstructing lost portions of the Spencer scroll. The Kanchi-in scroll, which was copied by Kempō, the second abbot of that temple, also includes some postscripts from his model. According to one of them, Kempō's model was made at the residence of the monk Toba Sōjō, and was in the collection of the Hōrin-in at Miidera, near Kyoto. This work was in turn modeled after a T'ang dynasty Chinese scroll, brought to Japan by a monk named Eun (798–869) of the Kyoto temple, Anshōji.[5]

A large number of iconographic drawings are known to have been stored at the Hōrin-in, a sub-temple at Miidera where Kakuyū, the legendary scholar-monk (1053–1140) lived. Known by the nickname Toba Sōjō (Abbot Toba) after he was made abbot of the temple, he is often associated with lively narrative paintings of the late twelfth century.[6] Although the attribution of these secular paintings to him is dismissed by most modern scholars, Kakuyū is known to have been an avid collector of iconographic drawings, some of which he may even have done himself.

The scroll in the Spencer collection contains superb drawings which can be dated to the first half of the twelfth century on the basis of their restrained, yet strong and supple line. This scroll is, in fact, the earliest of the three manuscripts of the constellations included here.[7] The full-faced, plump figures of the bodhisattvas and the unusual chain-mail armor worn by Seishuku (second from the right in the illustration) echo the art of T'ang China (618–906). Although there is no proof that this scroll was the model for the Kanchi-in version, this hypothesis is a distinct possibility. In any event, the Spencer scroll must have either been based directly on a Chinese work or on a close Japanese copy.

NOTES

1. Edward H. Schafer, *Pacing the Void: T'ang Approach to the Stars* (Berkeley, 1977), p. 10. For a good survey of Chinese astrology, see Joseph Needham, *Science and Civilization in China*, vol. 3 (London and New York, 1959), pp. 171ff, and Shigeru Nakayama, "Characteristics of Chinese Astrology," *Isis*, no. 57 (1966), pp. 442–454.
2. See the catalogue of sutras that he brought back from China. Sofū Sen'yōkai (ed.), *Kōbō Daishi Zenshū*, vol. 1 (Kyoto, 1910), p. 80.
3. See Ono Gemmyō (ed.), *Taishō Shinshū Daizōkyō Zuzō*, vol. 7 (Tokyo, 1933), pp. 815ff.
4. Schafer, *Pacing the Void*, p. 79, and Needham, *Science*, pp. 238–239.
5. Kempō also added a comment at the end of his copy that he thought the model scroll he used was based on a Chinese work brought to Japan by monk Jōkyō (died 866). The monks Enchin (the founder of Miidera, posthumously known as Chishō) and Jōkyō seem to have brought home similar scrolls. Kempō also includes an inscription which was found in his model stating that Enchin's Chinese work was made in 855.
6. The scrolls which are often associated with his name are the *Chōjū Giga* (*Frolicking Animals*) in the Kōzanji collection, and the *Shigisan Engi Emaki* (*The Legend of Shigisan*) in the Chōgosonshiji collection. See Tanaka Ichimatsu (ed.), *Shinshū Nihon Emakimono Zenshū*, vols. 4 and 3 respectively (Tokyo, 1976).
7. I am grateful to Yanagisawa Taka of the Research Institute of Art History, Tokyo, for dating this scroll on the basis of comparative studies with many other Buddhist paintings, such as the image of Fugen Emmei at Jikōji, Hiroshima, which was dedicated to that temple in 1153. See Sawa Takaaki and Hamada Takashi (eds.), *Mikkyō Bijutsu Taikan*, vol. 3 (Tokyo, 1984), Pl. 15 for a reproduction of this painting.

8
Venus and Ketu, from the *Kuyō Hiryaku* (*The Secrets of the Nine Luminaries*)

Mid-twelfth century, Late Heian period
Book with 56 pages
Ink and light colors on paper
Each page, H: 18.7 cm, W: 15.7 cm
Spencer no. 12

PUBLISHED: John M. Rosenfield and Elizabeth ten Grotenhuis, *Journey of the Three Jewels: Japanese Buddhist Paintings from Western Collections* (New York, 1979), no. 27; Yanagisawa Taka (ed.), *Bukkyō Kaiga*, in Shimada Shūjirō *et al.* (eds.), *Zaigai Nihon no Shihō*, vol. 1 (Tokyo, 1980), nos. 91, 92; Nakano Genzō, "Kanchi-in shozō Kuyō Hiryaku ni tsuite (The Kuyō Hiryaku—Iconography of the Deities of the Nine Luminaries—owned by the Kanchi-in)," *Museum*, 218 (1969), pp. 13–24.

The second work in the group of three manuscripts illustrating the celestial bodies is a small codex with seventeen illustrations. The figures represent Nine Luminaries, seven planets, and two imaginary planetoids, the lunar nodes called "Rāhu" and "Ketu." The Luminaries are illustrated according to two different iconographic traditions, with the first set accompanied by texts, and the second by a sort of appendix. The two groups are listed below in order of appearance; the figures from the second group (in the latter half of the book) are listed in parentheses.

The Nine Luminaries are the Sun, a woman in courtly costume, wearing a crown decorated with dragon heads, a horse, and a bird (a lion-headed man); the Moon, also a courtly woman with a similar headdress (a young woman in trousers and a tunic-like coat); Mars, a four-armed soldier holding weapons and dressed in armor with a donkey's head cap (an elephant); Mercury, a woman in courtly dress with a monkey on her head, holding a scroll and a brush (a dragon); Jupiter, a man in a flowing kimono-like robe, who sports a fish-tail and a boar's head on his head (a dragon-headed man in courtly robes); Venus, reproduced here, a female musician with a *biwa*—a lute-like instrument— and a rooster cap (a young woman astride a cock); Saturn, a grotesque, aging demon with a bull's-head cap (a half-naked man wearing a bull's-head cap, astride a bull); Rāhu, a three-headed, half-naked demon riding a bull and holding a small figure of a bodhisattva in one of his four arms (the figure for this "non-planet" was either lost from the second group or never illustrated there); and Ketu, shown here, even more grotesque and threatening than Rāhu (a panther-like spotted animal, not identified, although it could be Ketu).

Except for obvious differences between Mercury (woman/dragon) and Mars (warrior/ elephant), the iconography of the illustrations is fairly constant. A notable feature of the first set, however, is that the figures are humans, and the animals associated with them are relegated to minor positions, emerging, for example, only in their headgear. The figures in the second group on the other hand, have either been completely transformed into beasts, or are imaginary creatures with human bodies and the heads of animals.

The planets depicted in this codex are a far cry from the divine bodhisattvas represented in the *Astral Homa Rituals* (see no. 7). There is even a secular air about the figures, many of whom wear courtly robes, with ribbons fluttering about them. It is also notable that some of these figures are familiar to the West, which suggests that western elements had been introduced to Chinese astrology. Venus, for example, is depicted as a female musician, and Saturn, as an old man.

The difference in iconography that separates this codex from such works as the scroll of the *Astral Homa Rituals* may stem from two different traditions. First, the Buddhist images in the *Homa Rituals* manual are derived from iconographic types prevalent in the depictions of mandalas. On the other hand, the anthropomorphic representations of the celestial bodies may be based on descriptions from scriptural sources. For example, the *Shichiyō Jōsai Ketsu* (*Secrets for Shunning Disaster Through the Seven Planets*),[1] which was translated into Chinese (*Ch'i-yao jang-tsai-chüeh*) in the late ninth century by Chin-chu-cha, specifies that Venus should appear as a female deity, in yellow garments, wearing a rooster cap, and playing a biwa.

Also, the assertion of Chinese taste should not be ignored. Anthropomorphic representations of planets are not uncommon in China. Similar figures are found on Buddhist wall paintings recovered from caves in Tun-huang,[2] and on a silk hanging, now in the British Museum (dated to 897).[3] While these examples reveal a strong native Taoist influence on Buddhist icons, anthropomorphic paintings of the celestial bodies made outside of the Buddhist context also exist. The most famous is a Chinese handscroll, now in the Osaka Municipal Museum, which is often attributed to an early sixth-century painter, Chang Seng-yu.[4]

The Spencer book of *Nine Luminaries*, which was in the collection of the Kanchi-in at Tōji until the 1960s,[5] has been damaged; water and worm-holes have destroyed parts of the text. The missing text can be inferred, however, from other versions, most notably one in the Metropolitan Museum of Art, New York (dated to 1125),[6] another in the Museum of Fine Arts, Boston (dated to 1224),[7] and a late eighteenth-century copy of a work by the monk Kōnen (1120–1203) in the Kanchi-in.[8] These four works resemble each other closely and appear to derive from a common source. The author of the *Kuyō Hiryaku*, however, remains unknown. The text itself closely resembles the *Homa Rituals*, also included in this exhibition. It is stated at the beginning of the *Kuyō Hiryaku* that the secrets of stellar phenomena are difficult to understand, and that various treatises were consulted before compiling the book.[9]

After prayers are offered to Byakue Kannon (White-Robed Avalokiteśvara), emblem of piety, to overcome difficult astrological configurations, the auspicious and inauspicious influences of the planets and stars are revealed. Each planet is named in Chinese, then in Sogdian, Persian, and Sanskrit. Mantras ("true words") follow, written in Siddham characters. Some of the signs found under the influence of Venus, reproduced here, are said to benefit giving audience to noblemen, moving armies, planning business dealings, repairing houses, studying medicine, and sewing and washing garments. This is also said to be an excellent time to plan marriages. However, Venus has adverse effects on plans to construct tombs, arrange funerals, or visit sick people. The sick will not improve, prisoners will not be freed, runaways will be caught, and plans for robberies will fail. Those born under this star are intelligent and lucky. They respect their elders, behave in a filial manner toward their parents, and are loyal to their families and friends. They are high-spirited and high-minded, but not greedy. Armor and garments of white are recommended for the generals and officers who fight under this star.

No explanation of the horrendous figure Ketu is given in this codex, save for its mantras. Such scriptural sources as the *Bonten Kara Kuyō* (*The Hours of Brahmadeva and the Nine Luminaries*)[10] refer briefly to the disastrous influences exerted by this monster non-planet: there will be obstacles in obtaining offices, and a multitude of worries and illnesses. Rulers are advised not to venerate him. Ketu is shown in an ambiguous pose above a dragon, crouching but not quite sitting on it. He has three large, angry faces and three pairs of arms. The uppermost pair holds disks of the Sun (with a crow) and the Moon (with a quassia tree and a hare), and the center pair clutches a small human figure and a bemused-looking rabbit. Several snakes are entwined about Ketu's limbs (one is caught in his mouth), and his fat torso is adorned with a necklace of skulls. Ketu and his companion, Rāhu, are creations of Vedic Indian lore, according to which Rāhu drank the gods' forbidden wine and as a punishment was decapitated by Vishnu. Rāhu's head and torso flew around the sky, trying to devour the Sun and the Moon, who had reported his mischief to Vishnu. Rāhu's head, which represents the ascending node of the lunar eclipse, retained the original name, but his torso and tail, representing the descending node, came to be known as Ketu.

The drawings in this codex were originally much more colorful. Traces of blues and greens are still discernible in many places, and pale pinks are relatively well preserved. The drawings are unsigned and undated, but are reminiscent of other *zuzō* (iconographic drawings) dated to around 1165, with crisp, sharp ink lines that often begin with heavier touches.[11] If the date of the early or mid-twelfth century is accepted for this codex, it will be the second earliest dated work of the three versions of the *Nine Luminaries* currently in American collections; it is also far more refined and aesthetically superior to the other two examples. The figures in this codex reflect strong influences of T'ang dynasty Chinese elements, with their short, stout bodies, feminine full-moon faces, and elaborate costumes. This influence may also be seen in the corpulent naked bodies of Rāhu and Ketu. The armor worn by Mars suggests that the Chinese model for this book could have been a late T'ang work.[12]

NOTES

1. Takakusu Junjirō and Watanabe Kaigyoku (eds.), *Taishō Shinshū Daizōkyō*, vol. 21, no. 1308 (Tokyo, 1928).
2. Aurel Stein, *Serindia: Detailed Report of Exploration in Central Asia and Westernmost China*, vol. 2 (Oxford, 1921), Fig. 215.
3. Roderick Whitfield, *The Art of Central Asia, The Stein Collection in the British Museum I, Paintings from Dunhuang* (Tokyo, 1982), p. 323.
4. Partially reproduced in Osvald Sirén, *Chinese Painting: Leading Masters and Principles*, vol. 3 (London, 1956), Pls. 16–17. Yashiro Yukio "Gosei Nijūhasshuku Shingyō Zukan (Scroll of the Five Planets and the Twenty-eight Stellar Mansions)," *Bijutsu Kenkyū* 139 (1944), pp. 241–258. This painting is generally considered a T'ang copy, or sometimes a Sung copy. See Sherman E. Lee, *A History of Far Eastern Art*, 4th ed. (New York, 1982), p. 258. It is also the earliest known Taoist representation of the constellations. See Nojiri Hōei, *Hoshi to Tōhō Bijutsu* (Tokyo, 1971), pp. 133–144.
5. Nakano Genzō, "Kanchi-in shozō Kuyō Hiryaku ni tsuite (The Kuyō Hiryaku—Iconography of the Deities of the Nine Luminaries—Owned by the Kanchi-in)," *Museum* 218 (1969), pp. 13–24.

6. Shimada Shūjirō (ed.), *Zaigai Hihō*, vol. 1 (Tokyo, 1969), Pl. 35.

7. Shimada, *Zaigai*, vol. 1 (text), Fig. 4.

8. Ono Gemmyō (ed.), *Taishō Shinshū Daizōkyō Zuzō*, vol. 7 (Tokyo, 1933), pp. 769–773.

9. See Nakano, "Kanchi-in," pp. 21–24, for other scriptures which might have served as sources for the compilation of this treatise. He attributes its authorship to a Japanese (p. 23). But Morita Ryūsen attributes it to a late T'ang Chinese author. See his *Mikkyō Senseihō*, vol. 1 (Kyoto, 1974), p. 85.

10. *Daizokyo*, vol. 21, no. 1311.

11. Yanagisawa Taka (ed.), *Bukkyō Kaiga*, in Shimada Shūjirō *et al.* (eds.), *Zaigai Nihon no Shihō*, vol. 1, nos. 91 and 92.

12. For costumes, see Shen Ts'ung-wen (ed.), *Chung-kuo ku-tai fu-shih yen-chiu* (Hong Kong, 1981).

9

Five Figures from the *Nijūhasshuku* (*Scroll of the Twenty-eight Lunar Mansions*)

First half of the thirteenth century, Kamakura period
By the monk Anshun
One handscroll, ink on paper
H: 20.9 cm, L: 256.9 cm
Spencer no. 22

PUBLISHED: Ono Gemmyō (ed.), *Taishō Shinshū Daizōkyō Zuzō*, vol. 7 (1933), pp. 775–800.

The last of the Spencer Collection's three representations of the planetary bodies is known as the *Scroll of the Twenty-eight Lunar Mansions* (*Nijūhasshuku*; see no. 7); it is yet another series of secular personifications of the planets. The departure from standard Buddhist practice becomes apparent as one compares the figure at the extreme right in the group represented here, the twenty-fourth mansion (Ryūshuku), with the same figure in the handscroll of the *Astral Homa Rituals* (no. 7), where it is depicted as a bodhisattva. Despite this notable difference, the postscript and the note on its repair show that the *Scroll of the Twenty-eight Lunar Mansions* was made at a Buddhist temple and that the drawings were by a monk called Anshun (also known as Kyōōbō). The scroll was modeled after a work owned by the monk Jōen, whose name appears on a number of *zuzō* (iconographic drawings).[1] His name is also recorded on the portraits of patriarchs of the Shingon and Tendai sects, made in 1230 and kept at the Treasure House of Tōji.[2] Since the zuzō associated with this monk were all in the Kanchi-in at Tōji, it seems likely that Jōen worked at that temple.

The Spencer scroll was also at the Kanchi-in during the eighteenth century, when it was repaired at the order of the thirteenth abbot, Kenga (1684–1769). Kenga, who was deeply committed to the preservation of the numerous treasures in his charge, entered his name, age, and the time of repair at the end of many scrolls (see no. 5, scroll II). The present scroll was repaired in 1737, when he was 54 years old. In his postscript, Kenga notes that the missing parts at the beginning of the scroll had been replaced. The replacement was apparently lost or removed sometime before 1933, when the entire scroll (still in the collection) was reproduced, but without the first four figures.[3]

The twenty-eight lunar mansions (in Sanskrit, Naksatras) represent the moon's twenty-eight temporary resting places in the heavens. The belief in lunar lodgings was known in China even before the introduction of Buddhism from India and was mentioned in history books such as the *Lu-shih-ch'un-ch-iu* (which covers events between 897 and 221 B.C.) and the *Shi-chih* (edited in the first century B.C.). A tradition of representing the mansions in human form seems to have co-existed in ancient China with the Buddhist practice of depicting them as Buddhist gods, as can be seen in such works as the wall paintings in the caves at Tun-huang.[4] These paintings present the twenty-eight mansions as human or semi-human, together with other stellar figures depicted as Buddhist gods.

The most famous Chinese painting belonging to the non-Buddhist tradition of representing heavenly bodies is a handscroll (now in the Osaka Municipal Museum in

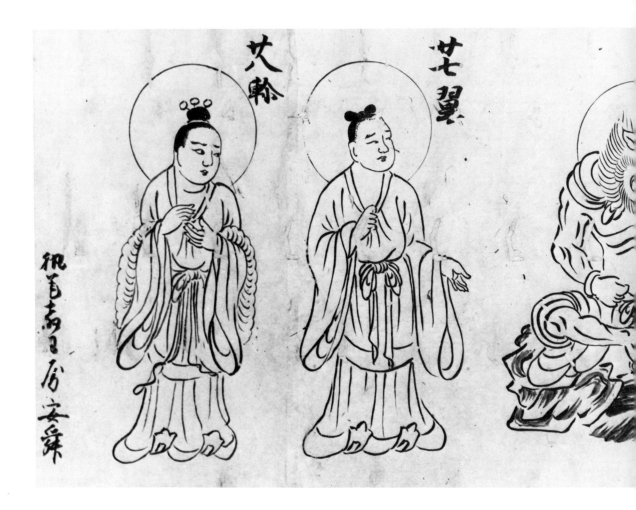

Japan)[5] which is usually attributed to the early sixth-century painter Chang Seng-yu. It depicts five planets and twenty-eight lunar mansions. A number of versions modeled after this scroll are in Chinese collections, but the only existing scroll which preserves all depictions of the twenty-eight mansions is a Japanese copy made centuries later by Tani Bunchō (1763–1840) in 1796.[6]

The Spencer scroll, executed in a quick, vigorous, ink sketch, is typical of zuzō, while the Chinese scroll is drawn in a precise, meticulous style. Nonetheless, the iconography is so similar in the two works that both must belong to an ancient Chinese tradition of representing the twenty-eight mansions as non-Buddhist deities. Of the mansions represented in these scrolls, some are endowed with the heads of animals—bull, tiger, lamb, and boar. One planet, Kyōshuku (number 11), is shown as a half-naked man emerging from a large vase. Other figures ride on large fish (number 13, Shitsushuku), or sit upon flying clouds (number 23, Kishuku). The last five mansions, reproduced here, are (right to left): number 24, Ryūshuku, riding on a dragon; number 25, Seishuku; number 26, Chōshuku, a tiger-headed man; number 27, Yokushuku; and number 28, Shinshuku.[7]

Each figure in the Osaka scroll and its copy by Bunchō is accompanied by a short text, but it describes only the horoscope and rituals to invoke or counteract the influence of a planet, and no reference is made to the mansion's appearance. The textual source for this iconographic tradition therefore remains unclear.

The Spencer scroll has no text. Only the names of the mansions and references to the positions that they hold within the group are given. This work, which is characterized by a powerful ink technique typical of works from the first half of the thirteenth century, is the earliest known Japanese rendition of this rare Chinese iconography.

NOTES

1. Nakano Genzō, "Sō shōrai Zuzō dempa (Transmission of Buddhist Iconography Imported from Sung China)," *Kokka* 1026 (1979).
2. Tokyo Kokuritsu Bunkazai Kenkyūjo (ed.), *Nihon Kaigashi Nenki Shiryō Shūsei* (Tokyo, 1984), p. 118.

3. Ono Gemmyō (ed.), *Taishō Shinshū Daizōkyō Zuzō*, vol.7 (Tokyo, 1933), pp. 775–800.

4. Roderick Whitfield, *The Art of Central Asia, The Stein Collection in the British Museum, I, Paintings from Dunhuang* (Tokyo, 1982), p. 27. Also see, for the painting dated 897, Osvald Sirén, *Chinese Painting: Leading Masters and Principles*, vol. 3 (London and New York, 1956), Pl. 71.

5. Sirén, *Chinese Paintings*, Pls. 16–17.

6. Yashiro Yukio, "Gosei Nijūhasshuku Shinkei Zukan (Scroll Painting of the Five Planets and the Twenty-eight Stellar Mansions)," *Bijutsu Kenkyū* 139 (1944), Pls. 11–12.

7. For a discussion of the twenty-eight mansions, see Joseph Needham, *Science and Civilization in China*, vol. 3 (London and New York, 1959), pp. 238–239, and p. 272 for a chart of Western denominations corresponding to the Chinese names.

10
Yugyō Shōnin Engi-e (*Records of Wayfaring Saints*)

Second half of the fourteenth century, Nambokuchō period
One handscroll, ink and light color on paper
H: 29.9 cm, L: 777.5 cm
Spencer no. 88

PUBLISHED: Louisa Cunningham, *The Spirit of Place: Japanese Paintings and Prints of the Sixteenth through Nineteenth Centuries* (New Haven, 1984), no. 3.

As with so many old *emaki* (illustrated narrative scrolls), the Spencer Collection's *Yugyō Shōnin Engi-e* has suffered from vandalism and careless repair. This short scroll consists of sixteen sheets of paper, all roughly uniform in length. It has no text, and the two painted scenes are abruptly joined at the ninth sheet. The first half of the scroll was originally the first episode in the ninth scroll of a ten-scroll set of the *Yugyō Shōnin Engi-e*, a work which depicted the lives and work of two monks, Ippen (1239–1289), the founder of the Jishū sect of Buddhism, and Taa (died 1319), the second Jishū patriarch. The latter half of the scroll was originally the fifth episode in scroll VII of the same set. At some unknown date, the set was broken up, and the pieces dispersed. Scrolls II, V, VI, and VIII are in the collection of the temple of Jōshōji in Onomichi, on the Inland Sea.[1] None of these, however, is in its original condition, and many parts of their texts are actually copies made at a later date.

Even though the scrolls are fragmented, their reconstruction is not too difficult, since at least fifteen sets of emaki on the same subject exist today. Ippen, one of the two heroes of the *Yūgyō Shōnin Engi-e*, holds a unique place in the history of Japanese Buddhism for his unwavering concern for the salvation of the poor and the downtrodden. A wandering preacher, Ippen advocated *odori-nembutsu* (the calling of Amida Buddha's name in dancing prayer), as he traveled through Japan on foot. The group that he founded, the Jishū sect, was an offshoot of the Jōdo ('Pure Land') sect. The Jishū discarded elaborate religious ritual, emphasizing instead religious ecstasy achieved through frenzied dancing and chanting; the sect itself persisted as a powerful spiritual force in Japan through the fifteenth century.

An intimate account of Ippen's life and his evangelical activities was celebrated in a twelve-scroll set of emaki, the *Ippen Hijiri-e* (*Scrolls of the Holy Man Ippen*), made in 1299 to commemorate the tenth anniversary of his death. Its text was compiled by Shōkai (died 1323), Ippen's disciple (who was rumored to have been his son), and the paintings were executed by En-i.[2] This emaki is filled with imagery based upon Shōkai's warm recollections of the great preacher, to whom he was deeply attached.

The Spencer scroll and the set to which it belonged can be placed within the large group of emaki, commonly known as *Yūgyō Shōnin Engi-e*, which also illustrate scenes from Ippen's life. Their inspiration and function, however, differed widely from Shōkai's work. The Spencer scrolls, which stem from a version edited between 1303 and 1307 by Sōshun—who was most likely a disciple of Taa—may be divided into two distinct parts: the first four scrolls follow Ippen's life and travels in a somewhat abbreviated sequence; the second part, which consists of six scrolls, is devoted to Jishū evangelism and a description of Taa's persecution. The second part usually begins with Taa's efforts to rally Ippen's followers after the latter's death in 1289; his life as the new leader of the group and his various trials are then detailed. The account concludes with Taa's retirement in 1303.

The text to Sōshun's version makes its aim blatantly clear: it is meant to show that Taa is the rightful heir to Ippen, countering a similar claim made by Shōkai in his scrolls. Clearly, a power struggle must have existed within the sect during its early years. Sōshun's scrolls also attempt to present the Jishū sect as a champion of the poor by emphasizing its works, among them the free distribution of food and the construction of roads. The scrolls were also intended as a theological text for the sect, which was in dire need of such a document (Ippen had destroyed most of his writings shortly before he died). This version, rather than Shōkai's, eventually became the official biography of Ippen and the basic theological framework for the group.

Colophons in some of the scrolls list certain "merits" to be gained by viewing these emaki. Apparently, many of them were carried by the traveling members of the sect to aid them in their evangelical work.[3] It is understandable, then, that this version of the Jishū story should have been in greater demand than Shōkai's version, and that so many copies of it were made.

The two scenes reproduced here are from the life of Taa. In 1298, he and his followers, who were traveling through the mountainous regions of central Japan, visited the temple of Zenkōji in Nagano. The striking composition reproduced here depicts their arrival at the temple gate; Taa, at the head of the group (at left), is conspicuously larger than his companions. A close look at Taa's followers, who parade behind him in two clusters, reveals that the figures at the top have more gentle facial features than those below; note in particular the figure whose face is wrapped in a cloth. These are the nuns; they are separated from their male colleagues (shown in the foreground), many of whom have dark shadows on their cheeks and chins. Segregation of the sexes was one of the sect's strict rules, aimed at keeping order within a closely knit group who were constantly traveling.

The text from the Spencer scroll is lost, but that of other scrolls goes on to explain that in the courtyard of the temple, the group prayed for seven days, performing odori-nembutsu and attracting a large crowd of onlookers.

The second scene reproduced here, originally the first episode in the ninth scroll of the set, depicts the group's visit to the Ise Shrine. Upon their arrival at this sacred Shinto shrine (in the tenth month of 1301), they were reminded by officials that the inner precinct was off-limits to Buddhist monks and nuns. Standing before the middle gate, Taa placed his hands together in prayer, and golden rays of light began to issue from them, astonishing everyone. After this miraculous incident, the group was allowed to proceed to the Naigū, or Inner Shrine. Just before they entered this holiest of areas, the monks and nuns bathed in the Isuzu River. In this scene, the gender of the figures is clearer. The men are on the far side of the small bridge; in the foreground, the nuns are delineated with breasts, gentler faces, and, above all, coy gestures and postures, expressing embarrassment and modesty before the other pilgrims who approach the site.

Pictorial techniques employed in this scroll are traditional emaki methods: figures move from right to left in a long horizontal space extending over three meters. Narratives are carried in rhythmic flow as the figures, in large groups or small clusters, move or stop. Buildings are viewed from angles, and the topmost parts of the scroll are partially shrouded in light mists and clouds, some in straight-edged bands, some with curly edges. Unlike most emaki on this subject, however, it is executed almost entirely in ink monochrome, with occasional touches of pale blue. Sharp contrasts between the dark areas, filled in with rich black ink, and the light greys and unpainted white areas create a unique beauty of a type that was beginning to capture the imagination of Japanese artists in the thirteenth century. The technique of Chinese ink monochrome painting, recently introduced to Japan, had inspired a few Japanese painters to experiment along similar lines. In this work the anonymous artist exhibits a fascination and some familiarity with the Chinese technique in such details as the exaggerated twists of tree trunks, the ink dots delineating foliage, and the swift, fluid outlines of modulated thickness. Above all, the use of light washes of ink, without outline, to model and define details of the landscape settings recalls details found in a small number of fourteenth-century Japanese landscape paintings executed in ink monochrome. The Spencer scroll and its companion pieces in the Jōshōji collection can be dated, on such stylistic grounds, to the second half of the fourteenth century.

NOTES

1. A few scenes from these scrolls are reproduced in Miya Tsugio, *Ippen Shōnin Eden, Nihon no Bijutsu*, vol. 56, ed. Staff of the National Museums of Tokyo, Kyoto, and Nara (Tokyo, 1971); Tanaka Ichimatsu (ed.), *Yugyō Shōnin Engi-e, Shinshū Nihon Emakimono Zenshū*, vol. 23 (Tokyo, 1979).
2. For this scroll, see Komatsu Shigemi (ed.), *Nihon Emaki Taisei*, Suppl., *Ippen Shōnin Eden* (Tokyo, 1978); Tanaka Ichimatsu (ed.), *Ippen Hijiri-e, Shinshū Nihon Emakimono Zenshū*, vol. 11 (Tokyo, 1975); and Miyeko Murase, *Emaki: Narrative Scrolls from Japan* (New York, 1983), no. 27.
3. Kadokawa Gengi, "Jishū bungei no seiritsu," Tanaka, *Ippen Hijiri-e*, pp. 15–31.

Episode 2　　　　　　　　　　　　　　　　　　　　　　*Episode 3*

11
Jyūgyū Zu (The Ten Oxherding Pictures)

Second half of the sixteenth century, Momoyama period
By an artist of the Kanō school
One handscroll, ink on paper
H: 24.2 cm, L: 111.0 cm
Spencer no. 52

The opening scenes of this handscroll, *The Ten Oxherding Pictures*, or *Jyūgyū-Z*, depict
a young oxherd and his ox in a rustic setting, and evoke thoughts of a simple, country
life. However, the last two scenes, which represent a rotund, smiling Hotei (Pu-tai in
Chinese)[1] holding a fan, and an empty circle (scenes 9 and 10), suggest that the subject
of the scroll has deeper meaning. The scoll illustrates, in fact, the *Ten Oxherding Songs*,
a Zen (Ch'an in Chinese) Buddhist parable in which the progressive stages of an individual's approach to Enlightenment are linked allegorically to an oxherd's search for his
run-away ox.[2] Arranged as though to suggest fans mounted on a handscroll, the ten

From right to left: Episodes 4, 7, 10, 8

scenes are actually painted within fan-shaped areas left blank in the large expanse of ink which covers the length of the scroll. The individual compositions are rendered in monochrome, and executed with a combination of crisp, expressive brushstrokes and areas of soft wash which attest to the artist's mastery of the ink painting technique.

In these scenes, intended to express the essence of Zen Buddhism, the oxherd represents Everyman, while the ox symbolizes the True Self, or Buddha Nature. In the parable, the boy and the ox start out as separate entities. As the boy progresses toward Enlightenment, their separation is diminished, little by little, and eventually the two are brought together, their unity in the Absolute symbolized by the circle of nothingness at the end of the scroll. Allegories such as the *Ten Oxherding Songs* were used by Zen masters to instruct their disciples. It was believed that such parables, meant to explain the increasing degrees of awareness preceding the enlightened state, might actually help a disciple achieve Enlightenment itself.

Many versions of the *Ten Oxherding Songs* were composed, the earliest during the eleventh century.[3] These drew on *kōan* (*kung-an* in Chinese) and other allegorical tales about cows and oxen recorded in Zen literature of the T'ang dynasty (618–906).[4] The tales, in turn, were probably inspired by the literature of ancient India.[5]

The most popular Chinese version was written by the Ch'an master P'u-ming (ca. A.D. 1050).[6] The ten progressive states of Enlightenment are represented in this work by a gradual transformation of the ox's color from black to white. Another version, written by the Ch'an master Kuo-an (ca. A.D. 1150) was introduced to Japan where it became extremely popular.[7] The woodcut illustrations which accompanied Kuo-an's text were often reprinted in Japan and served as models for at least one other known painted version of the *Ten Oxherding Songs*, now in the collection of the Shōkokuji in Kyoto.[8]

Although the sequence of the episodes is incorrect, the scenes represented in the Spencer scroll were based on the iconographic tradition established by the illustrations of the Kuo-an verson.

The Spencer scroll has been linked with the name of Kanō Motonobu (1476–1558), one of the leading masters of the Kanō school during the late Muromachi period, primarily because of a seal, placed at the end of the scroll, which resembles one used by Motonobu. However, this seal was also used by later Kanō artists, and the scroll is closer stylistically to works by Kanō school painters who lived a generation or two after Motonobu.

Vigorous drawings in ink, often using short, staccato strokes on drapery folds and foliages, convey the lively drama of the story. They also reflect the most popular style of ink painting in the late sixteenth century—expecially among the artists of the Kanō school, including the anonymous artist of this scroll. The original text and translation have been published by several scholars, all of whom have contributed to a better understanding of the symbolism in the Spencer handscroll.[9] The summary quoted below, by Heinrich Dumoulin, is used both for its brevity and clarity. The numbers correspond to the sequence of events in the original Kuo-an version.

1. (Scene 6 of the Spencer scroll.) The oxherd has lost his ox and stands alone on the vast pasture; but can the human being lose his Self?
2. (Scene 5 of the Spencer scroll.) He searches and catches sight of the tracks of the ox; there is a mediatory assistance, in which religious things like sutras and monasteries also play a part.
3. (Scene 4 of the Spencer scroll.) Following the tracks, he finds the ox; but this is still a distant, intellectual knowledge or intuition of the ox.
4. (Scene 2 and 7 of the Spencer scroll.) With fervent effort he tames the beast. . . .
5. (Scene 1 of the Spencer scroll.) . . . and sets it out to pasture under careful surveillance. These two stages (4 and 5) comprise practice in the Zen hall, the severe and painful practice until Enlightenment is grasped.
6. (Scene 3 of the Spencer scroll.) The practitioner finds complete certainty; the oxherd straddles the back of the ox and rides home triumphantly. . . . Now the two have become one; the oxherd in his freedom no longer has the need for the "ox" and forgets it.
7. (Scene 8 of the Spencer scroll.) The oxherd stands alone with the ox.
8. (Scene 10 of the Spencer scroll.) Now both the oxherd and ox have disappeared in the securing, embracing nothingness of a circle.
9. (Missing from the Spencer scroll.) When the oxherd reappears, everything around him is just as it is—the everyday life of the enlightened one.
10. (Scene 9 of the Spencer scroll.) And the oxherd enters the town and the marketplace and bestows goodness on all about him. The enlightened one lives with his fellow human beings and lives like them, but the benevolence he radiates has its source in his enlightenment.

NOTES

1. Hotei is believed to have been an incarnation of the Buddha of the Future, Miroku (Maitreya in Sanskrit).

2. For background information about Zen Buddhism, see Heinrich Dumoulin, *A History of Zen Buddhism* (New York, 1963).

3. Jan Fontein and Money Hickman, *Zen Painting and Calligraphy* (Boston, 1970), p. 113.

4. See, for example, *Ching-te chuang-teng-lu* (*A Record on Transmission of the Lamp*) by Tao-yuan, dating to A.D. 1004, published in *Taishō Shinshū Daizōkyō*, vol. 51, ed. Takakusu Junjirō and Watanabe Kaigyoku (Tokyo, 1928) no. 2078, pp. 204–467.

5. For example, Daisetz T. Suzuki described an early Hinayāna text which is parallel to the *Ten Oxherding Songs*. This sutra, entitled *On the Herding of Cattle*, explains in allegorical terms the eleven things required of a monk to be considered an exemplary Buddhist. See Daisetz T. Suzuki, *Essays in Zen Buddhism* (First Series) (London, 1927), p. 355.

6. Fontein and Hickman, *Zen Painting*, p. 116. Published in Shibayama Zenkei, *Jyūgyū Zu*, (Tokyo, 1954), pp. 17–82.

7. The earliest republished print in Japan may date to 1325. See Fontein and Hickman, *Zen Painting*, p. 116. Kuo-an version published in Shibayama, *Jyūgyu Zū*, pp. 83–124.

8. Published by Fontein and Hickman, *Zen Painting*, pp. 113–118, and described as "attributed to Shūbun." Japanese scholars, however, usually attribute the Shōkokuji scroll to Kanō Motonobu or give it a slightly later date. Another painted version of the *Ten Oxherding Pictures*, which is dated by inscription to 1278, has come to light and has been published by Shimbo Tōru in "Shinshutsu no Kōan-bon Jūgyū Zukan (Recently Discovered Paintings Depicting Zen Enlightenment Known as the Kōan Version Scroll of Jūgyū Zu)," *Bukkyō Geijustu*, no. 96 (May 1974), pp. 74–77.

9. See Fontein and Hickman, *Zen Painting*, pp. 113–118; Suzuki, *Essays*, pp. 347–366; M.H. Trevor, *The Ox and His Herdsman* (Tokyo, 1969); Sylvan Barnet and William Burto, *Zen Ink Paintings* (Tokyo, 1982); and Heinrich Dumoulin, *Zen Enlightenment: Origins and Meaning* (New York and Tokyo, 1979), pp. 154–156.

II
Heroes and Heroines of Classical Literature

IT is impossible to sum up in a few words or pages the role played by China in the formation of the civilization of ancient Japan, particularly its governmental and social systems and cultural development. Ancient Japan existed within an enormous pan-Chinese cultural sphere, and its own cultural history is punctuated by periodic efforts to free itself from the overwhelming power of Chinese influence.

The first such attempt with far-reaching consequences was the invention, around the ninth century, of a native writing system called *kana*. Although not regarded as suitable for official documents and communication, this phonetic system of writing—developed by selecting certain characters from the cursive rendition of Chinese script—freed the Japanese from their dependence on Chinese language and modes of expression. Also, by a curious twist of circumstance, it enabled women to become active participants in the great literary achievements of early Japan.

As Chinese language and literature were viewed as "masculine" and the property of cultivated gentlemen, women were discouraged from scholarly and literary pursuits. Murasaki Shikibu (died ca. 1016), author of the monumental novel, the *Genji Monogatari* (see nos. 20–22), described this situation succinctly in her diary, the *Murasaki Shikibu Nikki*. According to this record, her colleagues at court whispered accusingly behind her back, "What kind of lady is it who reads Chinese books?"[1] She also wrote of "eavesdropping" as a girl on the lessons in Chinese classics given to her brother, and learning the Chinese language more quickly than he. Upon discovering this, her father lamented, "What a pity she was not born a man!"[2]

The invention of kana completely altered this; discouraged from participating in Chinese-style literary activities, women seem to have been the first writers to take full advantage of the new script. Kana was instrumental in the evolution of *waka* (Japanese poetry), a brief, elegant form containing thirty-one syllables. Women became the major authors of waka, and are credited with initiating the fashionable pastime known as the "poetry contest," which became an all-consuming passion among Heian-period courtiers (see nos. 12, 13). Emotions and thoughts, both private and public, were expressed and exchanged through waka. Talent in its composition served as a stepping stone to greater opportunity and higher court rank for both men and women. Because its brief verses were relatively easy to compose, the Japanese soon came to believe that all beings—even beasts and insects—possessed poetic potential (see no. 16).[3]

Such was the importance of waka in ancient Japanese society that some of the most distinguished practitioners of the art were designated "Immortal Poets and Poetesses" *(kasen)*. Before long the portraits, both real and imaginary, of these poets became an important genre of painting (nos. 12–15). Another group of art works inspired by waka consists of a series of handsome calligraphy manuscripts, with poems written in elegant kana script on beautifully decorated paper (no. 17).

The development of prose literature also owes a debt to waka. What is considered Japan's first "novel," the *Ise Monogatari (Tales of Ise)* of the mid-tenth century (nos. 18, 19), belongs to a literary genre known as *uta-monogatari* (poem-tales), which consists of a series of waka linked by brief prose passages describing how the poems were composed. The first true novel of Japan, the *Genji Monogatari (The Tale of Genji)*, written at the beginning of the eleventh century, contains an enormous number of waka.

The Japanese propensity for fiction-writing was not derived from China; in fact, the Chinese have traditionally frowned upon fiction as a reflection of fantasy and the imagination, hardly an honorable instrument for ethical and moral instruction. Also native to Japan was the highly developed interest in and genius for illustrating stories in lively narrative paintings. The emergence of narrative painting occurred almost simultaneously with the birth of waka; then narrative painting developed in pace with prose narrative. Although we may not make too great an issue of the love-sick woman of the late ninth century who sent her lover a poem, accompanied by a sketch, now lost, of herself smoldering in the flames of love, she was the first Japanese on record to produce a truly narrative painting. Her poem reads, in translation:

> When this body of mine,
> So full of love for you,
> Is one day set on fire,
> How great will be
> The volume of smoke that rises![4]

From the mid-tenth century on, there is evidence which suggests that poetry, narrative prose, and illustration were the essential components of a "complete" literary work. Apparently, it was common practice to have a story illustrated soon after it was written.[5]

Although no painting from this remote age survives, it is likely that narrative painting was executed in a style which, to the mind of the contemporary Japanese, expressed an indigenous spirit and taste. The term *yamato-e* ('Japanese painting'), today often used indiscriminately, must be applied to these lost works. They depicted subjects which were dear to the hearts of the people, executed in a style which must have been clearly distinguishable from *kara-e* ('Chinese painting'). It is presumed that the latter type of work depicted strictly Chinese subjects, in Chinese style.

Yamato-e was used in books, hanging scrolls, handscrolls, and screens; these objects were often viewed by their owners when in the company of good friends. The ancient practice known as *etoki* (literally, "picture explanation and explainer") also added dimension to the art of illustrating literature. Etoki, which began as a Buddhist activity, contributed to the development of the unique Japanese *emaki*: handscrolls in which text and pictures are combined to tell stories. Etoki was an integral part of Buddhist life in China and Japan; even today at some temples narrators relate the tales and explain the illustrations of emaki. In Japan, it later became a secular practice as well.[6]

NOTES

1. Richard Bowring, *Murasaki Shikibu: Her Diary and Poetic Memoirs* (Princeton, 1982), p. 133.
2. Bowring, *Murasaki*, p. 139.
3. See the preface in H. H. Honda (trans.), *The Kokin Waka-shū* (Tokyo, 1970), p. 1.
4. This poem is included in the *Yamato Monogatari*, see Mildred M. Tahara (trans.), *Tales of Yamato: A Tenth-Century Poem-Tale* (Honolulu, 1980), pp. 33–34.
5. For a detailed description of this process, see Miyeko Murase, *Emaki: Narrative Scrolls from Japan* (New York, 1983), pp. 79–80.
6. A scene from the Azumaya chapter of the *Genji Monogatari Emaki* of the early twelfth century depicts a lady-in-waiting reading from a volume of text, while her lady studies a volume of pictures. See Komatsu Shigemi (ed.), *Genji Monogatari Emaki*, vol. I of *Nihon Emaki Taisei*, (Tokyo, 1977), pp. 36–37.

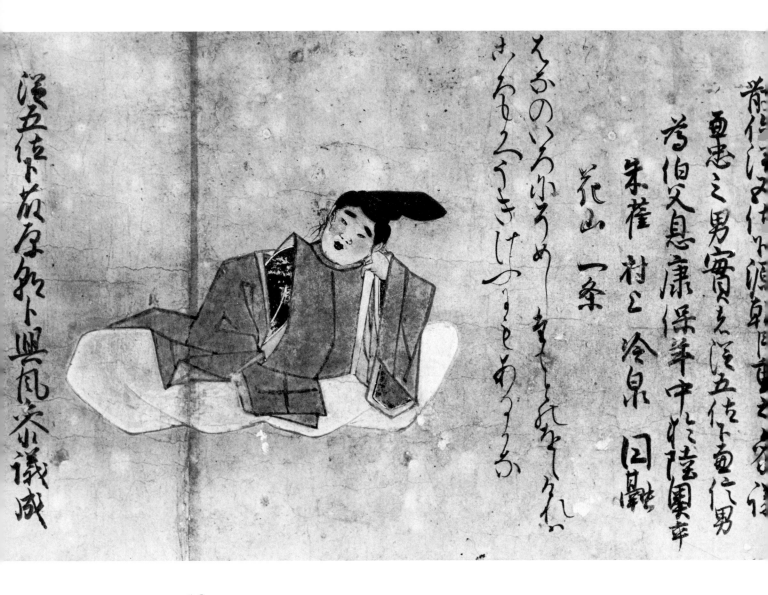

12

Minamoto no Shigeyuki and the Monk Sosei
from the Fujifusa version of the *Sanjūrokkasen Emaki*
(*Scroll of the Thirty-six Immortal Poets*)

Late sixteenth century, Late Muromachi to Momoyama period
One handscroll, ink and color on paper
H: 27.6 cm, L: 1341.41 cm
Spencer no. 28

The development of a phonetic system of Japanese writing *(kana)* freed the Japanese from their dependence on the Chinese language and modes of expression. The kana writing system, which came into use around the ninth century, was instrumental in the evolution of *waka*, the brief, thirty-one-syllable poetic form. During the Heian period emotions and thoughts of the aristocratic class were expressed and exchanged through waka. Talent in the waka art form helped gain recognition and rank for both men and women. In time, anthologies of superior waka were edited under imperial patronage, certain honors were bestowed upon the "superior" poets, and portraits of poets laureate were created to immortalize them. This type of poetry was so important in Japanese literature that it even can be said to have been the origin of the prose novel.

Composing waka soon became one of the most popular pastimes of the Heian court, primarily as the object of the "poetry contest," or *uta-awase*. During this period, tournaments were held for almost every artistic activity and the creation of any type of beautiful object. Painting competitions *(e-awase)*, for example, are mentioned in a chapter of the *Tale of Genji* which is also known as "E-awase."[1] Although it is not known exactly when the first uta-awase took place, the custom can be traced to the 880s and the games played among the women of the court.[2] (Aristocratic women were the first to take up waka as their mode of literary expression, while their male counterparts still clung to the traditional Chinese-style poetry.) In a classic poetry contest, poets were divided into two groups known as "the left" and "the right." Historical records indicate that, at first, both the contestants and judges at the tournaments were female; however, they were gradually replaced by male participants and male judges.

Tradition has it that Fujiwara no Kintō (966–1041), a renowned scholar, critic, and poet, and his fellow waka poet-critic, Prince Rokujō Tomohira (964–1009), developed a difference of opinion concerning the greatest waka composer of all time. Kintō nominated Ki no Tsurayuki (died 945), while Tomohira preferred Kakinomoto no Hitomaro (late seventh to early eighth century). To illustrate his view effectively, Kintō selected thirty-six poets (five of them female) and requested other lovers and connoisseurs of waka to evaluate and rank them. The majority agreed that Hitomaro was the best.[3] Subsequently, most popular listings of selected waka masters included thirty-six poets, with Hitomaro in the most honored position.

Thus, a sense of competition existed from the very beginning in selecting the immortal bards *(kasen)*. By about 1050, it was becoming customary to paint group portraits of the great poets, dividing them into two "teams" ("left" and "right"), and including written samplings of their best-known compositions within the painting.[4]

The oldest extant painting of kasen is a mid-thirteenth-century set of two scrolls known as the Satake version *(Satake-bon)* of the Thirty-six Immortal Poets *(Sanjūrokkasen)*, (originally it was part of the Satake Collection; in 1919 it was divided among various collectors).[5] Although the portraits in these scrolls are imaginary depictions of men and women who lived long before the work was painted, the interest in portraiture as a genre reflects the spirit of the Kamakura period. In fact, a long-standing tradition that attributes the Satake scrolls to Fujiwara no Nobuzane (1176–1269?), the most renowned portraitist of that era, has some historical basis.[6] During his lifetime, Nobuzane was the foremost artist of *nise-e* ("likeness-pictures") a new genre of painting that stressed capturing fleeting impressions of people, animals, and even inanimate objects in a sketch-like manner, often directly from life.[7] Nise-e came into being during the late twelfth century, when new cultural heroes were rising to the forefront of society, and an energetic, new spirit prevailed. Realism in the arts was one result of the new spirit, and nise-e is a prime example of this trend.

The Satake scrolls depict thirty-six men and women, seated and turning either to the left or the right. It is believed that the scrolls were modeled after an earlier emaki which divided the poets into two distinct competing groups.[8] While the sense of competition is not so apparent in the Satake scrolls, in many of the later works on the same subject, the poets are paired with opponents from the contesting group ("left" vs. "right"). Some of these pictures also include the names of judges, and the judges' decisions. These later paintings, which stress the interaction between poets, are usually called *uta-awase-e* (pictures of poetry contests), and those in which the emphasis is placed on the portrayal of each poet as an individual are called *kasen-e*. The distinction, however, is never clear-cut.

In the Spencer Collection are more than twenty sets of paintings of immortal poets—both in handscrolls and in albums. Five have been selected for this exhibition. The earliest dated work in this group is a kasen-e which includes thirty-two male poets and four female poets (no. 12). The figures are all seated, and they turn in various directions; one poet, Koō no Kimi, turns her back completely to us. Many of the poets are depicted in poses that suggest intense concentration and creative effort: some hunch their shoulders; others look up with mouths slightly open, as though to test the sound of their waka; still others bend their heads in deep reflection; one man seems to scratch his head. Minamoto no Shigeyuki, shown here, leans on one hand, grasping a scepter. Eyes unfocussed, he is lost in creative endeavor.

As in all standard kasen-e, next to each of the poets in the scroll is a short biographical note and one of his or her best-known poems (to our right). Shigeyuki, the thirteenth in the group, is described as a son of Kanenobu, adopted by his uncle, Kanetada. He served six successive emperors, from Suzaku (reigned 931–946) to Ichijō (reigned 987–1011), and died in Mutsu, in the north, while in service there. It is also known, from other sources, that although he eventually rose to the Fifth Order of court rank, he despaired over his social status; this sense of disappointment is often expressed in his plaintive poems. Perhaps to console himself, Shigeyuki took to the road, traveling from the southern island of Kyushu through the eastern provinces. His poem was included in the *Shūi Waka Shū (Collection of Gleanings)*, a twenty-volume anthology commissioned by a retired emperor Kazan (reigned 984–986) and compiled by Fujiwara no Kintō. It reads:

Hana no iro ni	How sad! When these sleeves
Someshi tamoto no	are stained by the color of the flowers.
Oshikereba	Again today, the seasons have
Koromo kae uki	changed, and new clothes
Kyō ni mo aru kana.	must be brought out—
	What a pity![9]

The last portrait in the scroll is that of Sosei, shown here, a priest-poet of the late ninth century. Sosei, the son of Bishop Henjō (also a member of the thirty-six) served as an officer of the palace guards under the lay name of Yoshimine no Harutoshi. Later, he renounced courtly life, took the tonsure, and became head priest of the Urin-in, a Tendai temple in Kyoto. Sosei is here depicted with shaved head and stiff monastic robes, indicating his priestly status. He sits with his back to his fellow poets, but turns his head toward the viewer. The three-quarter profile reveals a sweet, boyish mien with softly rounded cheeks and full, pursed lips. The selection from Sosei's poetic works is

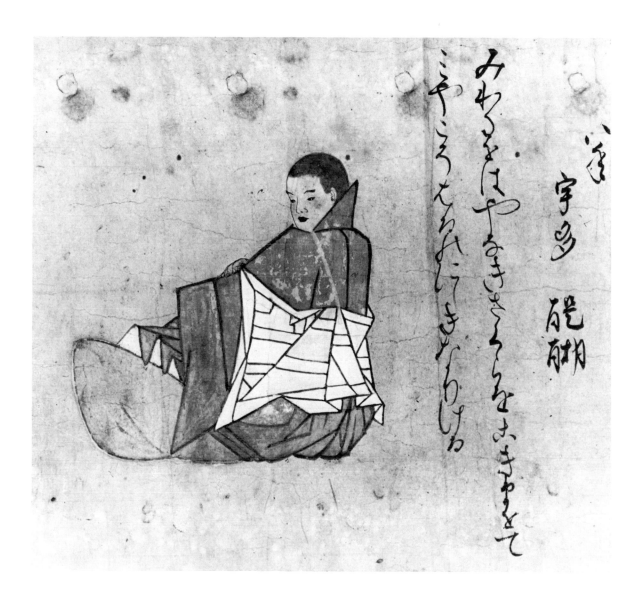

taken from the *Kokin Waka Shū (Collection of Poetry of Ancient and Modern Times)*, the first imperial anthology of poetry, commissioned by Emperor Daigo (reigned 897–930) in the early tenth century and compiled by Ki no Tsurayuki and three associates. It reads:

Miwataseba   Behold! the royal Capital,
Yanagi sakura o   Wrap't in the Spring's brocade, is gay,
Koki mazete   The willow leaves and cherry bloom
Miyako zo haru no   Mingled in fair array.[10]
Nishiki nari keru

At the end of the scroll are two colophons. One, by an unknown hand, states that the work, which came into his possession unexpectedly, was painted by Nobuzane. The second postscript asserts that the painting is without doubt by Nobuzane; this inscription is followed by the signature of Kanō Tan'yū (1602–1674), a leading master of the Kanō school of painting (see no. 47), and a seal reading "Morinobu," one of Tan'yū's acronyms. This signature and seal are, unfortunately, not authentic.

The portraits are executed in bright colors, applied in heavy layers and particularly brilliant on the women's garments. The women's robes are decorated with large gold designs, which reflect the fashions of the sixteenth century. Exaggerated facial expressions, sometimes verging on caricature, and the broad, sharply angled and conspicuous ink lines that delineate the details of costumes are also indicative of that time.

The Spencer scroll is an example of one of the variant forms of kasen-e that evolved during the many years when this art form enjoyed a great popularity. The poets are arranged, for example, in a completely novel order, one differing from that of the *Satake-bon* or most other kasen-e. Hitomaro is in his primary position at the head of the scroll, but the rest of the poets are depicted in a manner that lacks any hint of a contest, and one of the thirty-six poets has even been substituted for another poet.[11] Errors in the biographical notes and the inclusion of waka not found in most kasen-e also indicate that this scroll is a copy of the famous Fujifusa version, a Muromachi-period rendition of the kasen-e theme.[12]

The Fujifusa scroll was named after a courtier, Fujiwara (also known as Madenokōji) Fujifusa (1295–1380), to whom the scroll's calligraphy is attributed. This work is heavily damaged: the original was cut into small segments, only eleven of which exist today.[13] Not much is known about Fujifusa, but his father, Nobufusa (1253–1336), is also credited with having written the text for a kasen-e (the Nobufusa version). It, too, is fragmented,[14] but there are noticeable similarities between the two renditions.

The Spencer scroll is particularly important since it is the oldest complete scroll known today that belongs to the Fujifusa tradition of kasen-e.[15]

NOTES

1. See chapter 17 ("A Picture Contest"), Edward G. Seidensticker (trans.), *The Tale of Genji* (New York, 1976), vol. 1, pp. 307–317.
2. Minegishi Yoshiaki, *Uta-awase no Kenkyū* (Tokyo, 1958), p. 13.
3. For literary records on this matter, see Hasegawa Nobuyoshi, "Sanjūrokkasen no seiritsu," in *Sanjūrokkasen-e*, vol. 19 of *Shinshū Nihon Emakimono Zenshū*, ed. Tanaka Ichimatsu (Tokyo, 1979), pp. 40–44.
4. See the section on e-awase of the fifth year of the Eishō era (1050), in Nagazumi Yasuaki and Shimada Isao (eds.), *Nihon Koten Bungaku Taikei*, vol. 84 of *Kokon Chomon Jū* (Tokyo, 1968), p. 313.
5. Tanaka, *Shinshu*, vol. 19, and Miyeko Murase, *Emaki: Narrative Scrolls from Japan* (New York, 1983), pp. 127–133.
6. Recent scholarship has begun to take this traditional attribution more seriously. See Itō Toshiko, "Satake-bon Sanjūrokkasen Emaki no kōsei to seiritsu," Tanaka, *Shinshu*, vol. 19, pp. 61–62.
7. For examples of nise-e, see Murase, *Emaki*, pp. 123–126.
8. Itō, "Satake-bon," pp. 48–61.
9. For this poem, see Katagiri Yōichi (ed.), *Shūi Waka Shū: Teika-bon I, Koten Bunko*, vol. 199, (Tokyo, 1964), p. 23.
10. Asatarō Miyamori, *Masterpieces of Japanese Poetry, Ancient and Modern* (Tokyo, 1936), p. 204.

11. Kiyowara no Motosuke (c. 917–990) was replaced by Ariwara no Yukihira (c. 818–893). There are also poets whose names are misspelled: for example, Fujiwara no Kiyomasa, as Kiyotada, and Sakanoue no Korenori, as Minori. Also, about one-third of the poems included in this scroll differ from those in the Satake scrolls.

12. Mori Tōru, "Den Fujifusa hitsu no kasen-e ni tsuite (*Kasen-e* Painting attributed to Fujifusa)," *Yamato Bunka* 26 (June, 1958), pp. 37–47.

13. Mori, "Den Fujifusa." Some of them are in the Fujita Museum in Osaka, and others in private collections in Japan.

14. For reproductions of these fragments, see Tokyo National Museum, *Emaki* (Tokyo, 1974), nos. 76 and 77.

15. This scroll seems to have served as a model for a nineteenth-century kasen-e painting made by a renowned artist of the Nanga school, Tani Bunchō (1763–1840). This copy is reproduced in Tanaka, *Shinshū*, and Mori Tōru, *Uta-awase-e no Kenkyū: Kasen-e* (Tokyo, 1980). Other copies, including one by a Kanō master in the Mori Tōru collection, are also reported. See Mori, *Uta-awase-e*, note 2, p. 33.

13
Poetry Match of the Thirty-six Immortal Poetesses (*Nyōbō Sanjūrokunin Uta-awase*)

Mid-eighteenth century, Edo period
By Minamoto no Nobuyoshi
One handscroll, ink, gold and color on paper
H: 24.5 cm, L: 460.9 cm
Spencer no. 64

Women played a seminal role in the development of the *waka* genre of poetry (thirty-one syllable verse). In fact, women might have been the initiators of the poetry match, or *uta-awase*. However, when the first selection of *kasen* (Immortal Poets) (see nos. 12, 15) was made in the eleventh century, few female poets were among them. It was not until the Kamakura period that the Thirty-six Immortal Poetesses (Nyōbō Sanjūrokkasen) were selected and that all-female poetry matches (Nyōbō Sanjūrokunin Uta-awase) arose.[1] The earliest record of the "Poetry Match of Thirty-six Immortal Poetesses" dates to 1373.[2] A standard group of female poets-laureate pays homage to such literary giants as Lady Murasaki (died ca. 1016), author of *The Tale of Genji* (see nos. 20–22), and her brilliant contemporary, the essayist Sei Shōnagon. Otherwise, all five of the women traditionally included in the standard kasen group are incorporated, as well as others who lived from the ninth century to the late thirteenth, suggesting the mid-thirteenth century as the earliest possible date for the selection of the female poets.

The entire length of the Spencer scroll is decorated with delicate designs of flowers and grasses, painted near the top in gold ink. The thirty-six poets of the "left" and "right" groups are paired off, and each one is identified by name and accompanied by a representative poem. However, many of them are identified only by the court positions that they, or their male kinfolk, held—in ancient times, women were not referred to in public by their personal names. Each of the women is seated, turned either toward or away from her opponent. The delicate, doll-like figures are enveloped in voluminous court costumes of many layers in different colors, and behind them trail long streams of their jet-black hair. Poets of royal blood, like the Princesses Shikishi (shown here, second from right) and Saigū no Nyōgo, are seated on tatami mats behind curtains of state to distinguish them from the other women.

Following the figure of the last poet is a postscript: "This scroll was painted at the request of a certain person on a certain day in the ninth month." It is signed by Minamoto no Nobuyoshi, who is otherwise unknown.[3]

The limited possibility inherent in representing female poets must have been one of the reasons for the relative lack of popularity of this theme in painting. Only a few paintings of the *Nyōbō Kasen* exist today, and the Spencer scroll is one of those.[4] An almost identical scroll is reported to be in the collection of Yoshida Kōichi in Japan.[5] The poems are identical, and the calligraphy and style of the paintings are remarkably similar.[6] The postscript to the Yoshida scroll is also identical save that it is dated to a "certain day in the eighth month." On stylistic grounds, both the Yoshida and Spencer scrolls can be dated to the mid-Edo era (the mid-eighteenth century).[7]

Seated in the foremost position at the beginning of the Spencer scroll is Ono no Komachi (ninth century). Her legendary beauty and fame as a poet have obscured her real life story; many popular legends developed around her which were later adapted into Noh plays (see no. 32). It is said that Komachi refused to marry because she was determined to become the mistress of the ruler of Japan. But her hopes were never realized, and when she lost her youthful beauty she was forced to beg along the roadside. While refinement and grace characterize much of Komachi's verse, her waka carry an undertone of passion. The poem transcribed here is from the *Kokin Waka Shū* (*Collection of Poetry of Ancient and Modern Times*).

Iro miede	That which fades away
Utsurou mono wa	Without revealing its altered color
Yononaka no	—Is, in the world of love,
Hito no kokoro no	That single flower which blossoms
Hana ni zo arikeru.	—In the fickle heart of man.[8]

The melancholy air of Komachi's poem is reflected in her pose. Bowing her head, she gazes, downcast, at her opened fan. Delicate strands of black hair flow across her shoulders onto colorful layers of silk garments. At the edges of her outer robe, which is decorated with a swirling wave pattern, we catch glimpses of the multiple layers of under-robes. Komachi's dress was customary for women of the Heian court; her diminutive form literally swims in a sea of gorgeous fabric.

Facing Komachi, seated beneath a curtain, is the Princess Shikishi (ca. 1150–1201). As an indication of Shikishi's royal standing, she has been placed atop a thick tatami platform, flanked by a screen with flowing fabric panels, and she turns her back toward us. Daughter of the retired emperor Goshirakawa (reigned 1155–1158), Shikishi was named priestess of the Kamo Shrine in Kyoto in 1159, where she served for about ten years, until about age nineteen. Later in life, Shikishi became entangled in a struggle for supremacy between the warring Taira and Minamoto clans, and, disenchanted, decided to become a Buddhist nun. The waka by Shikishi transcribed in the Spencer scroll is from the chapter devoted to autumn themes in the *Shin Kokin Waka Shū* (*New Collection of Poetry of Ancient and Modern Times*):

Nagamureba	How cool the autumn wind!
Koromode suzushi	I seem to stand
Hisakata no	This twilight
Ama no gawara	on the Heavenly River's strand.[9]
no	
Aki no yūgure.	

The third poet is Ise (late ninth to early tenth centuries), a descendent of the Fujiwara line. The name Ise derives from the province in which the poet's father, Fujiwara no Tsugukage, served as governor. She herself served as lady-in-waiting to Lady Onshi, the consort of Emperor Uda (reigned 887–897). Ise's beauty was greatly admired by courtiers of her day, and she became romantically involved with several high-ranking figures. The first was Fujiwara no Nakahira, the brother of Lady Onshi. Emperor Uda was the father of her first child, a son who died at age seven. Years later, she gave birth to a girl. This child, whose father was Prince Nakatsukasa Atsuyoshi, grew up to become the famed poet Nakatsukasa, one of the traditional thirty-six immortal poets.

In the painting, Ise, enveloped in silk robes, turns away from Kunaikyō, her partner, casting her glance in the opposite direction.

The poem that represents Ise's verse is from the tenth-century anthology, the *Gosen Shū* (*Later Collection*). These waka were commissioned by Emperor Murakami in 951 and compiled by Ōnakatomi no Yoshinobu and four associates. Of the various poetic collections, the *Gosen Shū* contains the largest number of Ise's poems. The waka transcribed here reads:

Omoigawa	The River of Longing
Taezu nagaruru	flows on, never stopping.
Mizu no awa no	The froth on the water
Utakata hito ni	meets no one
Awa de kiemeya.	and dies away as ephemeral bubbles.[10]

Kunaikyō, the last poet shown here, daughter of Minamoto no Moromitsu (active 1168–1200), made her debut at a poetry contest sponsored by the retired emperor Gotaba in 1200. During the next few years, Kunaikyō participated in numerous poetic events. Soon after this, she died at an exceptionally young age.

The verse from Kunaikyō's poetry appears in the *Shin Kokin Waka Shū*:

Kakikurashi	Spring has come
Nao furusato no	here to this dark old village,
Yuki no uchi ni	Though buried still in snow,
Atokoso miene	where once I lived.[11]
Haru wa kinikeri.	

NOTES

1. The *Azuma Kagami*, the official chronicle of the Kamakura shogunal government, reports that portraits of female poets were made for the shogun Sanetomo but does not specify if they were of the "Thirty-six Immortals." See Kishi Shōzō (ed.), *Zen'yaku Azuma Kagami* (Tokyo, 1977), vol. 3, p. 204, the entry for the third year of the Kenryaku era (1213), third month, twenty-eighth day.
2. A scroll of the thirty-six female poets with the colophon dated to 1373 is reported to be in the Shōkōkan collection. See Kawamata Keiichi (ed.), *Shinkō Gunsho Ruijū* (Tokyo, 1929), vol. 10, p. 14.
3. Sorimachi identifies him as Kuzuoka Senkei (another, less likely reading of the name "Nobuyoshi"). See Shigeo Sorimachi, *Catalogue of Japanese Illustrated Books and Manuscripts in the Spencer Collection of the New York Public Library* (Tokyo, 1978), no. 64.
4. For other examples of female poets' portraits, see Mori Tōru, *Uta-awase-e no Kenkyū: Kasen-e* (Tokyo, 1970), pp. 74–77.
5. For a version in the Yoshida Kōichi collection, see Mori, *Uta-awase-e*, p. 228, fig. 6.
6. Only the first two figures are reproduced from the Yoshida scroll, however.
7. Mori, *Uta-awase-e*, p. 75.
8. Earl Miner (trans.), in *An Introduction to Japanese Court Poetry* (Stanford, 1968), p. 82.
9. H. H. Honda (trans.), *The Shin Kokinshū* (Tokyo, 1970), p. 91. In the transcription of the poem, the last word, *yūgure* (twilight), was changed to *matsukaze* (wind over pines).
10. At least three rivers named Omoigawa ("the river of longing") are known in Kyushu, and elsewhere. This poem is included in the *Gosen Waka Shū*, ed. Tsukamoto Tetsuzō (Tokyo, 1926), p. 302.
11. Honda, *Shin Kokinshu*, p. 8.

14
Four Poets from the *Kyūsoku Kasen-e* (*The Immortal Poets Taking a Break*)

Mid-seventeenth century, Edo period
By Hinaya Ryūho (1595–1669)
One scroll, ink and light color on paper
H: 28 cm, L: 773.5 cm
Signature: "Ryūho"
Seal: "Shōō"
Spencer no. 83

This scroll is an amusing parody on the theme of the "Thirty-six Immortal Poets," many of whom are depicted as members of a rather unceremonious crew. The poet Minamoto no Nobuakira, illustrated here, for example, is shown as an unkempt man leisurely stretching and yawning. Some of the renowned poets are absorbed in eating; others are snoozing, stretched full length on the floor. Still others seek diversion from the business of composing poetry and dance or kick a football. One of the female poets is busy repairing her make-up.

Hinaya Ryūho (1595–1669), the poet-painter who produced this outlandish scroll, inscribed the title, "Eighteen Sets of Haiku on Flowers and the Moon," in the opening section. This scroll and several others like it, however, are nicknamed *Kyūsoku Kasen-e (Pictures of the Immortal Poets Taking a Break)*, an expression derived from Ryūho's postscript, which states that he has portrayed the poets in a moment of relaxation. The postscript also explains that the poems by the Immortals of the "left group" allude to flowers, while those written by the "right group" are about the moon.

The *Kyūsoku Kasen-e* is probably the most daring and unconventional depiction of *kasen-e* or *uta-awase-e*, the courtly poetry matches. Not only are the poets depicted in informal or unexpected poses, but their poems, too, depart from the *waka* tradition. They are, in fact, *haikai*, verses of seventeen syllables each, which are better known in the West by the nineteenth-century appellation, *haiku*. With uncanny skill and a whimsical touch, Ryūho also wove each poet's name into the haiku as a pun. Note the Immortals' names within the following verses:

Gyoi no <u>mune</u>   The honorable message,
  <u>yuki</u> te mōsuya   The flower messenger
Hana no shisha.   has just gone to deliver.

Muneyuki sits at ease, courtier's cap on his head and long train trailing behind him.[1] Resting his chin on his hand, he gazes abstractly at his opponent, Nobuakira,[2] who yawns widely. Dressed in casual robes, his cap laid aside, Nobuakira is the archetypal image of the relaxing poet. Note the pun on his name in his verse:

Kokoro <u>nubu</u>	My heart is stretched
<u>akira</u> keki yo no	In this bright night
Tsukimi kana.	for moon-viewing.

The woman applying make-up in front of a mirror is Koō no kimi.[3] She delivers this poem:

Iro ya hana	In colors of flowers,
Tate yo<u>ko ō</u>ki	long and wide
<u>Mizu</u>goromo	is the Noh costume.

The verse refers to the Noh costume, with wide sleeves and long trousers, worn by her opponent Nakabumi.[4] His poem reads:

Tsuyu no <u>naka</u>	Do not step onto the
<u>fumu</u> na tsuki sae	dewy ground,
Kage bōshi	Moon is bright,
	casting shadows there.

In keeping with the whimsical nature of the scroll, Ryūho dispensed with the surnames of the poets and their biographies. The poets are shown in standard sequence, except the two masters, Toshiyuki and Muneyuki, whose places have been switched. Ryūho also heightened the sense of poetic competition by pairing the poets in an obvious manner—some face each other and others turn their backs on one another. Their names are positioned between each pair in columns.

The illustrations for this scroll belong to the genre of painting known as *haiga* (haiku pictures).[5] Ryūho was a pioneer of this genre, and the *Kyūsoku Kasen-e* possesses a light-hearted, spontaneous quality characteristic of haiga. Ryūho has painted his figures with free, fluent brush strokes, noting only essential details and achieving the effect of impromptu sketches. The poets' caricatured expressions enhance their relaxed and recumbent poses. Complementing the sketchy figures in light touches of color is Ryūho's rapidly brushed calligraphy, executed in the cursive style. This style is typical of Ryūho's painting, although he is known to have painted in other styles. His versatility is surprising, especially considering that he only began painting late in life—at age 60 or so.[6] In fact, Ryūho seems to have considered painting a hobby—a mere sideline to his predominant interest, haiku.

Born into a Kyoto merchant family named Nonoguchi, Ryūho adopted the appellative "Hinaya" ("doll shop") in keeping with the family business. Although he inherited the business, Ryūho was far from being a devoted shopkeeper. According to traditional accounts, he studied poetry with Karasumaru Mitsuhiro (1579–1638), a courtier with a wide range of artistic interests including poetry and calligraphy.[7] The story of Ryūho's association with Mitsuhiro may be apocryphal, but it is well established that Ryūho later became a disciple of the poet-calligrapher Matsunaga Teitoku (1571–1653). Teitoku was highly acclaimed for his waka, *renga* (linked verse), and haiku. Ryūho edited one of the first collections of haiku, the *Haikai Hokku Chō*, and, in 1636, issued a code of rules on its composition.[8] By the age of 47, Ryūho was so immersed in the literary world that he closed his family's doll shop and became a full-fledged haiku poet. In 1645, he moved east to Edo, and in 1650 again took to the road and traveled extensively until he died at the age of 75.

Ryūho painted different subjects in a variety of techniques: tales of miraculous occurrences, frolicking animals, Zen figures, trees and grasses, and even coy beauties. A theme that he turned to repeatedly, however, was that of poets, where his style of painting and subject matter also reveal great diversity. Some of his works, for example, are formal, classic depictions of the Immortals. However, Ryūho's creativity is most apparent in the "relaxing poets" theme, which he repeated in numerous paintings. At least one of these works, a scroll in the Mori Collection in Tokyo, is nearly identical to the Spencer scroll.[9] The wit and originality of the *Kyūsoku Kasen-e* no doubt appealed to many people, creating a demand for copies. Publication of a printed version attests to this.

This delightful scroll may be dated to about 1661, on the basis of stylistic similarities with another of Ryūho's haiku contest scrolls, dated to that year.[10]

NOTES

1. Minamoto no Muneyuki (died 939) was the son of a royal prince, and served as a court official. A friend of renowned poets, he participated in several famous poetry matches.
2. Minamoto no Nobuakira (909–970) was the son of Kintada, another of the Thirty-six Immortal Poets, and served as governor of Mutsu Province in the north.
3. A member of the court of the Late Heian period, Koō no kimi was married to Prince Shigeakira, a descendant of emperor Daigo (897–930).
4. Fujiwara no Nakabumi rose to the Fifth Rank in 977, and died soon after, at age 71.
5. For *haiga*, see Okada Ribei, *Haiga no Bi: Buson, Gekkei* (Kyoto, 1973).
6. Mori Tōru, "Kyūsoku Kasen-e ni tsuite (On the paintings of The Kyūsoku Kasen)," *Kokka* 852 (March 1963), p. 9.
7. Mori, "Kyūsoku Kasen-e," p. 9
8. *Ibid.*, pp. 33–35.
9. *Op. cit.*
10. *Op. cit.*

15

Kakinomoto no Hitomaro and Saigū no Nyōgo from the *Sanjūrokunin Uta-awase* (*Scroll of the Poetry Match of the Thirty-six Immortal Poets*)

Late seventeenth century, Edo period
Paintings by Genkyū
Text by several calligraphers
One album with 36 sheets of painting and 36 sheets of text, ink and color on paper
Each leaf, 24.2 cm x 20.4 cm
Spencer no. 147

Japanese albums of painting and calligraphy are usually designed in accordion shape, with sheets of paper called *shikishi* (literally, "colored paper") affixed to the folds. Such albums are opened from left to right, as are bound books of the Far East.

A large number of albums containing portraits of the Thirty-six Immortal Poets (*kasen*) have survived from the Edo period. These albums tend to follow two basic designs. Either the verse and portrait appear together on a single shikishi, or the poetry and portrait are on separate, facing leaves. The Spencer Collection's album is in the latter format, and consists of thirty-six poetry pages (recto) and thirty-six portrait leaves (verso).

Each poem sheet includes the poet's personal name (but not his surname), position in the contesting group of left or right, and one representative poem. No biographical notation is included. All of the poem sheets have decorative motifs, traditional since the Heian period—long leaves in silver and stylized mists in gold. A long, narrow strip of paper attached to the upper right-hand corner of each sheet is inscribed with the calligrapher's name and the first few words of the poem. These notes were written by a person called Yūken, who impressed his seal in black ink on the strips.

The first depicted in the album, shown here, is Kakinomoto no Hitomaro (late seventh to early eighth century), the pre-eminent poet of Japan. In his official capacity, Hitomaro never rose above minor rank; but as a poet he was celebrated in his own lifetime, and his fame greatly increased after he died. Not only was he chosen to head the Thirty-six Immortal Poets (see no. 12), he was also worshiped by young, aspiring poets, who conducted ceremonies in his honor and produced idealized portraits of their master. These images were patterned after an early twelfth-century portrait, painted for Awata Kanemori, which is now lost.[1] According to a famous anecdote, Kanemori saw Hitomaro in a dream and commissioned a painting of the poet as he had envisioned him—an old man holding paper in his left hand and a writing brush in his right, sitting under a blossoming cherry tree. This image was presented to Emperor Shirakawa (reigned 1072–1086) and served as the model for many Hitomaro portraits, including, perhaps, his image in the first representation of the Thirty-six Immortal Poets in handscroll format, now lost.[2] In the Spencer album, Hitomaro is shown as he appeared in the dream, seated and in robes of state, wearing a courtier's black lacquered cap. Intricate gold patterns ornament his gray robes, which are further highlighted by touches of bright red, indicating silk linings. A wispy, graying beard and wrinkled face suggest an elderly sage, while intelligent eyes and noble features bespeak his talent. This portrait is unusual in one important respect, however; the brush and paper Hitomaro holds in the dream sequence are not depicted. Painted with exacting, meticulous brushstrokes, this leaf is a consummate example of miniature art.

One of Hitomaro's most acclaimed poems, included in the *Kokin Waka Shū* (*Collection of Poetry of Ancient and Modern Times*, compiled in 905), is written in fluid *kana* script on the facing page.

> Honobono to
> Akashi no ura no
> Asagiri no
> Shima gakure yuku
> Fune o shizo
>   omou.

> Dimly, dimly
> In the morning mist that dawns
>   Over Akashi Bay,
> My longings follow with the ship
> That vanishes behind the
>   distant isle.

At the lower right-hand corner is the artist's signature, "Hokkyō Genkyū hitsu" (painted by Genkyū, the Hokkyō), Hokkyō being an honorary priestly rank granted to successful artists. The calligraphy is attributed by Yūken to a member of the renowned courtier family, Konoe Motohiro (died ca. 1732).

The second poet in the album is Ki no Tsurayuki (died 945), who always heads the right-hand group in standard kasen representations. Following this painting, the poets of the two groups alternate in the album, clearly expressing the spirit of the contest.

The nineteenth figure (the first poet on the reverse side of the album) is the female poet Saigū no Nyōgo (929–985) (cover). Saigū, a princess and priestess, and later a consort of the Emperor Murakami (reigned 946–967), is usually distinguished from other figures in kasen representations by being placed on a tatami mat shielded by a curtain in recognition of her exalted position. The daughter of Prince Shigeakira, she was chosen to be a *saigū*, a chief priestess of the Ise Shrine, at the age of eight. (It was then customary to select a virgin of royal blood to serve as chief priestess at this holiest of national sanctuaries.) She remained there for nine years, returning to Kyoto in 945, where three years later she was named a consort of the emperor.

In this album Saigū is shown posed atop a thick tatami, shyly peaking out from behind a richly decorated screen. Only her pale forehead, heavy eyebrows, and several strands of jet-black hair weaving between the layers of her silk robes are visible.

Saigū's poem is from the *Shin Kokin Shū* (*New Collection of Poetry of Ancient and Modern Times*), an anthology commissioned by retired Emperor Gotoba in 1201, and compiled by Fujiwara no Teika (1162–1241) and three associates.

> Sode ni sae
> Aki no yūbe wa
> Shirare keri
> Kieshi asaji ga
> Tsuyu o kake tsutsu

> Wet are my sleeves with tears
> Like autumn evening grass
> With dew
> Now that the Emperor is gone.[4]

The inscription attached to the upper-right hand corner of the page attributes the calligraphy to Daigo Fuyumoto (died ca. 1699), a courtier who served as chief counselor during the Edo period.

Although the oldest extant representations of the Thirty-six Immortal Poets, in the work known as the Satake scrolls (see no. 12), were models for kasen-e for generations, many variations of the theme developed in later periods. The choice of poems, the use of abbreviated identifications of the poets, and the poses struck by the figures in the Spencer album are, in fact, derived from a late thirteenth-century scroll known as the Narikane version, as its calligraphy is attributed (although without basis) to a courtier named Taira no Narikane. The Narikane scroll had already been cut apart by the Edo period;[5] only about ten fragments are reported to exist today. Fortunately, however, there is a complete copy in the collection of Tanaka Shimbi in Tokyo.[6] This copy carefully follows the original; for example, Hitomaro's portrait (which lacks writing implements) and the exaggerated pose of Saigū are found in the Spencer album. The Tanaka copy differs only in that it contains additional notes which divide the poets into two opposing groups.

The attribution of the text of the Spencer album to numerous courtier-calligraphers follows a popular practice of the late Edo period. Since many poems and novels were ascribed to Edo courtiers, in spite of their widely divergent styles, this attribution should not be taken seriously.

The artist of the album signed only his given name, and impressed his seal to the first and last illustrations (Hitomaro and Nakatsukasa). The *Koga Bikō*, a nineteenth century catalogue of Japanese paintings and painters, reports three artists who used the name "Genkyū." Two were trained in the Kanō school during the seventeenth century;[7] the third is listed as "Hokkyō Genkyū."[8] The latter Genkyū is also credited with the silk painting(s) of the Thirty-six Immortal Poets owned by the Mōri family. The author of the *Kago Bikō*, Asaoka Okisada (1800–1856), examined this work in 1820 and attributed the calligraphy of the silk painting to several calligraphers, including Konoe Iehiro (1667–1736), a son of Motohiro, to whom the text of the first poem in the Spencer album is attributed. The *Koga Bikō* also suggests that Hokkyō Genkyū was the student of a Sumiyoshi painter.

The meticulous, delicate treatment of figures in the Spencer album suggests a stylistic dependence on the conservative Tosa school or its offshoot, the Sumiyoshi school. Both schools produced numerous illustrations of the classics, rendered in the native yamato-e manner, using bright colors, stylized forms, and minute detail. A favorite theme of Tosa and Sumiyoshi artists was the group of Thirty-six Immortal Poets, which they customarily rendered with lavish detail, similar to that of the Spencer album. The Tosa school, descended from Tosa Mitsunobu (active 1469–1521), trained painters for the court. One artist born into this family, Tosa Jokei (1599–1670), left the family atelier in Kyoto and founded his own school in Edo, taking the new surname of Sumiyoshi. Jokei and his son Gukei (1631–1705) served the shogunate in Edo, producing fastidious renderings of classical subjects and lively genre scenes.[9]

The Narikane scroll in the Tanaka collection includes a notation by Gukei, who used another pseudonym, "Hirozumi." It should also be noted that Gukei's illustrations for an album of the *Hyakunin Isshu* (*Single Poems by One Hundred Poets*) display striking similarities to Genkyū's paintings in the Spencer album.[10] Genkyū probably was a student of Jokei or Gukei, and he doubtless used Gukei's copy of the Narikane scroll as a model when he created this album.

NOTES

1. For a full discussion of this legend, see Shirahata Yoshi, "Hitomaro zō ni tsuite (Portraits of Poet-Saint Hitomaro, a Historical Study)," *Bijutsu Kenkyū* 66 (June 1937), pp. 241–251.

2. Mori Tōru, "Sanjūrokkasen-e," *Sanjūrokkasen-e*, vol. 19, Tanaka Ichimatsu (ed.), *Shinshū Nihon Emakimono Zenshū* (Tokyo, 1979), p. 5.

3. For the translation of this poem, see Earl Miner, *Japanese Court Poetry* (Stanford, 1961), p. 99.

4. For the translation of this poem, see H. H. Honda (trans.), *The Shin Kokin Shū* (Tokyo, 1970), p. 212.

5. Several pieces of this scroll are reported in the *Kōko Gafu*. See Kurokawa Mamichi (ed.), *Teisei Zōho Kōko Gafu*, vol. 1 (Tokyo, 1910), p. 198.

6. Mori, "Sanjurokkasen-e," pp. 14–16.

7. Asaoka Okisada (ed.), *Zōtei Koga Bikō* (Tokyo, 1912), vol. 2, p. 1019; vol. 3, pp. 1843, 1977, and 1979.

8. Asaoka, *Koga Bikō*, vol. 3, p. 1506.

9. For Jokei and Gukei, see Doi Tsuguyoshi, "Sumiyoshi Jokei ni tsuite no ichi kōsatsu (A Study of Sumiyoshi Jokei)," *Kobijutsu*, 73 (January 1985), pp. 6–12; and Sakakibara Satoru, "Sumiyoshi Gukei kenkyū note (Research Notes on Sumiyoshi Gukei)," *ibid.*, pp. 29–49.

10. Shirahata Yoshi, *Kasen-e*, no. 96 of *Nihon no Bijutsu*, ed. Staff of the National Museums of Tokyo, Kyoto, and Nara (Tokyo, 1974), Fig. 95.

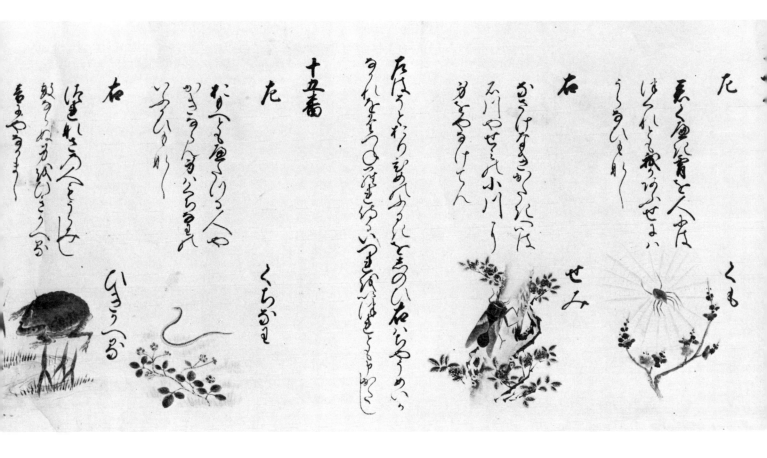

16
Mushi Uta-awase (Poetry Match of Insects)

Late seventeenth to early eighteenth century, Edo period
One handscroll, ink and color on paper
H: 30.3 cm, L: 840.7 cm
Spencer no. 163

The imaginative reinterpretation of classical themes gained unprecedented popularity during the Edo period. A perfect example is the *Mushi Uta-awase (Poetry Match of Insects)*—an amusing variant of the "Poetry Match of Thirty-six Immortal Poets." In this version, garden creatures are cast as the participants in the poetry contest. The text was by Kinoshita Katsutoshi (1569–1649), also popularly known as "Chōshōshi," an author and poet renowned for his wit and imagination.

The *Mushi Uta-awase* begins with a lengthy preface, which sets the stage for the match. The season is late autumn, the time, a moon-lit evening. The narrator, seeking shelter, enters a small garden hut surrounded by frost-covered acanthus reeds. Unable to sleep, he props himself up and observes a group of clustering insects and small animals. A cricket emerges from the clover at the edge of the garden, joins the crowd, and proposes that the insects hold a poetry contest, quoting the famous preface to the *Kokin Waka Shū* (*Collection of Poetry of Ancient and Modern Times*) of 905 that promises each sentient being the opportunity to become a poet.[1] Agreeing to this suggestion, the insects gather on the carpet of fallen leaves and select a toad as umpire. The fifteen poetic pairs are then matched, beginning with the cricket and his opponent, a wasp. Several of the participants are insects that easily conjure up poetic associations—a bell-cricket, firefly, and gold beetle. Others are more mundane—an earthworm, a fly, an ant, and a mosquito. Even lowly creatures like the flea and the louse are present.

In the Spencer handscroll, the poems and the judge's comments are illustrated by small, delicate pictures which show the creatures in their natural habitats. We see a cicada clinging to a tree trunk, a firefly hovering above a stream, and a butterfly next to a green caterpillar.

In a clever parody, rivaling Ryūho's painting of a *haiku* contest (no. 14), Chōshōshi incorporates the insects' names into the poems, either fully or in syllables, as in the final two matches, reproduced here. The fourteenth match, for example, pits a spider against a cicada and a snake against a toad. The spider (*kumo* in Japanese) is shown at the center of its web, which is woven in the fork of a branch with pink blossoms. The spider's verse reads:

Kimi kubeki	I told him
Yoi o hito niwa	What night he should come,
Tsugeredomo	But I have no idea
Waga ause niwa	What will happen when we meet.
Uranai mo nashi.	

The contesting poem by the cicada (*semi*) reads:

Nasake naki	So unresponsive is
Kataki kokoro wa	my frigid love.
Ishikawa ya	It is like the Stone River.
Semi no ogawa ni	I might as well throw
Mio ya nageten.	myself into the Semi River.

The toad umpire, who is evidently well-versed in classical literature, comments on the ancient literary sources which have inspired the two poems. The spider's poem, he notes, evokes a work by the fifth-century princess Sotōrihime, a renowned beauty,[2] while the cicada's piece follows a model established by the essayist Kamo no Chōmei (1153–1216).[3] Unable to decide on the winner, the toad declares the match a draw.

The last contest is between a snake and the toad himself. The snake (*kuchinawa*), positioned amidst a spray of flowers, composes the following verse:

Omoe domo	Separated from my love
Hedatsuru hito ya	by a wall,
Kaki naran	Nothing can be done.
Miwa kuchinawa no	I am the kuchinawa,
Yū kai mo nashi.	a discarded piece of rope.

The contribution of the toad (*hikigaeru*) is the last poem.

Tsuranasa no	My unrequited love,
Hito no urameshi	I am piqued about my unworthy self.

Kazu naranu	Yet, I shall not cry
Mi o hikigaeru	like a toad,
Ne ni ya nakamaji.	To change myself.[4]

The toad then states that he greatly admires the snake's poem, and rates it as comparable to the greatest masterpieces of the past. In great humility, he refers to his own creation as grains of sand mixed with gold. After profusely thanking all the creatures present, the bumpy, rotund toad disappears under the fallen leaves of bamboo.

Chōshōshi was the brother-in-law of the Momoyama military ruler, Toyotomi Hideyoshi, and lord of Obama Castle, north of Kyoto. After Hideyoshi's forces suffered a crushing defeat at the hands of the Tokugawa army in 1600, Chōshōshi took the tonsure and retired to the Higashiyama hills of Kyoto, devoting himself to literary pursuits.

Chōshōshi studied poetry under Hosokawa Yūsai (1534–1610), a military leader and poet, and counted a number of important literary figures and Confucian scholars as his associates. However, he became disenchanted with the poetic world of his day, which he felt was bound to convention, and began to compose light-hearted, even playful verse. His wit and predilection for unconventional themes is apparent in a set of four scrolls, the *Shishō Uta-awase (Poetry Matches of Four Types of Living Beings)*. In this work, insects, birds, beasts and fish are given human personae and cast as adversaries in four different contests.[5] The *Poetry Match of Insects* was probably the first of these. The view that all sentient beings have poetic potential had by then been widely accepted and undoubtedly inspired Chōshōshi's work. He was also undeniably influenced by popular stories in which animals represent humans—such as the tales about mice included in this exhibition (nos. 25, 26)—which came into vogue during the Muromachi period.

The intimate portrayal of insects, snakes, frogs, and other small forms of life in these tales greatly appealed to the diverse audiences of the Edo period, and many variant texts appeared. At least six other works are based on this theme—four painted and two printed versions.[6] The meticulous rendering of the illustrations in the Spencer scroll corresponds to those in a similar scroll painted by Sumiyoshi Jokei (1599–1670) in 1640. Jokei (originally known as Tosa Hiromichi) was trained in the elegant style of the Tosa school, and it is likely that the Spencer scroll was influenced by his illustrations.

NOTES

1. H. H. Honda (trans.), *The Kokin Waka-shū* (Tokyo, 1970), p. 1.
2. Sotōrihime, or Sotōshihime. The fifth daughter of the Emperor Ingyō (reigned 412–453), this princess's real name was Karuno Oiratsume, but she was nicknamed Sotōri or Sotōshi Princess (Beauty-Shining-Through-Dress). For her poem, which is included in the *Manyōshū*, see Ian Hideo Levy (trans.), *The Ten Thousand Leaves* (Princeton, 1981), vol. 1, pp. 82–83.
3. This poem was inspired by Chōmei's verse, which is included in the *Shin Kokinshū* (poem no. 1894). See H. H. Honda (trans.) (Tokyo, 1970).
4. *Hikigaeru* (toad) is used here as a pun on *hikikaeru*, to change or exchange.
5. Ichiko Teiji, *Chūsei Shōsetsu no Kenkyū* (Tokyo, 1956), p. 364.
6. Mori Toru, "Mushi Uta-awase-e" ("Illustrated Uta-awase of Insects"), *Kokka* 1043 (1981), pp. 32–49.

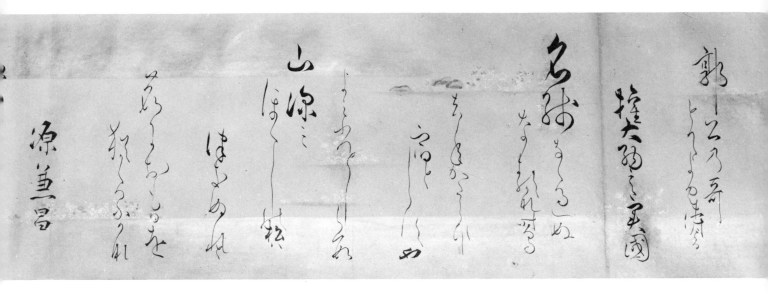

17
Two Poems from the *Senzai Shū*
(*The Collection of Poems of a Thousand Years*)

First half of the seventeenth century, Edo period
Calligraphy by Kojima Sōshin (1580 to ca. 1655)
One handscroll, ink, color, and gold on paper
H: 29.3 cm, L: 766.4 cm
Signature: "Shindokuken Sōshin sho"
Seals: "Shōsai," "Sōshin"
Spencer no. 84.

Against a background of long, horizontal bands of gold mist, accented by small clusters of flowers and rocks, nineteen poems from the *Senzai Shū*—the seventh imperially commissioned poetry anthology—were written in a flowing script, in rich black ink. This exquisitely decorated handscroll bears the signature and two seals of the calligrapher Kojima Sōshin (1580 to ca. 1655). Born in Kyoto, Sōshin was a student of Hon'ami Kōetsu, founder of the Rimpa school (1558–1637, see no. 35),[1] and was connected with Kōetsu's small community of artists and craftsmen at Takagamine, north of the city. Later, he instructed Ogata Sōken (1621–1687) (whose sons were the Rimpa school masters Kōrin and Kenzan) in the art of calligraphy. Relatively little is known about his life, but it is possible that he was inspired by the writing style of the Heian period calligrapher Ono no Tōfū (896–966), since he owned a part of the *Saigū no Nyōgo Shū* (*Collection of the Poems of Saigū no Nyōgo*) attributed to that early master.[2] A number of handscrolls with Sōshin's calligraphy, decorated in a manner similar to that of the Spencer scroll, exist today.

During the late sixteenth and the seventeenth centuries, poems from the imperially commissioned anthologies of *waka* (thirty-one syllable poems) of the Heian and Kamakura periods became popular subjects among the leading calligraphers and artists of Kyoto. There had been renewed interest in ancient courtly traditions among the Kyoto aristocracy, and a desire, perhaps, to assert a "cultural" independence from the powerful Tokugawa military regime in Edo. The Kyoto merchants and artisans—among them such innovative and influential masters as Kōetsu—were also deeply interested in the aesthetic traditions of the Heian period, Japan's "Golden Age." The *Senzai Shū*, compiled ca. 1188 by Fujiwara no Shunzei (1114–1204), contained twenty volumes with a total of 1286 waka.[3] It is not known how Sōshin chose the poems for his scroll, as they do not appear to be thematically connected, and do not follow the original order. The first of the two waka shown here is poem 162 from Book III. The title reads "Composed as a poem about a cuckoo," and names the author, Gon no Dainagon Sanekuni (1140–1183):

Nagori naku   Without regret
Suginu naru kana   The cuckoo passes by,
Hototogisu   Not knowing this as the place
Kozo kataraishi   Where we met last year.
Yado to shirazu ya.

The second poem, which we are told is by an anonymous poet, is number 199, also from Book III:

Yama fukami   The torch lights do not reach,
Hogushi no matsu wa   Into the deepening mountains.
Tsukinuredo   Yet, my thoughts still
Shika ni omoi o   linger on the deer.
Nao kakuru kana

Sōshin's elegant calligraphy reflects Kōetsu's style in its deliberate contrast between thick and thin ink lines, juxtaposition of strongly brushed Chinese characters, or *kanji*, with thin, flowering *kana* (Japanese script) letters, and the exposed brush tip that often appears in the opening or closing strokes of the characters. However, it lacks the smoothness and rhythmic harmony of Kōetsu's works; instead, the approach is rather self-conscious and mannered, executed with a nervous, sharply fluctuating brush. The visual effect of the dark, rich ink against the shimmering gold background of the underpainting is one of refined richness and has decorative appeal.

The underpainting, on which the lines of calligraphy are carefully arranged so as not to obscure the delicate flower and rock motifs, reflects the aesthetic influence of the early Rimpa school and the designer-painter Tawaraya Sōtatsu (active ca. 1600–1640, see no. 35). The small, rounded rocks are painted in blue and green pigments which pool, or run into one another in the technique called *tarashikomi*. However, the overall composition and use of colors with gold appear to be inspired by decorative arts of the time, including lacquer, textile design, and screen painting. Indeed, a Sōshin handscroll of poems from the second imperial anthology, the *Gosen Shū* (in the Harvard University Art Museum,[4] contains not only a length of underpainting which strongly resembles that of the Spencer scroll, but also a section decorated with designs of flowing water, upon which float beautifully painted folding fans and chrysanthemum blossoms, motifs clearly reminiscent of Edo period textile design. These delicate underpaintings are

sometimes attributed to an artist of the Sumiyoshi school, which, like the Tosa school, specialized in the traditional Japanese (*yamato-e*) painting style.[5]

The Spencer scroll bears no date or mention of Sōshin's age at the time of production. However, it closely resembles another handscroll by Sōshin in the Freer Gallery of Art, Washington, D.C. dated to 1652 and another scroll, dated to 1655, immediately preceding his death. The underpaintings of these scrolls are almost identical to that of the Spencer *Senzai Shū*. It appears likely, therefore, that he produced it in the last few years of his life.

NOTES

1. For discussion of Sōken's background and his art, see Yamane Yūzō, "Ogata Kōrin and the Art of the Genroku Era," trans. Rei Sasaguchi, *Acta Asiatica*, no. 15 (December, 1968): pp. 71–74.
2. John M. Rosenfield, Fumiko E. Cranston, and Edwin A. Cranston, *The Courtly Tradition in Japanese Art and Literature* (Cambridge, Mass., 1973), p. 305.
3. Kubota Jun and Matsuno Yōichi (eds.), *Senzai Waka Shū* (Tokyo, 1969).
4. See Rosenfield, *The Courtly Tradition*, pp. 190–191, for catalogue entry on the *Gosen Shū* scroll.
5. Kuboki Shōichi, *Kojima Sōshin Waka-kan*, in Komatsu Shigemi (ed.), *Nihon Meiseki Sōkan* (Tokyo, 1979), vol. 27, p. 60.

18

Two chapters from the *Ise Monogatari Emaki* (*Scroll of the Tales of Ise*)

Late sixteenth century, Momoyama period
Three handscrolls, ink, color and gold on paper
H: 14.6 cm, L: 865.5 cm (scroll I), 962.4 cm (scroll II), 1061 cm (scroll III)
Spencer no. 46

PUBLISHED: Akiyama Terukazu, *Emakimono*, vol. 2 of *Zaigai Nihon no Shihō*, Shimada Shūjirō, ed. (Tokyo, 1980), Pl. 34 and p. 139; Barbara Ruch *et al.* (eds.) *Kaigai Shozō Nara Ehon (Nara Ehon from Outstanding Foreign Collections)* (Tokyo, 1979), Pl. 62; Itō Toshiko, *Ise Monogatari-e* (Tokyo, 1984), pp. 94–121.

These small handscrolls, with thirty-two polychrome illustrations, contain textual and poetic excerpts from sixty-two chapters of the mid-tenth century literary classic, the *Ise Monogatari*, or *Tales of Ise*. An example of the *uta-monogatari* (literally, "tales and poems") genre of Heian fiction, the *Ise Monogatari*, whose author is unknown, includes 209 *waka* (thirty-one-syllable verses) linked by brief passages of narrative prose. The uta-mono-gatari evolved from the custom of attaching fictional or historical headnotes to waka poetry, and the *Ise Monogatari* is the earliest known example of this type of work. Although its 125 tales[1] are not chronologically ordered and there is no unifying storyline, many of them appear to be based on the adventures and amorous exploits of the Heian courtier-poet Ariwara no Narihira (825–880). However, in most of the tales the hero is simply identified as "the young man." Of the several versions of the *Ise* that still exist, the text known as the *Teika-bon* (after the late Heian–early Kamakura period poet Fujiwara no Teika, 1162–1241) evidently was the source for the Spencer Collection's text.[2]

Like the Shining Prince of Murasaki Shikibu's *Genji Monogatari* (*Tale of Genji*, see nos. 20–22), written perhaps half a century later, the "young man" of the *Ise Monogatari* episodes apparently is the prototype of the consummate courtier-lover of the Heian period: handsome, sensitive, fashionable, and skilled in the arts, especially in composing poetry. His love-affairs are with women of varying ages and from different levels of society, so it is not surprising that these tales were a popular subject for narrative illustration from the Heian period on. Chapter 17 ("E-awase") of the *Tale of Genji* refers to an illustration of one of the *Ise* tales, describing it as "a bright, lively painting of contemporary life with much . . . to recommend it."[3] This statement argues for the existence of polychrome *Ise* illustrations at least as early as the beginning of the eleventh century, but, unfortunately, no Heian works on this subject are known to have survived.

The earliest illustrated version of the *Ise* (ca. 1250), a fragmented monochrome scroll with lines of Sanskrit text printed over ink-line drawings, is divided among a number of museums and private collections.[4] The earliest dated scroll in color is a beautiful fourteenth-century work from which only seven painted scenes remain; it is now in the Kubosō Memorial Museum of Fine Art in Osaka Prefecture.[5] There is evidence suggesting that rules for representing *Ise* scenes had developed during the late Heian period, and were perpetuated throughout the Kamakura and Muromachi periods by professional and amateur artists who may have relied upon model books for reference. By the early

sixteenth century, a more or less standard type of *Ise* illustration had evolved, and contemporary literature refers to *Ise* paintings both in *emaki* (handscroll) and *shikishi* (album leaf) forms.[6]

Several of the scenes in the Spencer scrolls are similar to the other extant *Ise Monogatari* scroll paintings of the late Muromachi–Momoyama periods.[7] Apparently all of these works were by amateur artists and are characterized by thickly applied, bright colors and a charmingly naive treatment of figures and landscapes. The Spencer scrolls are unusual because they contain scenes which have not been found in any earlier emaki. Sections of the scrolls apparently were divided and remounted sometime after they were made, so that the scenes do not always follow the sequence of the *Ise* text. Some scenes also appear to be missing.

The Spencer scrolls can be categorized, on the basis of their height, as *ko-e* (small picture) works. Ko-e are associated with narrative painting from the late Muromachi through the early Edo period.[8] The illustrations are relatively uncomplicated and exhibit a sprightly charm. However, a degree of sophistication does emerge in certain elements, such as fabric designs, architectural details, and in the miniature screen paintings, in both color and monochrome ink, that decorate interior scenes. Pigments vary from relatively light to thick and opaque, and the use of gold and dots of heavy white pigment add brilliance and a touch of opulence. The upper and lower borders of each scene are bounded by cloud patterns rendered in blue. The figures are doll-like, executed according to the ancient *hikime-kagihana* (lines-for-eyes, a-hook-for-the-nose) tradition of classical

yamato-e (native Japanese style) figure painting. Landscapes and animals are painted with fluctuating ink outlines filled in with heavy washes of pigment and, occasionally, some delicate fine-lined detail. Most of the tales are accompanied by one painted scene, such as Plate I, for Chapter 67. An exception is Chapter 23, which is illustrated in three scenes (sections 16 through 21 of scroll I).[8]

Chapter 23 tells the story of a young couple, beginning when they were children and "played together beside a well."[9] After their marriage, the husband enters into a liaison with another woman. Astonished that his wife displays no resentment over the affair, he is convinced that she, too, has taken a lover. One night, after pretending to leave home to visit his mistress in Takayasu, he spies on his wife from behind a bush. She has made herself up beautifully, and, gazing into the distance, recites the following poem:

Kaze fukeba	When the winds blow,
Okitsu shiranami	White waves rear up in the offing.
Tatsutayama	Shall you be crossing
Yowa ni ya kimi ga	Tatsutayama
Hitori koyuran.	Quite alone by night?[11]

Upon hearing this, the husband realizes his love for his wife and ceases his visits to his mistress. When he does happen to pass by her house, he finds that this woman, who "had at first taken great pains to make a good appearance,"[12] has abandoned all pretense of good manners. When he observes her filling her rice bowl "to overflowing" with her own hands (shown here), he is quite disgusted and severs their relationship completely.

The second tale shown (Pl. I) is from scroll II (Chapter 67). Here the texts of Chapters 67 and 68 are combined and are followed by the illustration for Chapter 67. The story is a simple one: a gentleman and his companions take a pleasure trip to Izumi. On the way they pass Mt. Ikoma and spend the morning gazing at new-fallen snow. One of their group recites the following poem:

Kinō kyō	It was through reluctance
Kumo no tachimai	To reveal the woods in bloom
Kakurou wa	That yesterday and today
Hana no hayashi o	Clouds soared and swirled
Ushi to narikeri	And the mountain hid itself.[13]

The painting, which seems to have little relation to the tale, is a genre-type scene, painted in vibrant colors. Men, women, and children are shown strolling and playing in the snow; in the center of the picture two young men roll an enormous snowball with their staves. The young man to the far left (one of the travelers?) holds a blossoming branch that evokes early spring, probably a reference to the poem. The strong reds and oranges of the costumes, and the touches of white pigment for snow, animate this simple but charming painting. This particular rendition of Chapter 67 is unusual, and did not appear in any of the earlier versions of the *Ise Monogatari*.[14] A recent study of the *Ise* iconography shows that the cycle of illustrations increased during the late sixteenth century, and that it also began to include pictures with no apparent relation to the text.[15]

Stylistically, the paintings in the Spencer scrolls date to the late sixteenth century, in the Momoyama period. Bright colors and touches of gold on the costumes and architectural interiors reflect the sumptuous tastes of this era. Some of the retainers are portrayed wearing flat-topped, broad-brimmed hats, made popular by the Nambans (literally, "Southern Barbarians")—the Europeans who began visiting Japan during the mid-sixteenth century. Furthermore, the paintings include interior scenes with large, prominently displayed floral arrangements known as *rikka*, which are absent from the same episodes in earlier *Ise* illustrations. These scenes reflect the great vogue that the art of flower arranging began to enjoy during the Momoyama period; they also exhibit the popular flower-arranging technique of the time, one which favored large, sumptuous and schematized compositions (see no. 40).

NOTES

1. The different recensions of the *Ise Monogatari* contain varying numbers of "tales" or chapters. See Helen Craig McCullough, *Tales of Ise: Lyrical Episodes from Tenth-Century Japan* (Stanford, 1968), pp. 182–193.
2. The *Teika-bon* category itself encompasses a variety of close recensions, their compilation being attributed to the hand of Teika or to members of his family. The earliest extant *Teika-bon* manuscript is believed to date to the early Kamakura period. *Ibid.*, p. 187.
3. Murasaki Shikibu, *The Tale of Genji*, Edward G. Seidensticker (trans.) (New York, 1982), p. 312.

4. For reproduction of extant fragments, see Itō Toshiko, "Hakubyō Ise Monogatari emaki ni tsuite," *Yamato Bunka* 53 (November, 1970), pp. 35–58.

5. Nihon Keizai Shimbun, *Kubosō Collection: Tōyō kobijutsuten* (Tokyo, 1982), no. 2. For detailed description see Miyeko Murase, *Emaki: Narrative Scrolls from Japan* (New York, 1983), pp. 81–87.

6. Charles Franklin Sayre, *Illustrations of the Ise Monogatari: Survival and Revival of Heian Court Culture*, Ph.D. thesis, Yale University, 1978, pp. 200–201.

7. *Ibid.*, p. 202.

8. For ko-e, see Umezu Jirō, "Suzuriwari emaki sonota: ko-e no mondai (On the Suzuriwari Zōshi Picture-Scroll)," *Kokka* 828 (March, 1961).

9. This chapter appears to have been one of the more popular of the *Ise* tales, and it served, among other things, as the inspiration for the Nō play *Izutsu* by Zeami Motokiyo (1363–1443). For the English translation of this play, see Nippon Gakujutsu Shinkō-kai (ed.) *The Noh Drama: Ten Plays from the Japanese* (Tokyo and Rutland, Vt., 1955), pp. 91–105.

10. McCullough, *Tales of Ise*, p. 87.

11. *Ibid.*, pp. 88 and 212.

12. *Ibid.*, p. 89.

13. *Ibid.*, p. 115.

14. Sayre, *Illustrations*, pp. 259–260.

15. Itō Toshiko, *Ise Monogatari-e* (Tokyo, 1984), p. 9.

19
Saga-bon Ise Monogatari (Saga Book Tales of Ise)

Dated 1608, Early Edo period
Two bound books, printed in ink on paper
Published by Suminokura Soan (1571–1632)
H: 27.1 cm, W: 19.3 cm
Spencer no. 268
Provenance: Awa no Kuni Bunko

This two-volume version of the *Ise Monogatari* (see also no. 18), was printed in 1608 with movable wooden type and woodblock illustrations on colored papers. It was the result of collaboration among three notable figures from the artistic-literary circles in Kyoto during the early Edo period: the wealthy merchant, official, and art connoisseur Suminokura Soan (1571–1632), his friend and mentor, the artist-calligrapher Hon'ami Kōetsu (1558–1637), and the scholar-courtier Nakanoin Michikatsu (1558–1610). The full-page illustrations, the work of an unknown artist, are among the earliest examples of secular woodblock prints in Japan. These volumes were also among the earliest in a series of printed books known as *Saga-bon*—a term which refers to Soan's private press in the Saga district of Kyoto—and contain forty-nine illustrations of the tenth century prose-and-poetry narrative. Both text and pictures were printed on paper of five different colors—pink, blue, green, purple, and white.

Suminokura Soan was a patron of the arts and a devotee of classical literature.[1] Born to a family of physicians, scholars, and warehouse owners, the young Soan became involved in projects that his father initiated such as the building of the Takasegawa Canal in Kyoto, and the improvement of waterways, such as the famous Hozu Rapids. Soan's family was also active in the lucrative spice and medicinal herb trade with Vietnam and other southeast Asian countries and had accumulated great wealth, which enabled Soan, among other things, to amass a famous library. As a respected scholar, calligrapher, and tea master, Soan moved in Kyoto's cultivated circles.

Although the history of printing in Japan can be traced to the eighth century, printing projects were costly and were usually sponsored by the court or temples.[2] The *Saga-bon* volumes, printed with a new, movable type introduced from Korea only a few years earlier, was the first printing project organized and financed entirely by a private citizen. Soan's books, which began to appear in Kyoto around 1604, included such classics as the *Genji Monogatari (Tales of Genji*, see nos. 20 and 22), an illustrated *Sanjūrokkasen (Thirty-Six Immortal Poets*, see nos. 12 and 25), and texts of *utai* (chants) from Nō theatre dramas of the Kanze school (see no. 35).

The *Saga-bon Ise Monogatari* was reprinted nine times during the two years following its publication in 1608. The books in the Spencer Collection are apparently from one of the first editions, as the second volume concludes with a postscript and written seal of Michikatsu (who died in 1610), along with a reference to mid-summer. Editions printed after 1608 carry a different postscript and have no written seal.[3] *The Tales of Ise*, which had long been considered essential to a cultivated person's education, were enjoying renewed interest at court during this time. The Emperor Goyōzei (reigned 1587–1611), who also commissioned movable-type printed versions of Japanese and Chinese classics, took a special interest in the *Ise*. Himself a classical scholar, he delivered lectures on the *Ise* and *Genji Monogatari*, and wrote scholarly essays on them.[4] It seems likely, then, that the cultural ambiance of Kyoto influenced Soan's choice of subjects for his publishing venture.

The calligraphy of the *Ise* volumes is elegant and expressive, written in a fluid combination of Japanese script (*kana*) and cursive Chinese script. Calligraphy expressed in movable type has its limitations, but, since the actual pieces of type varied in size—from a single letter or character to two- or three-letter elements—the printed script conveys the impression of an elegant, flowing script in which one letter frequently flows into the next. The calligraphy model for the *Ise* text is often attributed to Kōetsu, but more recent studies favor a re-attribution to Soan himself.

Apparently, one painter of the period, Tawaraya Sōtatsu (died ca. 1641), was involved with the *Saga-bon* project—although not directly. He, along with Kōetsu, founded the Rimpa school, and produced models for stamp designs which were used in books printed and published at Saga (see no. 35). Sōtatsu and his associates also produced a number of *Ise* paintings in album leaf and fan format, but these are stylistically unrelated to the printed *Saga-bon* pictures and are generally dated to a later period in his career.[5] The printed pictures exhibit stylistic elements characteristic of the Tosa school of narrative painting (see nos. 21 and 22). Recent scholarship has drawn comparisons between the *Saga-bon* scenes and miniature paintings by such early Edo period Tosa masters as Mitsuyoshi (1539–1613).[6] The *Saga-bon* arrangements of figures, architecture, and landscape elements are reminiscent of those found in the *Genji Monogatari* album leaves—exquisitely detailed polychrome and *hakubyō* (ink-line drawings)—created by Tosa artists.

Another two-scroll set of *Ise* pictures, bearing the seal of Tosa Mitsunori (1583–1638),[7] depicts the same episodes as those in the *Saga-bon* version. The compositions are identical, suggesting that Mitsunori was inspired by the printed pictures, which could have been designed by an older member of his family. During this period there was a veritable sea of *Ise* iconographic types, and the artist of the *Saga-bon Ise* may have attempted to create a standard pictorial cycle and uniform compositions for the tales. In fact, *Ise* pictures of later years, whether in handscroll, book, or screen format, often adhere to the imagery he established.

A red rectangular seal reading "Awa no Kuni Bunko" ("Library of the Province of Awa") was impressed after the postscript of the Spencer *Saga-bon Ise*, indicating that these books once belonged to the famous collection owned by Lord Hachisuka of Awa Province (modern Tokushima Prefecture), in the southeast of Shikoku Island.

Chapter 12 of Volume I of the *Ise Monogatari* is the subject of the illustration reproduced here. In this brief tale, an amorous young man runs off with a young girl, but is apprehended by a group of provincial officials. He hides the girl in a clump of bushes and flees, but the officials, thinking that he must be nearby, decide to set fire to the surrounding plain in order to flush him out. The young girl overhears this plan and calls out in terror:

> Musashino wa   Do not set fire today
> Kyō wa na yaki so   To Musashi Plain,

Wakakusa no	For my beloved husband
Tsuma mo komoreri	Is hidden here,
Ware mo komoreri.	And so am I.[8]

The pursuers find the girl and capture her lover, too.

In the picture, we see the young couple dressed in court garments, kneeling in the windblown foliage. The searcher in the foreground appears to glance in their direction. The turbulence of the scene is echoed by the ominous clouds scudding overhead. The figures are stylized, but the artist has managed to convey a sense of agitation and movement within the simple arrangement of forms.

The scene from Volume II is taken from Chapter 69. This episode, which involves the seduction of the Virgin Priestess of the Ise Shrine, is one of the longer stories from the narrative and contains three poems. In this episode, a courtier is sent off to Ise province as an Imperial Huntsman. At the Ise Shrine—the holiest shrine of ancient Japan—he encounters the Virgin Priestess, who has been told to treat him "better than the ordinary run of imperial representatives."[9] On the second day of his stay, the young man makes certain overtures to the Virgin, who agrees to meet him at his bedchamber around 11 o'clock that night.[10]

Publication of the *Saga-bon Ise Monogatari* made this classic work more widely available to those members of Kyoto society who were interested in the study and revival of Heian culture. In later years, other classics of Japanese literature with woodblock print illustrations were printed.

NOTES

1. Hayashiya Tatsusaburō, *Suminokura Soan* (Tokyo, 1978).
2. For the early history of printing in Japan, see David Chibbett, *The History of Japanese Printing and Book Illustration* (Tokyo, New York, and San Francisco, 1977); and Mosaku Ishida, with English adaptation by Charles S. Terry, *Japanese Buddhist Prints* (New York, 1964).
3. For reproduction of different postscripts, see Kawase Kazuma, *Saga-bon Zukō* (Tokyo, 1932); also for the discussion of the *Saga-bon Ise*, see Charles Franklin Sayre, *Illustrations of the Ise-Monogatari: Survival and Revival of Heian Court Culture*, Ph.D. dissertation, Yale University, 1978.
4. Higo Kazuo (ed.), *Rekidai Tennō Ki* (Tokyo, 1972), pp. 499–504.
5. Yamane Yūzō, "Den Sōtatsu hitsu Ise Monogatari Zu shiki-shi ni tsuite (Study on the Ise Monogatari Shikishi, attributed to Sōtatsu)," *Yamato Bunka*, 59 (March 1974), pp. 216–27; this article is quoted in summary in Yoshiaki Shimizu and John M. Rosenfield, *Masters of Japanese Calligraphy, 9th–19th Century* (New York, 1984), p. 233.
6. Sayer, *Illustrations of the Ise-Monogatari*, p. 274.
7. This book is reproduced in Itō Toshiko, *Ise Monogatari-e* (Tokyo, 1984), pp. 184–188.
8. Helen Craig McCullough (trans.), *Tales of Ise: Lyric Episodes from Tenth-Century Japan* (Stanford, 1968), p. 78.
9. *Ibid.*, p. 115.
10. *Ibid.*, p. 116.

20

Four scenes from a *Hakubyō Genji Monogatari Emaki* ("White Drawing" Handscrolls of the Tale of Genji)

Dated 1554, Muromachi period
By Keifukuin Gyokuei
Six handscrolls, ink on paper
H: 9.8 cm, L: 1043.8 cm (scroll I), 620.5 cm (scroll II), 1125.1 cm (scroll III), 637.6 cm (scroll IV), 785.1 cm (scroll V), 1052.6 cm (scroll VI)
Spencer no. 37

PUBLISHED: Akiyama Terukazu, *Genji-e*, no. 119 of *Nihon no bijutsu*, ed. Staff of the National Museums of Tokyo, Kyoto and Nara (Tokyo, 1976); Akiyama Terukazu, "Genji-e no Keifu," in Akiyama Ken *et al.* (eds.), *Genji Monogatari*, vol. 7 of *Zusetsu Nihon no koten* (Tokyo, 1978); Barbara Ruch *et al.* (eds.), *Kaigai Shozō Nara Ehon (Nara Ehon from Outstanding Foreign Collections)* (Tokyo, 1979), Pl. 63; Julia Meech-Pekarik, "The Artist's View of Ukifune," in Andrew Pekarik (ed.), *Ukifune: Love in the Tale of Genji* (New York, 1982); Miyeko Murase, *Iconography of the Tale of Genji* (New York and Tokyo, 1983).

This charming series of illustrations executed in the *hakubyō* (literally, "white drawing") manner in ink on paper, depicts scenes from the *Genji Monogatari (Tale of Genji)*, the most celebrated work of Japanese fiction. In six scrolls of diminutive height, this *emaki* follows the sequence of events from the eleventh-century prose narrative in fifty-five illustrated sections, each of which is accompanied by a chapter heading and a brief text. The text consists, for the most part, of poems exchanged between the figures in the scenes. There are also brief explanatory notes in prose.[1] The poems reveal the central theme of each chapter, and set the atmosphere for the illustrations.

The illustrations themselves exhibit a delightfully naive approach, a characteristic of a number of monochrome handscrolls from the Muromachi period. The meticulous hakubyō technique, which reduces painting to the austerity of the black ink line, appears to have been perfected in Japan during the second half of the thirteenth century.[2] Hakubyō drawings differ from monochrome ink paintings of the Muromachi and later periods in that they do not utilize ink washes or fluctuating brush lines to define planes and three-dimensional forms. Instead, shapes and volume are delineated entirely by outlines executed without modulation. No doubt this technique was inspired in part by the premium which Chinese art placed upon the purity of the ink line; however, hakubyō may have evolved as artistic possibilities were recognized in the ink line underdrawings made before pigment was applied to polychrome paintings. The austere, yet haunting beauty of hakubyō's gossamer-thin lines, and forms punctuated by stark black highlights, must have appealed to connoisseurs of art as even more evocative of the elegant and graceful atmosphere of courtly life than the brilliant colors of polychrome painting.

Both text and paintings in this set of scrolls are attributed to Keifukuin Gyokuei, daughter of the Kyoto courtier and regent Konoe Taneie (1503–1566), in an inscription on the frontispiece of the first scroll. A colophon on the sixth scroll, written by the artist herself, dates the emaki to 1554:

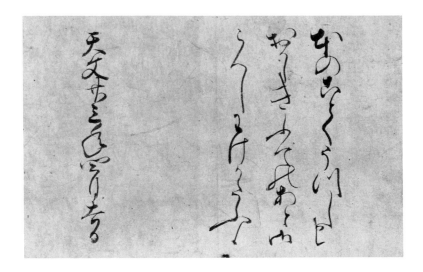

I have copied it just like the original [so that] the pleasing traces of the brush are difficult to distinguish [from those in the original work]. Temmon 23 [1554], the fourth month, an auspicious day.

The *Genji Monogatari*, like the *Ise Monogatari* (see nos. 18, 19), was a highly popular subject for narrative illustration from late Heian times onward. Written around the year 1000 by Murasaki Shikibu, a noblewoman from a minor branch of the powerful Fujiwara family, the novel traces the life and loves of the incomparable Prince Genji and two generations of his descendants in highly evocative and descriptive literary style. The "Shining Genji," whose career takes the reader through forty-one of the tale's fifty-four chapters, is a personification of the Heian ideal—learned and highly sensitive to the beauty of the natural world. His physical beauty is such that it inspires in others "a shudder of delight and [sense of] foreboding"[3] that it may all too soon pass away. The

novel is primarily about the many romantic adventures of the prince, beginning with his secret love affair with his stepmother Fujitsubo, and ending with his ill-fated marriage to the young "Third Princess" and the tragic death of his favorite lover, Murasaki. Following the death of Genji, the narrative turns to the lives of his son Yūgiri and the amorous intrigues of Kaoru, offspring of an illicit relationship between the Third Princess and the son of Genji's closest friend, and Niou, Genji's grandson.

The earliest example of an illustrated *Genji* is a work dating to the early twelfth century,[4] parts of which are held by the Gotō Museum, the Tokugawa Reimeikai, and several other collections in Japan. The paintings from this set are beautiful examples of the brilliantly colored *tsukuri-e* (literally, "built-up pictures") style of painting that evolved during the latter half of the Heian period. Tsukuri-e, which utilized conventionalized figures and a strong schematic approach to color, scenery, and architectural elements, is both evocative and highly decorative. Although no earlier *Genji* pictures exist, comparisons of these paintings with later works and literary references to lost *Genji* paintings clearly indicate that, by the late twelfth century, certain rules for illustrating episodes from the famed novel had been firmly established.[5]

During the thirteenth century, the *Genji* continued to inspire illustration; however, the only *Genji* pictures from this period are the exquisitely delineated ink drawings currently in the Yamato Bunkakan in Nara and the Tokugawa Reimeikai in Tokyo. This set of drawings, a distinct ancestor of the Spencer monochrome scrolls, was executed in the classic hakubyō style, with striking contrasts between areas of solid black and fragile ink lines against a stark white background.

Hakubyō narrative painting of later periods cannot match the "white drawing" works of the thirteenth century, but the genre did survive into the sixteenth and seventeenth centuries, and appears to have been popular among amateur artists. Hakubyō works produced during the late Muromachi period include several versions of the *Genji*, for the most part technically naive small-scale drawings, but decorative and executed with exuberance. The outlines in these works—including the Spencer *Genji*—vary from relatively soft and broad to thin, sharp brushstrokes which lack the tension and tautness

characteristic of earlier hakubyō painting. Ink tones range from a washy grey to dark black; the frequent application of pearl-grey ink softens the stark contrast between black ink and white paper and increases the decorative quality of the illustration. Men and women are pear-faced and doll-like, and basically interchangeable. Some are identified by inscriptions written close to their figures. Floral and foliage motifs, fantastically conceived, are often disproportionately large in comparison to the figures, a characteristic of pictorial art from the late Muromachi period.[6] Floral motifs in the Spencer *Genji* scrolls also exhibit the influence of a dyed textile pattern, known as *tsujigahana* (crossed-flowers), which became popular in the second half of the sixteenth century and is specifically associated with Momoyama-period taste.[7] Like the motifs in tsujigahana-dyed fabrics, the flowers that grow in riotous profusion in many of the *Genji* scenes are frequently shaded with a delicately applied dark ink wash, with parts of the foliage completely filled in with ink or wash for decorative contrast. In these scrolls, ink washes are also used for atmospheric effect in landscape elements.

The first scene reproduced here is from section 10 of the first scroll, illustrating Chapter 10, "Sakaki" ("Sacred Tree").[8] It shows Prince Genji paying a visit to the Lady Rokujō,

a former lover, who is preparing to depart for the shrine at Ise with her daughter. With one hand, Genji pushes a branch of the sacred tree *Sakaki* beneath the sharply angled blinds separating him from Lady Rokujō. Beyond the veranda stands a brushwood fence, above which flowers, autumn grasses, and leaves emerge, and in the "reed plain of melancholy beauty"[9] a *torii* (shrine gate), can be seen.

A scene from scroll III, section 7, represents Chapter 28, "Nowaki" ("Typhoon").[10] An autumn storm has wreaked havoc with Genji's residence, and, since the house is in some disarray and folding screens have been put aside, the visiting Yūgiri catches his first glimpse of his "stepmother," the beautiful Murasaki. In the illustration, Genji and Murasaki are shown seated indoors, close to a rolled-up blind. Standing beyond a small garden of wind-dishevelled flowers, Yūgiri turns his head to look in their direction. Beyond his figure we see another garden where three young girls are setting out insect traps among the plants.

Another scene, section 3 of the fifth scroll, juxtaposes an indoor and outdoor scene in a particularly striking composition. It represents Chapter 38, "Suzumushi" ("Bell Cricket"), in which Genji's young wife, the Third Princess, becomes a nun as a private

penance for her clandestine love affair with Kashiwagi, the son of Genji's closest friend.[11] During the summer while the lotuses are in bloom, holy images are dedicated for the Princess's chapel; in autumn, Genji has his garden arranged to "look like a moor"[12] and he and his son pay a visit to the Princess on the eve of the full moon. During his visit, Genji, Yūgiri, and others indulge in an impromptu concert. In the illustration, the imaginatively realized lotus pool is set next to two sharply angled fences enclosing autumn flowers and plants, which also grow at the corner of the veranda.

The final scene reproduced here is from Chapter 45, "Hashihime" ("The Lady at the Bridge"), the first of the so-called "Ten Uji Chapters" that make up the last section of the *Genji Monogatari*. In this popular episode, Kaoru, Genji's illegitimate son, visits Genji's brother, the Eighth Prince, and his lovely young daughters Ōigimi and Naka-nokimi.[13] Kaoru manages to catch a glimpse of the two princesses as they play musical instruments in their chambers, unaware that they are being observed. In the painting, the girls are shown at the far right. One raises the plectrum of her lute, while the other bends her head over her *koto* (a thirteen-stringed instrument).

The illustrations in the Spencer handscroll are stylistically extremely close to other hakubyō narrative paintings produced around the mid-sixteenth century—several of which also depict scenes from the *Genji Monogatari*. However, the Spencer paintings are among the finest examples of the late hakubyō technique; the charming, childlike figures of courtiers and ladies, placed amidst flowers and plants of the different seasons, evoke gentle pathos and call to mind a bygone, halcyon era. The artist's claim to have made her drawings "indistinguishable" from those in her model was not a boast.

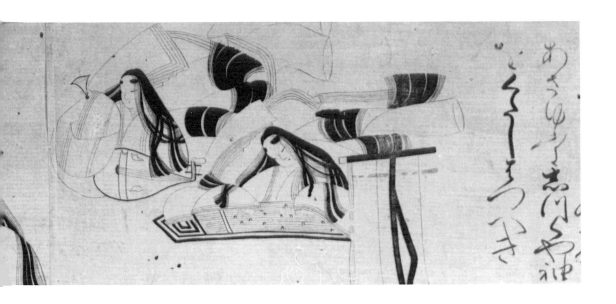

NOTES

1. For detailed discussion, description and analysis of this emaki, see Sarah E. Thompson, *A Hakubyo Genji Monogatari Emaki in the Spencer Collection*, unpublished M.A. thesis, Columbia University, 1984.

2. For similar examples of Muromachi-period hakubyō scrolls, see Shimbo Tōru, *Hakubyō Emaki*, no. 48 of *Nihon no Bijutsu*, ed. Staff of the National Museums of Tokyo, Kyoto and Nara (Tokyo, 1970).

3. Murasaki Shikibu, *The Tale of Genji*, trans. Edward G. Seidensticker (New York, 1977), p. 138.

4. Komatsu Shingemi (ed.), *Nihon Emaki Taisei*, vol. 1 (Tokyo, 1977); Miyeko Murase, *Emaki: Narrative Scrolls from Japan* (New York, 1983), nos. 9, 10.

5. For the early history of *Genji* paintings, see Miyeko Murase, *Iconography of the Tale of Genji* (New York and Tokyo, 1983), p. 10.

6. Saburō Mizoguchi, *Design Motifs*, trans. Louise Allison Cort, *Arts of Japan 1* (New York and Tokyo, 1973), p. 86.

7. See discussion on the use of tsujigahana motifs in other illustrated handscrolls in Thompson, *A Hakubyo Genji*, pp. 124–125; also see Itō Toshiko, *Tsujigahana: The Flower of Japanese Textile Art*, trans. Monica Bethe (Tokyo, 1981).

8. Seidensticker, *The Tale of Genji*, pp. 185–187.

9. *Ibid.*, p. 186.

10. *Ibid.*, p. 465.

11. *Ibid.*, p. 668ff.

12. *Ibid.*, p. 671.

13. *Ibid.*, p. 785.

21

"Sakaki" ("Sacred Tree") and "Kashiwagi" ("Oak Tree"), Chapters 10 and 36 of the *Genji Monogatari* (*Tale of Genji*)

Beginning of the seventeenth century, Momoyama period
Attributed to the circle of Chōjirō
Two books with painted covers, ink, color and gold on paper
H: 25.3 cm, W: 17.1 cm ("Sakaki"), 17.3 cm ("Kashiwagi")
Spencer nos. 49b and 50

PUBLISHED: Akiyama Terukazu, *Emakimono*, vol. 2 of *Zaigai Nihon no Shihō*, Shimada Shūjirō, ed. (Tokyo, 1980), Pls. 28–29 and pp. 137–138.

Glowing, jewel-like colors and billowing scalloped-edged clouds of gold lend a rich, iconic quality to the painted covers of two small volumes containing text from the *Genji Monogatari* (see no. 20). These paper-bound volumes with handwritten text in *kana* script, once belonged to a set of books comprising the fifty-four chapters of the classical romantic prose narrative. There are no illustrations in the books; the only paintings are on the covers (front and back) of the volumes. On the front covers of the books are small slips of orange paper, pasted in the upper left-hand corner, which bear the titles for the chapters "Sakaki" (Chapter 10) and "Kashiwagi" (Chapter 36). From the Momoyama period on, small-scale *Genji* paintings, often produced in album format, were popular, and complete illustrated sets of the tale became favored dowry gifts for young girls.[1] It is possible that the two books in the Spencer Collection were originally part of such a set.

The cover scenes were taken from episodes within each chapter. The painting on the front of the "Sakaki" volume depicts a nobleman approaching the blinds of a room within which a woman is seated. In his hand he holds a small sprig or branch. In the garden, flowers bloom next to a brushwood fence, but behind the veranda a leafless tree can be seen. It is autumn, in the Ninth Month. A half-moon hangs in the night sky, surrounded by ornamental golden clouds. This scene depicts an early episode from the chapter, in which Prince Genji pays a visit to a former lover, the Lady Rokujō. Genji approaches the building in which the lady and her daughter are staying.

> "May I at least come up to the veranda?" he asked, starting up the stairs.
> The evening moon burst forth and the figure she saw in its light was handsome beyond describing.
> Not wishing to apologize for all the weeks of neglect, he pushed a branch of the sacred tree in under the blinds.[2]

This scene (also illustrated in the Spencer *Hakubyō Genji Monogatari Emaki*, no. 20) is one of the most frequently depicted of the *Genji* episodes.

On the back cover of this volume is a winter scene at the emperor's palace: two courtiers and two gorgeously clad women, one of whom is partially shielded by the curtains of a dais, are seated in a room together. Outside, a pine tree and rocks are dusted with snow, and ice forms on a pond or river. The two male figures are Genji and Prince Hyōbu, the brother of the imperial consort Fujitsubo, Genji's secret love.

Prince Hyōbu has arrived to take his sister back to her family residence, and Genji has come to see them off. Together, they compose poetry. Fujitsubo, who is clad in a white robe with floral motifs over layers of colored garments, is seated on the dais.

The paintings on the "Kashiwagi" volume depict two incidents which were often combined in other *Genji* paintings.[3] The front cover depicts a man in courtier dress— Tō no Chūjō, one of Genji's closest friends—facing an ascetic from Mt. Katsuragi, who has been summoned by Tō no Chūjō to exorcise spirits believed to be causing the illness of his son Kashiwagi. Kashiwagi is in truth suffering pangs of love and guilt; he has been involved in a secret affair with the Third Princess, the young wife of Prince Genji. But Kashiwagi declines rapidly and none of the holy men called in are able to restore his health.

The scene on the back cover shows the ailing Kashiwagi, clad in a sumptuous robe, reading a letter from the Third Princess. A young woman kneels beside him, holding a lighted taper for him to read by.

Each of these paintings exhibits the style of polychrome illustration practiced by artists of the Tosa school—heirs to the *yamato-e* (native Japanese) tradition—during the Momoyama and Edo periods. This approach relied not so much on the flexibility of ink brushwork as it did on the harmony of fine-lined details, colors, and gold. The Tosa outline, uniform and fragile, might lack the tensile strength of that of the Kanō school, but it was perfect for the miniaturist's art, the concern in these paintings being surface rather than movement or depth. Architectural details, although they owe their basic outlines to the *fukinuki-yatai* (literally, "blown-off roof") device of yamato-e, have become a part of the overall decorative scheme of the paintings. Tiny faces bear minimalized and anonymous features—the *hikime-kagihana* (lines-for-the-eyes, a-hook-for-the-nose) basic to the yamato-e style. The courtiers in Tosa paintings are schematized— their figures consisting of voluminous yet structured robes from which doll-like heads and tiny white hands emerge: idealized humans inhabiting an idealized past.

During the Momoyama and early Edo periods, the two most notable exponents of this exquisite painting technique, Tosa Mitsuyoshi (1539–1613) and his successor Tosa Mitsunori (1583–1638), produced series of *Genji* illustrations in the small album format. Both artists worked with brilliant colors and gold. The Kyoto National Museum owns an important album from the Tosa school containing fifty-four leaves of *Genji* paintings, which provides material for comparison with the Spencer book covers.[4] Thirty-six of these paintings carry the "Kyūyoku" seal adopted by Mitsuyoshi after he took that priestly name, twelve leaves have no seal or signature, and the remaining six (which duplicate six of Mitsuyoshi's scenes) are signed by a virtually unknown artist called Chōjirō. Since that artist's works bear certain stylistic similarities to Mitsunori's paintings, it has been suggested that the youthful-sounding name of "Chōjirō" may have been used by the Tosa artist before he adopted the name "Mitsunori."[5] The paintings on the covers of the Spencer albums strongly resemble the "Chōjirō" works, particularly in such details as the plump faces and landscape elements. The compositions are also less tightly constructed than those by Mitsunori, and lack the painstakingly executed details that distinguish Mitsunori illustrations.

On a stylistic basis, it would appear that the artist of the Spencer paintings worked in the Tosa school at the time Chōjirō was active. Chōjirō may have taken over the illustration of the Kyoto album at about the time of Misuyoshi's death, and was probably

active toward the end of the Momoyama era. It is likely that the Spencer book covers were produced during those years.

Two different calligraphers were responsible for the text in these volumes. In an inscription at the end of the "Sakaki" volume is the name Saionji Shōkō (the Minister Saionji), and in the "Kashiwagi" volume is the name Kazan-in Naifu (Keeper of the Privy Seal, Kazan-in). The name Saionji Sanekatsu also appears in the "Sakaki" volume, but as each of the inscriptions was written in a hand that differs from that of the text, it is likely that these attributions were made after the original set of books was produced.

NOTES

1. Miyeko Murase, *Iconography of the Tale of Genji* (New York and Tokyo, 1983), p. 16.
2. Murasaki Shikibu, *The Tale of Genji*, trans. Edward G. Seidensticker (New York, 1977), p. 187.
3. *Ibid.*, pp. 637–639.
4. Takeda Tsuneo, "Tosa Mitsuyoshi to saiga: Kyoto Kokuritsu Hakubutsukan *Genji Monogatari* zujō o megutte," *Kokka* 996 (December 1976), pp. 11–40. For a discussion of another small *Genji* painting attributed to Chōjirō, see *New York Burke Collection: Nihon Bijutsu Meihinten*, Tokyo National Museum exhibition catalogue (Tokyo, 1985), no. 38.
5. Virtually nothing is known about this artist and the development of his oeuvre. Chōjirō may have been a name used by Tosa Mitsunori when he was a pupil of Mitsuyoshi, before his painting style reached its maturity.

22
"Hahakigi" ("The Broom Tree") and "Suetsumuhana" ("Safflower"), Chapters 2 and 6 of the *Genji Monogatari Emaki* (*Handscrolls of the Tale of Genji*)

Mid-seventeenth century, Edo period
Calligraphy by Minamoto no Toshinaga ("Hahakigi"); Nishiike Suemichi ("Suetsumuhana")
Three handscrolls, ink, color, and gold on paper
H: 35.4 cm ("Hahakigi"), 35.3 cm ("Suetsumuhana," second scroll), 35.2 cm ("Suetsumuhana," third scroll)
L: 1123.1 cm ("Hahakigi"), 1475.1 ("Suetsumuhana," second scroll), 1735.5 cm ("Suetsumuhana," third scroll)
Seal: "Moriyasu," "Sugihara Shōun" (?)
Spencer no. 67

PUBLISHED: Akiyama Terukazu, *Emakimono*, vol. 2 of *Zaigai Nihon no Shihō*, Shimada Shūjirō (ed.) (Tokyo, 1980), Pl. 23 and pp. 134–135; Mieyko Murase, *Iconography of the Tale of Genji* (New York and Tokyo, 1983), pp. 329–330.

In a dazzling display of gold and rich color, and in remarkable detail, these three handscrolls relate sections of two chapters from the eleventh-century literary classic, the *Genji Monogatari*, or *Tale of Genji* (see nos. 20–21). The labels on the covers of these scrolls indicate that they originally belonged to an *emaki* (illustrated narrative handscroll) of over 100 scrolls that reproduced the complete text. The "Hahakigi" scroll bears the character for autumn, suggesting that it was the third in a set of four handscrolls. The two "Suetsumuhana" scrolls are marked with the characters for "middle" and "lower," indicating that this chapter was illustrated in three scrolls. Several different calligraphers and artists were apparently responsible for these sumptuous works. A colophon from the "Hahakigi" scroll cites Minamoto no Toshinaga as calligrapher, while the scribe named in the "Suetsumuhana" scrolls is Nishiike Suemichi. The artists are unknown, but each of the scrolls is stamped with a seal which may have belonged to the mounters of these works. A round seal on the "Suetsumuhana" scrolls reads "Moriyasu," and a rectangular seal on the "Hahakigi" scroll may read "Sugihara Shōun."

The *Genji Monogatari* of Murasaki Shikibu enjoyed a long history of narrative illustration from the twelfth century on, and while many *Genji* paintings dating to the late Muromachi period were executed in the *hakubyō* (ink-line "white drawing") manner (see no. 20), artists of the Tosa school (see no. 21) began to produce *Genji* paintings in miniature detail and brilliant color and gold. It was during this period, too, that the iconography of *Genji* scenes was codified and written down in a manual. The earliest existing manuscript of a *Genji* painting manual, known as the *Genji Monogatari Ekotoba* (in the collection of the Osaka Women's College), appears to date to the sixteenth century. This book, however, may be a copy of an older version.[1] Not all painters adhered to such manuals—the Spencer scrolls, for example, do not seem to follow any set formulas— but the books no doubt helped to guide artists who were not familiar with the entire novel.

Many of the brightly colored *Genji* paintings that exist today date to the Momoyama and Edo periods. Patrons were the scholarly aristocracy, the military, and the wealthy merchant class, among whom there was a revival of interest in native classical tradition. Artists of various schools, including the official Kanō painters and members of the innovative Rimpa school, illustrated scenes from the *Genji*; the illustrations were produced on large folding-screens, fans, and *shikishi* (small squares of paper).[2]

The Tosa school, heir to the classic tradition of painting Japanese subject matter, perfected a polished, highly detailed approach to polychrome *Genji* illustrations. As the various schools of painting became more eclectic, however, Kanō artists—among them the great master of the Momoyama period, Kanō Eitoku (1543–1590)—frequently combined elements of their so-called Chinese ink-painting techniques with elements borrowed from the Tosa style of illustration.[3] Tosa artists, in turn, were influenced by the Kanō style in their treatment of landscape motifs and their use of large-scale decorative formats such as folding and sliding screens. The Spencer scrolls are excellent examples of the eclectic style of the early Edo period, although the artist appears to have been strongly influenced by the Kanō school. For example, certain landscape elements in the garden scenes—especially the angular, multi-faceted rocks and boulders delineated in ink and filled in with color—are in the Kanō style. Many of the tiny paintings-within-paintings on sliding and standing screens also are "Kanōesque," with strongly articulated ink outlines and bird-and-flower or "Chinese-landscape"-inspired subject matter.

These *Genji* scrolls display a richness of color and a lavish use of gold—suggesting that the work was commissioned by a wealthy patron. (So lavishly is the gold applied as a ground that these scrolls are noticeably heavier than others.) Billowing clouds of golden mist flecked with powdered gold, and gold patterns in the dark blue of garden streams add to the sumptuous quality of the paintings. In interior scenes, furnishings are so carefully depicted one can see the tiny lacquer designs on boxes, mirror stands, and other objects. In outdoor settings, a lush variety of flora stands out in exquisite relief against the gold background and billowing clouds (Pl. II). Some plants are drawn in an ink outline that fluctuates in width and is filled in with color, in the Kanō school manner. Figures are rather stiffly rendered.

The first scene depicted here is the third painting from the "Hahakigi" scroll. In this episode from the second chapter of the novel, Prince Genji is spending the night at the residence of the governor of Kii. After the household has retired, Genji, "not pleased at the prospect of sleeping alone,"[4] overhears a conversation in the adjoining room and realizes that Utsusemi, the young wife of the governor of Iyo (the father of his host) is within. Intrigued, he opens the door between their rooms and makes his way toward her.

> A curtain had been set up just inside, and in the dim light he could make out Chinese chests and other furniture scattered in some disorder. He made his way through to her side. She lay by herself, a slight little figure. Though vaguely annoyed at being disturbed, she evidently took him for the woman Chūjō [her attendant] until he pulled back the covers.[5]

In the "Suetsumuhana" chapter, Genji enters into a love affair with the "Safflower Lady," an impoverished noblewoman somewhat lacking in beauty and sophistication. Genji pities her and later takes her into his house as one of his concubines.

The scene from the third "Suetsumuhana" scroll shows Genji and his young ward and future favorite, the child Murasaki, playing together.

> She drew charming little sketches, coloring them as the fancy took her. He drew a lady with very long hair and gave her a very red nose [a portrait of the unattractive Safflower Lady], and though it was only a picture it produced a shudder.[6]

The detail in this scene is so meticulous the red dot on the nose of the figure in the drawing can be discerned. Musical instruments are propped against the wall, and a *go* board stands beneath shelves in an alcove—objects which bespeak Murasaki's accomplishments as a cultured and refined girl.

This *Genji Monogatari Emaki* must have been one of the most expensive and lavishly designed sets of scrolls produced during the Edo period. Not only does it reproduce the entire novel, its profusely detailed and decorative paintings are the most comprehensive cycle of *Genji* illustrations known. Other scrolls belonging to the set are known to exist—the first scroll of the "Suetsumuhana" chapter is in the collection of the temple Ishiyamadera in Kyoto.[7] A group of six scrolls, representing Chapter 9, "Aoi" ("Heart-vine"), which once belonged to the Nambu family in Mutsu province (modern Iwate prefecture), still exists in Japan.[8]

In 1980, the text and paintings (six scrolls) for Chapter 10, "Sakaki" ("Sacred Tree"), from this set were discovered in Paris;[9] however, these have since been separated and dispersed to various collections. Examination of these paintings and the Spencer scrolls reveals slight differences in the delineation of facial features and, more noticeable, land-

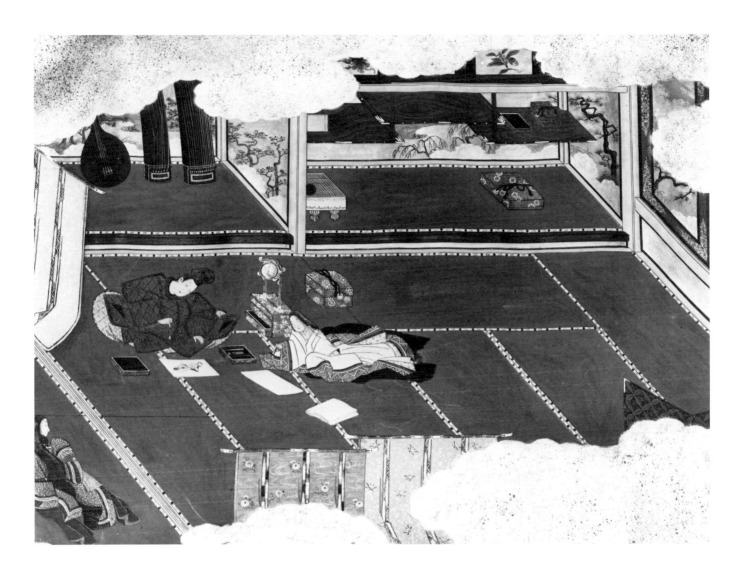

scape elements, indicating that several different hands were involved in the production of the complete work. The calligraphy is fluid, and the paper is decorated with sprinkled gold patterns and designs of flowers and leaves painted in gold. The inscriptions in the "Hahakigi" and the "Sakaki" scrolls read "Uma no kami Minamoto no Toshinaga hitsu." Little is known about Toshinaga's life other than that he held the title of "Master of Horse" (*Uma no kami*). The "Suetsumuhana" scrolls in the Spencer collection are signed "Kamo no Agata nushi Nishiike Mokunosuke Suemichi hitsu," which indicate that the calligrapher came from the Nishiike family, who held the hereditary title of honor at the Kamo Shrine in Kyoto. It is known that Yottsuji Suetaka (1630–1668), the calligrapher of the "Suetsumuhana" scroll in the Ishiyamadera collection, received the title of "Chūjō," or captain, in the year 1647.[10] Since his signature includes the same title, this *Genji Monogatari Emaki* may have been created about 1650.

NOTES

1. See Miyeko Murase, *Iconography of the Tale of Genji* (New York and Tokyo, 1983), pp. 19–27.

2. For different types of formats of *Genji* paintings, see Akiyama Terukazu, *Genji-e*, no. 119 of *Nihon no Bijutsu*, ed. staffs of the National Museums of Tokyo, Kyoto, and Nara (Tokyo, 1976).

3. A pair of *Genji* screens in the imperial collection attributed to the premier master of the Momoyama period, Kanō Eitoku, features the influence of Tosa school painting. See Akiyama Terukazu, "Genji-e no keifu," in Akiyama Ken *et al.* (eds.), *Genji Monogatari*, vol. 7 of *Zusetsu Nihon no Koten* (Tokyo, 1079), p. 130, fig. 128. For a screen version by Tan'yū (1602–1674), the major Kanō artist of the seventeenth century (also in the imperial collection), see Yamane Yūzō (ed.), *Nihon Byōbu-e Shūsei*, vol. 5 (Tokyo, 1979), Pls. 81–82.

4. Murasaki Shikibu, *The Tale of Genji*, trans. Edward G. Seidensticker (New York, 1982), p. 41.

5. *Ibid.*, p. 42.

6. *Ibid.*, p. 130–131.

7. Murase, *Iconography*, p. 330.

8. Kyoto National Museum, *Genji Monogatari no Bijutsu (The Tale of Genji in Arts)* (Kyoto, 1975), no. 20.

9. Galerie Janette Ostier, *Les jardins d'or du Prince Genji: Peintures japonaises du XVIIe siècle* (Paris, 1980).

10. Murase, *Iconography*, p. 330; see also Akiyama Terukazu, *Emakimono*, Zaigai Nihon no Shihō, vol. 2, Shimada Shūjirō (ed.) (Tokyo, 1980), pp. 134–135.

Plate I. "Sacred Tree," Chapter 10 of the *Tale of Genji*

Plate II. "The Safflower," Chapter 6 of the *Tale of Genji*

Plate III. Chapter 67 of the *Tales of Ise*

Plate IV. *Night Attack by the Soga Brothers*

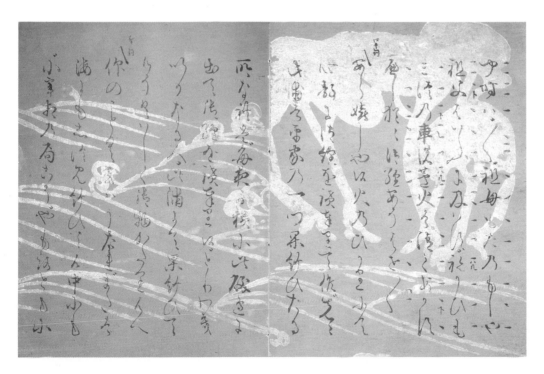

Plate V.
Michimori,
Saga-bon Utai Book, I

Plate VI. *Exemplary Conduct of Ancient Chinese Emperors*

Plate VII. *The Tale of Peach Boy*

Plate VIII.
*The Success Story
of a Mouse*

Plate IX. *The Tale of Bunshō*

Plate X. Hachiman Shrine Festival

Plate XI. Portraits of Six Ladies of the Pleasure Quarters

Plate XII. Ladies' Pastimes in Spring and Autumn

Plate XIII. Shang Yuan Fu-jen, from the Scroll of Chinese Immortals

Plate XIV. Geisha Masquerading in a Niwaka Festival (Utamaro, no. 1)

当時全盛美人揃

玉屋内

花紫
せきや
てりく

哥麿筆

Plate XV. Courtesan Hanamuasaki of Tamaya (Utamaro, no. 10)

Plate XVI. A Courtesan of Shinagawa (Utamaro, no. 8)

Plate XVII. A Courtesan (Utamaro, no. 13)

Plate XVIII. Third Station, Kawasaki (Hiroshige, no. 48)

Plate XIX. Thirty-fourth Station, Futakawa (Hiroshige, no. 60)

Plate XX. Thirty-sixth Station, Goyu (Hiroshige, no. 61)

23
Giō Monogatari (*The Tale of Giō*)

Late sixteenth century, Momoyama period
Two handscrolls, ink, color and gold on paper
H: 32 cm, L: 1116.4 cm (scroll I), 1124.4 cm (scroll II)
Spencer no. 58

If the *Genji Monogatari* and *Ise Monogatari* (see nos. 20 and 18) are the masterpieces of ancient Japanese romantic literature, the *Heike Monogatari* (*Tale of the Heike*)—from which the story in the scrolls of the *Giō Monogatari* is derived—is the pinnacle of epic literature based on historical fact.[1] Written by several authors in the early thirteenth century, the *Heike Monogatari* traces in twelve chapters the rise and fall of the Heike, also known as the Taira clan. The tale spans the years between 1131 and 1221, focussing on the clan's most glorious days—from the time that the family's archpatriarch, Kiyomori (1118–1181), assumed the premiership (1167) to the total defeat of the Heike in the battle of 1185, at the hands of the family's archrivals, the Minamoto clan.

The theme and tone of the book, which was written less than half a century after the tragic defeat of the Heike, is brilliantly set in the famous opening passage:

> The bell of the Gion Temple tolls into every man's heart to warn him that all is vanity and evanescence. The faded flowers of the sala trees by the Buddha's deathbed bear witness to the truth that all who flourish are destined to decay. Yes, pride must have its fall, for it is as unsubstantial as a dream on a spring night. The brave and violent man—he too must die away in the end, like whirl of dust in the wind.[2]

The *Heike Monogatari* was originally written to be read to the accompaniment of a *biwa* (a lute-like instrument), by traveling storytellers who would select a few appropriate chapters or episodes from the book.

The tale's origin and its reliance on narration seem to have affected the tradition of *Heike* illustration. While romantic literature like the *Genji Monogatari* and *Ise Monogatari* appear to have been embellished with illustrations almost from the time of their creation, there is nothing to suggest that the *Heike Monogatari* was accompanied by artwork. In fact, the documentary material on *Heike* iconography is sparse, and extant works reveal little of what might have constituted a complete cycle of *Heike* illustrations.[3]

A little-known fourteenth-century diary, the *Kōya Nikki* (*Diary at Mount Kōya*), by a monk-poet named Ton'a (1289–1372), includes a reference to a set of six scrolls illustrating episodes from the last chapter of the *Heike*, that Ton'a had viewed. He believed that the paintings were by the great master Fujiwara no Takanobu (1142–1205),[4] but nothing has been found that would verify Ton'a's attribution. A late seventeenth-century set of thirty-six handscrolls, now in the Okayama Museum, depicts many episodes from the book, suggesting that an extensive iconographic tradition had indeed existed earlier.[5] However, earlier *Heike* pictures tend to differ altogether from these late paintings. In illustrating the *Heike*, earlier painters, like the narrators of the tale, often singled out popular heroes and heroines as subjects for independent sets of scrolls or books—an example being the scrolls of the *Gio* episode included here. The earliest extant paintings which might be called "*Heike* pictures" date from the Kamakura period, and in fact illustrate the lives of the characters rather than the episodes described in the book.[6] Otherwise, most *Heike* pictures, produced from the late sixteenth century through the Edo period in handscrolls or on fans and folding screens, illustrate famous battle scenes.

The *Tale of Gio* and other subplots from the *Heike Monogatari* also were popular subjects for the Nō and Kōwaka repertories in later years (see Section IV). The main theme of the Gio episode, which is from the first chapter of the *Heike*, reflects the general philosophy of the book: human fortune and destiny are evanescent and ephemeral. It begins with the author's appraisal of Kiyomori during his most glorious moments at court, as premier and father-in-law of an emperor.

> Now as Kiyomori, the Priest-Premier, held in his palm both heaven and earth, his rule grew yearly more extreme and eccentric. Moreover, he closed his heart to the criticisms and jibes of his people.[7]

The episode described in this tale occurred after Kiyomori took the tonsure at the age of fifty-one, fearing that he was suffering from a terminal illness and hoping to obtain the buddha's sanction for a longer life. At this time, he indulged in an affair with a beautiful *shirabyōshi* dancer named Gio (a name literally meaning "Ruler of the Arts").[8] For a time, Gio enjoyed Kiyomori's undivided affection, until one day another *shirabyōshi* named Hotoke ("Buddha"), age sixteen, arrived at Kiyomori's mansion uninvited. Kiyomori was at first outraged at the boldness and aggressiveness of the younger entertainer, and refused to see her. Giō, generous hearted and confident of her position, persuaded him to let the dancer perform. Struck by Hotoke's beauty and talent, Kiyomori decided to replace Giō with the newcomer. Dismayed, Hotoke protested, but her pleas on Giō's behalf went unheeded, and the once-favored dancer, her younger sister, and her mother were expelled from the palace.

The first of the *Giō* scrolls depicts in six scenes the events leading up to the heartless expulsion of Giō. The second scroll, in five scenes, illustrates Kiyomori's further humiliation of Giō, and her eventual decision to take vows. The scene reproduced here depicts Giō's degradation when she is summoned to Kiyomori's palace, a full year after her expulsion, to entertain Hotoke, who is bored with her leisure hours. Kiyomori, in priestly garb, is with Hotoke, visible through delicately painted blinds. Giō, at the right, holds a fan as, to her chagrin, she is ordered to dance for Hotoke.

After this incident, Giō contemplates suicide but instead determines to take the vows of a nun. Her sister and mother also decide to become nuns, joining her to pray for a better life in Amida Buddha's Paradise. One night, Hotoke pays a sudden visit to Giō's cottage and, confessing her concern over Giō's misfortune—which could be her own one day—seeks Giō's forgiveness. Hotoke then joins the other women in prayers for entry into the Pure Land, and the four nuns end their lives in peaceful mountain seclusion.

The *Giō* scrolls are fine examples of the popular genre of narrative painting that was produced from the late Muromachi period, in the sixteenth century, through much of the Edo period. Although regarded as a misnomer and an expression which escapes precise definition, the word *Nara-e* (Nara pictures) is often used to categorize this large group of paintings, made in either book or handscroll format. These works perpetuated the brilliant tradition of *emaki* of earlier periods, although in somewhat amateurish, if charming, styles (see Section III for other examples of Nara-e). They were usually executed in bright colors, with a great deal of gold ink and foil—especially the early works, which were probably bought by affluent patrons. In these works, including the example here, youthful figures of men and women have slender, oblong faces, and their brightly colored costumes are rendered in stylized patterns. The Spencer *Giō* paintings, in spite of their naiveté and amateur quality, vividly convey the pathos of the tale. Also typical of sixteenth-century Nara-e are the heavily painted, dense blue mists used to frame scenes, and interior views enlivened by gold screens with large-scale designs of flowers and grasses in bright colors. The plants and trees adorning the outdoor settings are often disproportionately large, as in the scene reproduced here. The *Giō* scrolls should be dated to the Momoyama period, in the late sixteenth century.

NOTES

1. Hiroshi Kitagawa and Bruce T. Tsuchida (trans.), *The Tale of the Heike* (Tokyo, 1975).
2. Kitagawa, *The Tale of the Heike*, p. 5.
3. For some examples of Heike pictures, see Nagazumi Yasuaki *et al.* (eds.), *Heike Monogatari*,

vol. 9 of *Zusetsu Nihon no Koten* (Tokyo, 1979), and Takeda Tsuneo and Muramatsu Sadataka, *Heike Monogatari Emaki*, vol. 13 of *Bessatsu Taiyō* (Tokyo, 1975).

4. Ōta Tōshirō (ed.), *Zoku Gunsho Ruijū* vol. 18/2 (Tokyo, 1924), p. 1247.

5. For some scenes from this set, see Takeda, *Bessatsu Taiyo*.

6. These are the *Heike Kintachi Emaki* (*Pictures of the Heike Nobleman*) of the early fourteenth century in the Kamakura period. See Tanaka Ichimatsu, "Heike Kintachi Sōshi ni tsuite (A Heike-Kintachi-Soshi Picture-Scroll)," *Kokka* 665 (August, 1947), pp. 279–285, and the *Takafusa-kyō Tsuyakotoba Emaki* (*Lord Takafusa's Love Songs*). See Miyeko Murase, *Emaki: Narrative Scrolls from Japan* (New York, 1983), pp. 71–75.

7. Kitagawa, *The Tale of the Heike*, p. 21.

8. Literally meaning "white beat," shirabyōshi is a dance performed by lowly female entertainers, which became especially popular after the mid-twelfth century.

III

Heroes and Heroines of Popular Tales

Z_EN, the spartan brand of Buddhism introduced to Japan from China at the end of the twelfth century, exerted a sweeping influence over the *samurai* (warrior) class during the Muromachi period. Converts to this new faith, among them shoguns, high-class warriors, and monks, encouraged the promulgation of all things Chinese, including knowledge of the Chinese language, Chinese literature, and the Chinese manner of painting in monochrome ink. Zen played a primary role in the formation of new aesthetics, inspiring such arts as the tea-ceremony. However, the popularity of the faith and the new aesthetics had an adverse effect upon the traditional arts. The art of *emaki* (illustrated narrative handscrolls) was seriously affected by these new developments; it managed to survive, but only by undergoing a metamorphosis.

Subjects for the emaki of the Muromachi period were often drawn from a genre of literature called *otogi zōshi*, short stories which began to appear at about this time. The term otogi zōshi, which is difficult to translate, roughly means "tales told by a companion." The word "otogi" originally referred to the practice of telling stories to ward off evil spirits at dusk or to ease bedtime loneliness. Warlords of the Muromachi and Momoyama periods are known to have employed story-tellers, who not only entertained them with amusing tales but also educated them, for most men-at-arms had little formal education. After peace was established, warriors acquired a greater level of education and sophistication, and the chief beneficiaries of otogi were women and children.

Narrowly defined, the term "otogi zōshi" refers to a group of twenty-three short stories written during the Muromachi period and published in the early eighteenth century under that name.[1] Among these twenty-three tales are the

Bunshō Sōshi and *Ōeyama Shutendōji* included here (nos. 24 and 27). Broadly defined, the term designates any of the short stories written from the Muromachi period through the early eighteenth century.

As a literary genre, otogi zōshi serves as a link between the literary tradition of the aristocratic Heian and Kamakura periods and the new tendency of Edo-period literature to express plebian taste. Given its background, it is easy to understand why otogi zōshi covered a wide range of subject matter, story plots and ideas, many of which are amusing and even comical or fantastic. They are often didactic and laden with superstition, as they were intended to ensure the happiness and success of those who read or listened to them. Otogi zōshi were written in simple, colloquial language, suitable for narrating sessions. Their authors remain anonymous, although evidence suggests that most were court nobles and Buddhist monks, while some were warriors and women. The influence of literary classics is quite apparent: some popular episodes from well-known works were incorporated into the tales. Such heroes as Ariwara no Narihira, a purported protagonist of the *Ise Monogatari* (nos. 18, 19) and the epitome of manhood, spawned many imitations.

Many otogi zōshi were illustrated by anonymous painters, whose works are often grouped under the term *Nara-e* (Nara pictures) or *Nara Ehon* (Nara picture book), terms which are also difficult to define. It is generally agreed that, despite the name, which made its first appearance in 1909,[2] the illustrated books and scrolls in this category were produced in Kyoto rather than Nara. Many were produced and purchased for special occasions, and were given as dowry and New Year's gifts. Pigments used in the paintings were often high-quality, expensive mineral products, and the paper used for the text was often beautifully decorated with designs in gold and silver. In its broadest sense, the term Nara-e refers to books and scrolls with text and illustrations which were produced by anonymous artists from the Muromachi through the mid-Edo period. Yet it is not easy to precisely define a Nara-e style. Current scholarship agrees on a number of characteristics: Nara-e is colorful, often embellished with gold foil (occasionally copper foil); its technique and style are frequently uninspired and unsophisticated, yet the works are almost always charming; and Nara-e paintings tend to be eclectic, revealing their artists' varied backgrounds and training.

A number of scrolls and books in this catalogue may be classified as Nara-e; they include renditions of classical literature (nos. 18, 23), auspicious stories (no. 24), tales of mice (nos. 25, 26), an encyclopedia of fantastic animals (no. 30), histories of good and evil Chinese emperors (no. 31), and dramas (nos. 32, 33, 36, and 37).

The art of illustrating popular tales, and Nara-e, regardless of its literary content, may be regarded as the rightful successors to the traditional art of narrative painting in Japan.

NOTES

1. Chieko Irie Mulhern, "Otogi-zōshi. Short Stories of the Muromachi Period," *Monumenta Nipponica*, vol. 29 (Summer 1974), pp. 181–198, and Ichiko Teiji, *Chūsei Shōsetsu no Kenkyū* (Tokyo, 1956).

2. The first usage of this word can be traced only to the *Bungei Hyakka Jiten* (encyclopedia of the arts) which was published in 1909. For examples of illustrated otogi zōshi and Nara-e, see Okudaira Hideo (ed.), *Otogi Zōshi Emaki* (Tokyo, 1982); Nara Ehon Kokusai Kenkyū Kaigi (ed.), *Zaigai Nara Ehon* (Tokyo, 1981); Ichiko Teiji (ed.), *Zusetsu Nihon no Koten*, vol. 13, *Otogi Zōshi* (Tokyo, 1980); Yoshida Seiichi and Akai Tatsurō (eds.), *Taiyō Koten to Emaki Series*, III, *Otogi Zōshi* (Tokyo, 1979); and Takasaki Fujihiko, *Otogi Zōshi*, no. 52 of *Nihon no Bijutsu*, ed. Staff of the National Museums of Tokyo, Kyoto, and Nara, (Tokyo, 1970).

24
Bunshō Sōshi (*The Tale of Bunshō*)

Early seventeenth century, Edo period
Three volumes, ink, color, gold and silver on paper
H: 28.1 cm, W: 21.4 cm, each
Spencer no. 91

These three volumes of the *Tale of Bunshō*[1] are typical examples of the type of illustrated book, popularly known as *Nara Ehon*, that was produced during the early Edo period. The covers are decorated with plum blossoms, pine, and bamboo, drawn in gold on dark blue paper; the text is illustrated with colorful, miniature paintings. In this set of books the twenty-three images are divided among the three volumes as follows: nine images in the first book, six in the second, and eight in the third. A number of the paintings are double-page compositions.

The story recorded and illustrated here is one of the most popular tales of the Edo period. Our hero, Bunshō, was a menial laborer from an impoverished family, who served the Shinto deity of the Kashima Shrine, in the coastal area northeast of modern Tokyo. As a test of Bunshō's sincerity and devotion, the Great Priest of the shrine ordered him to leave the sacred precinct and embark upon his own career. After his departure, Bunshō worked as a salt-maker and, aided by his steadfast devotion to the great god of Kashima, achieved spectacular success. However, as he and his wife were childless, they returned to the shrine to beg the great deity to grant them children. With the god's blessing, they were soon graced with two daughters of exceptional beauty and talent. Many lords vied to gain their affections, and a captain of the imperial court married the older girl and took her to the capital (Pl. IV). The younger sister became an imperial consort and gave birth to an imperial prince. Bunshō himself was then appointed Minister of State and later, at the age of 70, he was promoted to the rank of Senior Councilor.

As in many so-called Nara Ehon, the pictures in the Bunshō books are painted in bright colors—oranges, white, greens and blues—with gold outlines used to emphasize the most significant characters. Figures of both men and women have the appearance of charming dolls; wide bands of light blue mist and cloud are bounded in white lines, and speckles of gold add a rich lustre to the paintings.

Of the many tales of the day which were regarded as auspicious, the story of Bunshō occupied a special place in the hearts of the Edo citizenry. In 1841, a popular novelist, Ryūtei Tanehiko (1783–1842), began a collection of his essays, the *Yōshabako* (*Box to Use and Discard*), with the remark,

> In times past, following the customary "first calligraphy" in the New Year, women and children performed their "first reading," a reading of the *Bunshō Sōshi*. This tradition is still observed by some of the great families . . .[2]

The Bunshō story, which may have originated in the Muromachi period, with possible roots in the oral folk tradition, seems to have become particularly well-loved during the early years of the Edo era. In addition to the obvious reasons for the tale's popularity, Kashima was a center of the salt-making industry during the Edo period, which may have contributed to its appeal. Salt is not only an indispensable commodity in everyday life, it is given a sacred quality in the native Shinto religion of Japan. Even today, salt is used in various purification rituals: it is placed at the entryways of shops and restaurants and sprinkled on people as they return home after a funeral. Illustrated books and handscrolls of the Bunshō story were seen as both educational and entertaining because of the tale's didactic message and happy ending; they became popular gifts for New Year celebrations and weddings. Many editions of this story exist, as illustrated books, handscrolls, printed books, and folding screens.

NOTES

1. For a translation of this tale, see James T. Araki, "Bunshō Sōshi: The Tale of Bunshō, the Saltmaker," *Monumenta Nipponica*, vol. 38, no. 3 (Autumn, 1983), pp. 221ff.
2. *Yōshabako* is reprinted in Nakatsuka Eijirō (ed.), *Nihon Zuihitsu Zenshū* (Tokyo, 1927), vol. 10.

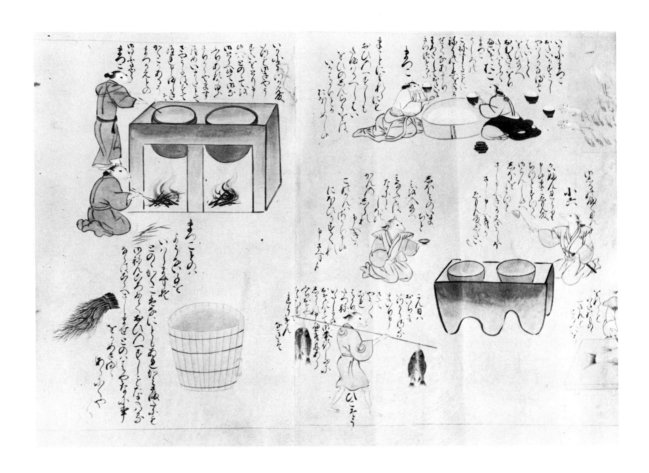

25
Nezumi no Sōshi (*The Story of a Mouse*)

First half of the seventeenth century, Edo period
Three handscrolls, ink, color and gold on paper
H: 32.7 cm (scroll I); 32.5 cm (scroll II); 32.6 cm (scroll III)
L: 9.71 m (scroll I); 9.51 m (scroll II); 4.05 m (scroll III)
Spencer no. 65

PUBLISHED: Nara Ehon Kokusai Kenkyū Kaigi (ed.), *Zaigai Nara Ehon* (Tokyo, 1981), no. 18;
Barbara Ruch *et al.* (eds.), *Kaigai Shozō Nara Ehon* (*Nara Ehon from Outstanding Foreign Collections*)
(Tokyo, 1979), Pl. 68.

Tales of animals and humans have been popular throughout the history of Japanese art
and literature. They are particularly important within the genre of popular short stories
called *otogi zōshi*, which were written for the most part during the Muromachi period.
Known as *irui-mono* (tales of non-humans), these stories reveal elements from a variety
of sources—religious tales, folktales, and other, orally transmitted stories.[1] The famous
preface to the *Kokin Waka Shū* of 905, a poetic anthology of *waka* (thirty-one-syllable

verse), also played a role in forming this genre of literature by proclaiming that all beings—whether human or animal—possess poetic potential (see no. 16).[2]

The category of non-human beings includes such lowly creatures as insects and shellfish. Birds, trees, flowers, and fish fall under this broad definition, as do even inanimate objects. However, it is notable that irui chosen as subjects for these tales are all familiar creatures from everyday life; wild beasts and mythological creatures are excluded. Irui tales also tell of the "humanization" or anthropomorphization of non-humans, and the consequences, which frequently involve marriage between irui and human beings. The anthropomorphization of non-humans was a natural outcome of certain Japanese religious beliefs: both Shintoism, Japan's native faith, and Buddhism proclaim that all things in the world, whether animate or inanimate, possess souls. It is therefore understandable that many of the charming and humorous tales of irui also contain moral instruction with Buddhist overtones.

Tales of mice (nezumi)—told in two of the emaki (illustrated narrative handscrolls) included here—are typical of the irui genre. Mice were endowed with a dual nature and contradictory symbolic characteristics.[3] They bring calamity to man, yet they are thought to possess mystical powers that can bring man good fortune; by the same token, they are regarded as messengers of the god of wealth. Many primitive cultures have similar folk beliefs about these tiny creatures, but mouse tales are not found among works of classical literature of the aristocratic Heian period. They only began to appear as folktales during the Kamakura period, and enjoyed a sudden rise in popularity during the Muromachi period; mouse stories were considered especially appropriate literary fare for New Year celebrations because of the association of mice and affluence. Even today, people in many provinces of Japan continue to make offerings of rice cakes to mice on New Year's Day to ensure wealth and happiness for the year to come.

This set of three handscrolls, with text and twelve illustrations, relates the tale of a mouse named Nezumi Gon no Kami. Wishing for release from the world of beasts,[4] Gon no Kami decides to accomplish this—if not for himself then at least for his descendants—by marrying into a higher stratum of existence, that of humans. After relating his plans to friends and relatives, he sets off to visit the Kiyomizu Shrine in Kyoto, which was renowned for its powers of intervention in the affairs of men and women. Among the other pilgrims at the shrine is a beautiful young woman.. She is also from a wealthy family, which decides the issue for Gon no Kami: the two become engaged and soon are married in a celebration attended by both mouse and human retainers, in rich surroundings. The humans, however, are unaware of the true nature of the masquerading rodents, who are depicted in human costume.

In the section from scroll II illustrated here, mouse retainers are busy in the kitchen preparing for the wedding ceremony feast of Gon no Kami and his bride. The mouse cooks and helpers also labor over ovens, grills, chopping blocks and storage shelves. Their running commentary on the cooking and the gossip they exchange are written alongside their painted figures. The cook at the extreme right, for example, is identified as an "Official of Broth" named Koroku. Brandishing a ladle in his hand, he urges his colleague at the left to taste his broth to see if it needs more salt. Throughout the scrolls, characters and major landscape and architectural settings are identified by written captions. Many mouse characters are given humorous names, some of which are outrageous combinations of respectable-sounding court titles, with comic appellations like "Hole

Digger." This type of sub-text, which records not only conversation but also monologues and the private thoughts of characters in narrative paintings, was occasionally used in earlier emaki of the twelfth and thirteenth centuries.[5] These sub-texts became quite common in narrative painting of the Muromachi period and enlivened *etoki* (picture explanation) sessions—the reading aloud of the text to an audience.

The remaining episodes of scrolls II and III relate a tragi-comic turn of events as Gon no Kami's true nature is revealed. Delighted with his good fortune, Gon no Kami decides to return to the Kiyomizu Shrine to offer grateful thanks for his happiness. However, during his absence, his wife, who has become suspicious about his true identity, sets a rope trap. Gon no Kami comes home and is caught in the trap in the garden; irrefutable proof of his true nature, his tail, is exposed. Overcome by this discovery, the wife flees with her maid.

In the third and final scroll, the mouse's sorrow is complete when he learns that his wife has been married again, this time to a human. He decides to become a Buddhist monk and renounce the world. The final scene of the scroll depicts the tonsure ceremony of Gon no Kami at a mouse monastery, presided over by Buddhist mouse-monks in religious robes.

Among the many different stories of mouse–human marriages, this particular version seems to have been especially popular. A number of nearly identical scrolls are known to exist today; one is in the Tokyo National Museum and another in the Suntory Museum of Tokyo.[6] These scrolls are so similar that their texts even contain identical errors.[7] One notable difference between these works and the Spencer set is that the Spencer emaki lacks the concluding episode found in the versions in Tokyo; this describes Gon no Kami's journey to Mt. Kōya, the mountain sacred to Japanese Buddhists, where he devotes the remainder of his life to prayers to the various buddhas. This episode must have also been included in the Spencer emaki, since the present third scroll is unusually short for a regular handscroll—less than half the length of the two other scrolls in the set. The final scene in the third scroll ends abruptly after the name of a mouse is given in an inscription, a fact which suggests that the remaining sections were detached at this point.

The version of the *Nezumi no Sōshi* in the Tokyo National Museum is stylistically dated to the sixteenth century, in the late Muromachi period, not long after the tale was actually written.[8] The Spencer emaki resembles the Tokyo National Museum version in painting style, yet it must be dated much later, to the first half of the seventeenth century; several of the women's kimonos depicted in the scrolls are decorated with the large, bold designs that were popular at that time. The scrolls also contain certain details not found in the Tokyo National Museum version. It seems likely that the two renditions of the *Nezumi* story were taken from a common prototype, as it is doubtful that the earlier Tokyo emaki served as a model for the later work.

Architectural elements, exterior and interior glimpses of gardens, cloud patterns, costume details and the mice's postures in these scrolls are all deftly executed. The attention to detail, visible in the miniature paintings on folding screens and the skillful rendering of the mice in their natural forms, suggests that the paintings were done by an artist well-versed in narrative illustration. Although some colors are heavily applied, as on the tatami mats and flowering cherry blossoms, the artist's palette is generally pale and gives an impression of a sketch or study. Faces of human women, which in most finished paintings tend to be painted in opaque white, are only lightly brushed in with tawny pink; mountains and hills in landscape settings and in miniature screen paintings are painted in bluish ink, rather than heavy blues or greens. In fact, there is a strong possibility that this work was intended as an artist's "memo" rather than a finished product ready for sale, particularly since the sheets of paper joined to make up the scrolls vary greatly in width. Some of the sheets are a mere three centimeters wide, and the quality of paper also varies greatly from section to section.

NOTES

1. Chieko Irie Mulhern, "Otogi-zōshi. Short Stories of the Muromachi Period," *Monumenta Nipponica*, vol. 29 (Summer 1974), p. 194, and Ichiko Teiji (ed.), *Zusetsu Nihon no Koten*, vol. 13, *Otogi Zōshi*, pp. 77ff. The earliest and the most famous example of the painting of non-humans is the twelfth-century scroll, the *Chōjū Giga* (*Frolicking Animals*). See Komatsu Shigemi (ed.), *Nihon Emaki Taisei*, vol. 6, *Chōjū Jimbutsu Giga* (Tokyo, 1977).
2. See the preface, H. H. Honda (trans.), *The Kokin Waka-shu* (Tokyo, 1970), p. 1.
3. Ōshima Tatehiko, *Minzoku Bungei Sōsho*, vol. 12, *Otogi Zōshi to Minkan Bungei* (Tokyo, 1967).
4. According to Buddhist cosmography, the universe consists of six realms of existence: those of gods, men, fighting spirits, beasts, hungry ghosts and demons of Hell. By being reincarnated into the next highest realm, a being's opportunity of final enlightenment was improved. Thus Gon no Kami, of the world of beasts, aspired to make a great leap ahead to the realm of humans.
5. Among the extant emaki which have such texts-within-texts, the earliest and the most famous one is the *Kegon Engi*. See Komatsu Shigemi (ed.), *Nihon Emaki Taisei*, vol. 17, *Kegon Shū Soshi Eden* (Kegon Engi), (Tokyo, 1978) and Miyeko Murase, *Emaki: Narrative Scrolls from Japan* (New York, 1983), no. 26.
6. For the version in the Tokyo National Museum, see Okudaira Hideo (ed.), *Otogi Zōshi Emaki* (Tokyo, 1982), no. 30, and for the Suntory Museum version, see Ichiko Teiji, *Otogi Zōshi*, pp. 137–143, and Yoshida Seiichi and Akai Tatsurō (eds.), *Taiyō Koten to Emaki Series*, III. *Otogi Zōshi* (Tokyo, 1979), pp. 25–37.
7. Nara Ehon Kokusai Kenkyū Kaigi (ed.), *Zaigai Nara Ehon* (Tokyo, 1981), p. 54.
8. *Ibid.*

26
Nezumi no Sōshi Shusse Monogatari (*The Success Story of a Mouse*)

Second half of the seventeenth century, Edo period
One handscroll, ink, color and gold on paper
H: 34.4 cm, L: 2100 cm
Spencer no. 118

PUBLISHED: Nara Ehon Kokusai Kenkyū Kaigi (ed.), *Zaigai Nara Ehon* (Tokyo, 1981), no. 19; and Barbara Ruch *et al.* (eds.), *Kaigai Shozō Nara Ehon* (*Nara Ehon from Outstanding Foreign Colllections*) (Tokyo, 1979), Pls. 36–37.

The tale of a mouse named Nehyōe, his misadventures away from home and his eventual return to his home and family, is considered to be an offshoot of an earlier work, the *Nezumi no Sōshi* (no. 25),[1] a "mouse tale" which had been extremely popular in the early seventeenth century. The tale of Nehyōe also must have been inspired by such rags-to-riches stories as the *Tale of Bunshō* (no. 24); these fanciful tales in scroll or book form were popular New Year's gifts as well as casual reading material. Indeed, a three-line postscript to this scroll states that the work should be viewed at the beginning of spring (the New Year).

Although the title of the scroll, written on a small piece of paper attached to the cover, reads *Nezumi no Sōshi Shusse Monogatari Emaki* (*An Illustrated Scroll of the Success Story of a Mouse*), the scroll itself tells of both the high rank that is awarded to the mouse and the wealth attained by a human who helps Nehyōe during his period of hardship. The story actually endorses a popular belief that mice are messengers of the god of wealth and bring good fortune.

The scroll of the tale of Nehyōe begins by introducing the protagonist, a white mouse who lives in a pagoda at Tōji, in Kyoto. He is—as most heroes are—handsome, rich, and educated in both academic and military matters. He wishes to be married, and, with a bat acting as a go-between, is paired with a princess, the beautiful and talented daughter of a wealthy mouse. A section of the opening scene, shown here (see Pl. V), depicts a view of the kitchen in the wealthy mouse's home as the household prepares for the wedding celebration. Mouse cooks and servants are busy preparing fish, making rice cakes, filling red-lacquered wine jugs trimmed in black (at the lower left), and heaping rice into bowls.

Time passes, and Nehyōe's wife bears him several children. During her final pregnancy she feels a great longing for the taste of goose, and she asks her husband to procure some fresh meat from the right shoulder of the bird. Nehyōe complies by going into the garden and biting into the shoulder of a feeding goose. The startled bird soars into the air, carrying an equally startled Nehyōe, and flies far away into the east. Finally, the goose alights in Hitachi province, northeast of Edo. So far away from home, the stranded Nehyōe asks every creature he meets how he might return to his family. In the scene illustrated here, he is seen wandering about the countryside, close by a flowering cherry tree. Playful pairs of animals gamboling in the background accentuate his solitary state. Gazing at the flowering cherry, Nehyōe is reminded of his own distant

home, and he begins to compose poems about it. Unfortunately, in this painting, the body of the mouse has lost some of its white pigment, as have some of the cherry blossoms.

At last Nehyōe befriends a human couple, Saemon and his wife, who are sympathetic to his plight and wish to help him. One day, when Saemon has to make a journey to Kyoto, he takes Nehyōe along, and Nehyōe is finally reunited with his wife and children. The grateful mouse heaps gifts of gold, silver and other precious treasures upon Saemon, who, because of his kindness, acquires even greater wealth later on. Nehyōe, who has overcome hardship with perseverance and fortitude, is awarded the rank of Lieutenant General by the Wolf Emperor.

The protagonist in other versions of this tragi-comic success story is sometimes called by the slightly different name of Yahyōe; this name appears in a similar and almost contemporary book rendition in the Harvard University Art Museum, Cambridge. Although most of the scenes in the two versions are quite similar, the Spencer scroll is distinguished by its many illustrations of the mouse's journey to the north, and his voyage over open fields and rough seas as he clings precariously to the breast of the flying bird. As in the scene reproduced here, depictions of nature in this scroll are often poignant and romantic.

The paintings in this scroll also differ from the amateurish, popular works of the so-called *Nara-e* genre. They are refined and accomplished illustrations, painted in a sumptuous and rich array of colors, with gold and silver ink lavishly applied to costumes, household furnishings, ground mists, and tree trunks. The soft fur and feathers of animals and birds are also delicately highlighted with gold ink. The scroll was probably made to be given as an expensive New Year's gift.

The Spencer scroll illustrations also differ from other narrative paintings of the Edo period in that the strong ink outlines which were often applied over colors to accent the contours of landscape elements are absent. Here, thick green pigment has flaked off the gentle, rounded hills and mountains, revealing evenly drawn, thin ink-line underdrawings. Delicate wildflowers are also painted in brilliant colors without a trace of ink outline. It seems likely that the artist of this scroll was influenced by works of the decorative Rimpa school of painting, begun by Sōtatsu (died ca. 1641, see no. 35) in the early 1600s.[2] The unknown artist's predilection for depicting women's kimonos with ornamental tie-dyed designs helps us to date this work to the second half of the seventeenth century.

NOTES

1. Nara Ehon Kokusai Kenkyū Kaigi (ed.), *Zaigai Nara Ehon* (Tokyo, 1981), p. 56.
2. Howard A. Link and Tōru Shimbo, *Exquisite Visions: Rimpa Paintings from Japan* (Honolulu, 1980).

27
Ōeyama Shuten Dōji (The Giant Drunkard of Ōeyama)

End of the seventh century, Edo period
By Kaihō Yūchiku (1654–1728)
Three handscrolls, ink, color, and gold on paper
H: 32.4 cm, L: 1552.2 cm (scroll I), 2024.4 cm (scroll II), 1747.2 cm (scroll III)
Seal: "Motosada"
Spencer no. 96

These three scrolls, with their thirty-three paintings and thirty-four sections of text, illustrate the famous tale of Minamoto no Yorimitsu (948–1021), also known as Raikō, killing the giant demon Shuten Dōji, who lived at Ōeyama, southwest of Kyoto.[1] "Shuten Dōji" (literally, "drunkard boy"), the monster of this tale, is variously described as an ogre, an abductor of maidens, and a gigantic cannibal disguised as a human—20 feet tall with flaming red hair, whose feet and hands were covered with hair, like a bear's. At the end of the eleventh century, this ogre is said to have established himself at Ōeyama in Tamba Province, where his unruly cronies created havoc throughout the countryside and abducted beautiful maidens from the capital.

To rid the country of this evil band, the emperor enlisted Minamoto no Yorimitsu (Raikō), who forthwith assembled five companions: Usui Sadamitsu (954–1021), Urabe Suetake (950–1022), Watanabe no Tsuna (954–1024), Sakata no Kintoki (active ca. 1000) and Fujiwara no Yasumasa (died 1036). To prepare for his difficult task, Raikō then visited three Shinto shrines—Iwashimizu Hachimangū in Kyoto, Sumiyoshi in Osaka, and Kumano in Wakayama—to receive the blessings of the gods. On their way to Ōeyama, Raikō and his fellows encountered three celestial beings who proved to be the gods of the shrines he had visited. The deities gave two gifts to the companions. The first was a wine which would render Shuten Dōji dead drunk, causing him to lose his magical powers; the second was a magic golden cap. Following the three gods' directions, Raikō and his companions found the garishly decorated palace of the ogre, where they were treated to a banquet of human flesh and blood (shown here). In exchange, Raikō offered his magic wine to the demon and his household, putting Shuten Dōji into a deep sleep, which revealed his true demoniacal appearance, and rendering his cronies helplessly drunk and ill. As Raikō and his men chopped off the ogre's head, the sky suddenly darkened and thunder roared; the giant head jumped high into the air and fell upon Raikō's helmet, but his life was saved by the magic golden cap shown here. The story ends happily with the release of all the captive ladies, and the citizens of the nation resume their lives of peace and tranquility.

The paintings in these scrolls, executed in a rather rugged and broad style using bright colors, depict gory scenes of violence and carnage in graphic detail. The vividness of the painting makes up for a lack of subtlety in the technique. The horror of the repulsive banquet scenes and bloody fighting clashes with such details as the delicate flowers, which, according to the text, adorned the ogre's palace all year round.

Each section of painting is marked with the small rectangular seal of the artist, which

reads "Motosada." This is one of the many sobriquets of the painter Kaihō Yūchiku (1654–1728), a grandson of Yūshō (1533–1615), one of the leading masters of the Momoyama period, and a son of Yūsetsu (1598–1677), an artist to whose studio a set of scrolls in this exhibition is attributed (no. 34). Yūchiku's claim to fame rests entirely on the 1724 portrait of his grandparents, a work whose lengthy colophon provides basic biographical information on Yūshō.[2] Although this painting bears a seal of Yūsetsu, the consensus today is that both the painting and the colophon were copied by Yūchiku from his father's original.

Yūchiku's life and oeuvre can be partially reconstructed from what is known of his father. After the great master Yūshō's death in 1615, the family's fortune declined precipitously, and Yūsetsu turned to painting ready-made pictures to earn a living. The great majority of Yūsetsu's works, both those recorded in literature and those that are extant, are narrative paintings. Although Yūchiku seems to have followed in his father's footsteps, little is known about him today. This particular work shows little of his father's influence, except in such small details as the broad, slow-curving ink outlines which define rocks and mountains. These are done in an exaggerated, mannered imitation of his father's ink-painting technique. He does not seem to have been trained in the monochrome ink tradition, and the pristine, aristocratic quality that characterized his father's works is lost in Yūchiku's painting.

The tale of the abominable drunkard involves actual historical figures and is based on the fact that its protagonist, Raikō, was known for his spectacular prowess in the military arts. Yet the escapade that may have inspired this fantastic tale is not known. The exact date of the tale's origin is unknown as well, but the story seems to have evolved from a mixture of ancient, orally transmitted legends of a monster devil and tales of heroic exploits. The tale apparently enjoyed a measure of popularity even before the second half of the fourteenth century, when the earliest exant *Shuten Dōji* emaki was made.[3] During the Muromachi period, it became the most popular of the many tales about warriors and their adventures. So well known was the *Shuten Dōji* story that it spawned another version, set at Ibukiyama in Ōmi province (modern Shiga prefecture), northeast of Kyoto.[4] Subsequently, it became customary to distinguish the late version as *Ibukiyama Shuten Dōji*, in which greater emphasis is placed on the ancestry and upbringing of the giant ogre, who is described as a foundling who was reared in the wild. The tale of *Shuten Dōji* also became an important part of the repertories of the Nō (see nos. 32, 33), puppet, and Kabuki theatres. In the eighteenth century, it was one of the twenty-three "most popular tales" that were published together under the rubric of *otogi zōshi*.

For some unexplained reason, members of the Kanō school of painting seem to have preferred the Ibukiyama version of the story, which they painted on scrolls and screens, emphasizing strong ink brushwork. These works reflect their training in the Chinese style of painting, which appealed to their military patrons. It is also possible that the Kanō tradition of using the Ibukiyama tale began because one of the school's august ancestors, Kanō Motonobu (1476–1559), was believed to have painted it.[5] Other painters, like Yūchiku, whose art was more closely dependent on an indigenous *yamato-e* technique of narrative painting that used bright colors as opposed to ink line, illustrated the Ōeyama version of the tale, which was perhaps preferred by the more tradition-bound clientele of Kyoto.

NOTES

1. F.V. Dickens (trans.), "The Story of Shiuten Doji from a Japanese Makimono in Six Ken or Rolls," *Journal of the Royal Asiatic Society of Great Britain and Ireland*, vol. 17 (n.d.).

2. Kawai Masatomo (ed.), *Yūshō/Tōgan*, vol. 11 of *Nihon Bijutsu Kaiga Zenshū*, ed. Tanaka Ichimatsu *et al.* (Tokyo, 1978), pp. 120–121.

3. It is in the collection of the Itsuō Museum in Osaka. See Okudaira Hideo (ed.), *Otogi Zōshi Emaki* (Tokyo, 1982), no. 2.

4. For example, one emaki of this tale is in the Suntory Museum collection in Tokyo. See Sakakibara Satoru, "Suntory Bijutsukanbon 'Shutendōji Emaki' o megutte, I (Shutendōji Emaki Owned by the Suntory Museum of Art, Part I)," *Kokka* 1076 (1984), pp. 7–26; Part II, *Kokka* 1077 (1984), pp. 33–61.

5. *Ibid.*, pp. 33–39.

28
Tale of Momotarō (The Tale of Peach Boy)

By Isen-in, Kanō Naganobu (1775–1828)
Two handscrolls, ink, colors and gold on silk
H: 31.9 cm, L: 893.7 cm (scroll I), 933 cm (scroll II)
Signature: "Isen-in Hō-in Fujiwara Naganobu hitsu"
Seal: "Genshōsai"
Spencer no. 202

This pair of handscrolls illustrates one of the most famous and well-loved Japanese tales for children, the story of Momotarō, the Peach Boy.[1] Twenty painted scenes follow the exploits of this remarkable and resourceful hero, who collects a group of companions—a pheasant, a monkey, and a dog—to conquer the inhabitants of the Island of Ogres, and returns home victorious and laden with treasure. The story abounds with brave deeds, and Momotarō, the dashing boy, represents the ideal hero for young and old alike. The tale of Momotarō became quite popular during the Edo period, and has remained so.

The tale begins with the traditional phrase, "Long, long ago . . . ," and goes on to tell how one day the aging wife of a poor, elderly woodcutter found a large peach floating in a river (shown here). At home, when she and her husband opened the peach, they discovered a young boy nestled inside the pit. The couple believed the child to be a gift from the gods, and they adopted the boy as their own son, naming him Momotarō, the First Son of the Peach.

Momotarō grew to be big and strong, and he excelled in feats of strength. One day he decided to leave his parents and go to the Island of Ogres, to conquer the evil creatures who terrorized the good people of the countryside. Along the way, Momotarō met a dog, a pheasant and a monkey, all of whom joined him as traveling companions (see Pl. VII). With their help, Momotarō vanquished many of the ogres and returned home with a great store of treasure (shown here).

Kanō Naganobu, also called Eishin, the artist of these scrolls, signed the end of both scrolls with the inscription "Isen-in Hōin Fujiwara Naganobu hitsu"; he also included his seal, "Genshōsai." As the first son of Kanō Korenobu (1754–1808), Naganobu followed his father's style, specializing in richly decorative bird and flower paintings. Eishin later succeeded his father as head of the Kobikichō branch of the Edo-period Kanō school. He served as an official painter to the Tokugawa shogunate, and was given the honorary rank of *hōgen* in 1802. In 1816, he was promoted to the rank of *hōin* and adopted the name of Isen-in. On the basis of these facts we may assume that the two *Momotarō* scrolls date to a period between 1816 and 1828, the year of his death.[2] Naganobu's style is for the most part decorative, with an emphasis on bright colors and complex compositions; the *Momotarō* scrolls, which were executed with a very free, sketchy brush, stand out as refreshingly different from his more dry and academic works. The light, wet ink washes delineating mountains and hills create an impression of pale and misty settings; washes of pale colors and gold provide an atmosphere of pristine serenity, even in scenes depicting the evil-looking ogres.

These charming illustrations of the Momotarō tale exhibit subtlety and refined taste, characteristics rarely found in works for children. Ink, colors, and gold are used with restraint. Even the violent fighting scenes are depicted in a subdued manner without gory details such as those graphically painted in the *Ōeyama* scrolls (no. 27). The large

empty spaces left on the silk between the painted scenes suggest that they were originally intended to be filled in with written text. The use of such expensive materials as silk, gold, and high-quality mineral pigments, and the restrained nature of the painting technique suggest that the scrolls may have been intended for an aristocratic patron, perhaps a young member of the shogunal family that Naganobu served.

Because of its obvious didactic message regarding good and evil, and because the protagonist serves as a peace-maker between the dog and monkey, arch-enemies who become his devoted companions, the fairy tale of Momotarō became part of the education of the young for generations. However, the origins and history of the Momotarō story remain obscure; no documentary references to the Peach Boy story before the Edo period have yet been found. It is known that in its earliest form the tale apparently approached the matter of the boy's birth in a much less fantastic manner: instead of a baby, the peach found by the old woman contained a potent aphrodisiac.[3] The distant ancestor of the tale seems to have had a variety of "roots;" it belongs to a popular genre of myth that centers around "tiny" children and others born under extraordinary circumstances, such as Oyayubi Tarō (the Thumb Boy), Issun Bōshi (the One Inch Boy), and Kaguya Hime (the Shining Princess). These little children were representatives from the realm of benevolent spirits, who descended from the celestial world to benefit good people and punish the evil. Many other Asian myths involve similar "birth stories" connected with fruits and water. The peach, a symbol of longevity and immortality, is

considered a protector against evil forces. It is most familiar to us through the Chinese legend of Hsi-wang-mu (the Queen Mother of the West), who watches over this potent fruit.

It is possible that the tale was written in the sixteenth century, when the Japanese were being awakened to the existence of riches outside their country; they may well have dreamed of achieving the remarkable good fortune that the story bestows on Momotarō.[4]

The story of the little Peach Boy, with its didactic notes, was well appreciated by the adult population of Edo society, which lived by a strict Confucian code of morality enforced by the shogunal regime. The earliest known illustrations of this tale, dating from the early eighteenth century, were woodcuts; the tale itself was included in the popular repertories of the puppet (Bunraku) and Kabuki theatres of the Edo period.

NOTES

1. Eric Sackheim (trans.), *Momotaro* (Tokyo, 1963).
2. Hosono Masanobu, *Edo Kanō to Hōgai*, vol. 52 of *Book of Books, Nihon no Bijutsu* (Tokyo, 1978), p. 53.
3. Shimazu Hisamoto, *Nihon Kokumin Dōwa Jūnikō* (Tokyo, 1948), p. 40. Also see Namekawa Michio, *Momotarō Zō no Henyō* (Tokyo, 1981).
4. Shimazu, *Nihon Kokumin*, p. 50.

29
Hyakki Yakō Zu (*Night Parade of One Hundred Demons*)

Mid-nineteenth century, Edo period
Text and painting attributed to Okada Tamechika (1823–1864)
One handscroll, ink, color and gold on paper
H: 35 cm, L: 1239.9 cm
Spencer no. 112

In five paragraphs of text and five sections of painting, this handscroll records the horrifying experiences of a young man who witnesses grotesque demons parading at night through an old house. The text of the scroll sets the time and place as the closing years of the Jishō era (1177–1180) in the western section of Suzaku Street in Kyoto. The period specified in the text is meant as a reference to a famous unhappy episode in the history of the capital city and the imperial court. Beset by hostile and militant Buddhist monks, Kiyomori, patriarch of the ruling military Taira family, forced the imperial court to abandon the old capital and move to the city of Fukuhara in June of 1180. The move was extremely unpopular and unsuccessful, and Kiyomori was obliged to return to Kyoto in November of that year.

The unnamed owner of the old mansion in this tale, a gentleman holding the title of Chūnagon (Middle Counsellor), followed the court to the new capital, leaving his Kyoto mansion in the care of an old retainer. The Spencer scroll opens with a view of the interior of the large, once elegant and luxurious house, in which two men are sitting and conversing: a young man and the old retainer he has come to visit. According to the story, the young man, having been persuaded to stay overnight, becomes a terrified witness to the wild antics of prancing demons, who create a hellish racket until dawn, then disappear as suddenly as they had materialized.

A number of the demons in the scroll have recognizably female faces, but beastly claws emerge from beneath their robes. According to the text, one particularly frightening-looking woman was engaged in her toilet in front of a "mirror eight feet in diameter. While she was painting her teeth black,[1] she gave a big grin that was frightening enough to cause [one to] faint . . ." Other creatures are the spirits of musical instruments, such as bells, lute, flute and *koto* (a thirteen-stringed instrument): in this guise they produce an alarming commotion and terrifying noises. Still others are Buddhist ritual objects come to life—"living" banners, cymbals, drums, and handscrolls. Yet others are common household utensils which have taken on a grotesque and shocking appearance, such as an old umbrella, shoes, straw sandals, cooking pots and large kettles.

This tale of imaginary demons is rooted in both the universal fear of darkness and the ancient Japanese belief that alien spirits and monstrous creatures ran riot in the darkness of night. Ancient Japanese literature refers to a number of supposedly real incidents of men witnessing the activities of night demons; some court rules actually forbade nightly excursions for fear of such encounters.[2] Mixed with the ancient fear of darkness is another old Japanese belief that used, worn household utensils can turn into evil spirits and lead humans astray.

The tale of one hundred demonic creatures upsetting the quiet of the night inspired the popular imagination. At the turn of the century, a catalogue of old paintings reported that as many as seven handscrolls illustrating this subject were in existence.[3] The oldest was dated to the early fourteenth century, and the latest to the mid-nineteenth century. All were attributed to generations of Tosa painters. Several other scrolls on this subject, not included in the catalogue, are also known today; the oldest of the extant scrolls depicting the "one hundred night demons," dated to the sixteenth century,[4] is in the collection of the Shinjuan temple in Kyoto.

The scroll from the Spencer Collection, although late in date, is unique among the various interpretations of the one hundred demons theme, because it is the only known *Hyakki Yakō* scroll to contain text. The painted scenes are also remarkably similar to those in the Shinjuan version, even to the minute, idiosyncratic details of the brush strokes. It seems that the artist of the Spencer scroll attempted to make an intelligent restoration of the original format of *Hyakki Yakō* depiction by using the Shinjuan version as a model. He divided the one continous composition that constitutes the Shinjuan scroll into five sections, inserted paragraphs of text, and shifted some of the scenes so that they formed a logical unity with the sections of text. For the same purpose, he transplanted two demon figures that he found in the second half of the Shinjuan version to the opening section of his own scroll. Such a systematic and intelligent reinterpretation of a model is quite in keeping with the practices of Okada Tamechika (1823–1864), the artist to whom this scroll is attributed. It is also conceivable that someone like Tamechika, with his strong antiquarian interests, was able to discover a textual source for the one hundred demons theme, which he used to reproduce the original arrangement of *Hyakki Yakō* scrolls. The text of the Spencer scroll is written in a clear but fluid *kana* script typical of the writing style used by Tamechika during the later years of his life.[5]

Okada Tamechika, also known as Reizei Tametaka,[6] was deeply concerned with the revival of the ancient *yamato-e* style of native painting and the art of *emaki*, at a time when both were largely ignored by most Japanese painters. He made efforts to revive these indigenous art forms, producing many copies of older emaki. Born the third son of a minor Kanō painter, Kanō Nagayasu, Tamechika was profoundly influenced by the volatile political climate in Japan during his youth, when the nation was split into factions fighting to preserve the shogunal regime, on the one side, and to restore imperial sovereignty on the other. His youthful admiration for the ancient yamato-e style may have been partly stimulated by his disillusionment with the tradition-bound training of the Kanō school; however, he was also affected by the political and artistic goals promoted by two older artists who are often cited in reference to "Fukko Yamato-e" ("Revivalist Yamato-e"): Tanaka Totsugon (1760–1823) and Ukita Ikkei (1795–1859). Tamechika began making copies of old emaki while in his teens, and he studied yamato-e and the ancient costumes and other details that formed the backbone of this artistic mode throughout his adult life.

Tamechika was also influenced by his religious mentor, the priest Gankai (1823–1873) of Mt. Hiei, for whom he painted many Buddhist icons. Through his friendships with court nobles he obtained commissions to execute large screen paintings for the imperial palace and important Buddhist temples. His patrons also included military lords in service to the shoguns. Tamechika's broad artistic and social contacts seem to have irked both the pro- and anti-shogun factions, and in 1862 he was forced to take refuge at

Kokawadera, south of Osaka. He spent the remainder of his life "underground," assuming several aliases, until he was finally assassinated near Nara by a band of warriors sympathetic to the imperial court.

Tamechika changed his signatures to reflect his promotions in courtly rank.[7] The signature in the scroll exhibited here refers to the rank of "Shikibu Shōjō" (Junior Secretary at the Ministry of Ceremonials), a position which he was granted in 1855. Unfortunately, however, the constrained writing style and the small characters found in this signature do not appear to conform to Tamechika's calligraphic hand; it must have been added by someone at a later date.

NOTES

1. This curious custom called *haguro*, blackening the teeth with liquid obtained from a mixture of iron and other minerals, was an important cosmetic practice for both men and women of ancient Japan. Young women applied haguro on their teeth only after matrimony, as it symbolized fidelity.
2. For literary references to the night demons, see Komatsu Shigemi, "Hyakki Yakō Emaki no nazo," Komatsu Shigemi (ed.), *Nihon Emaki Taisei*, vol. 25, *Nōe Hōshi Ekotoba, Fukutomi Sōshi, Hyakki Yakō Emaki* (Tokyo, 1979), pp. 126–128; for other examples of this tale, see Stephen Addiss (ed.), *Japanese Ghosts & Demons: Art of the Supernatural* (New York, 1985), pp. 15–23.
3. Kurokawa Mayori (ed.), *Kōko Gaku*, in *Kurokawa Mayori Zenshū* (Tokyo, 1910–1911), vol. 9, pp. 60–63.
4. Komatsu Shigemi, *Nihon Emaki*.
5. For example, see no. 66 in the Tokyo National Museum exhibition catalogue, *Reizei Tametaka* (Tokyo, 1979).
6. For his life and works, see Tokyo National Museum exhibition catalogue, and Itsuki Seishō, *Reizei Tametaka no Shōgai* (Kyoto, 1956).
7. Matsumura Masao, "Tamechika rakkan nempu," *Kokka* 844 (July 1962), pp. 318–328.

30
Sankai Ibutsu (Strange Creatures of Mountains and Seas)

Early seventeenth century, Edo period
Two books, ink, color and gold on paper
H: 30.2 cm, W: 22.0 cm, each
Spencer no. 61

The *Sankai Ibutsu* is a two-volume book with 47 pages of text and an equal number of illustrations arranged in a recto (text) verso (paintings) order. Each illustration depicts an exotic creature in a minimally defined landscape setting; the brief sections of text describe each creature and its natural habitat. Both rare and familiar mammals, birds, reptiles, and fish are shown. Some exhibit bizarre aberrations; we see, for example, a rooster with an abnormally elongated neck, a bird with multiple heads, a one-legged crane, a headless elephant with flaming wings, and a tiger who takes dance-like steps on its two hind legs. Many of the creatures are hybrids of different classes of the animal kingdom, such as a winged fish, a rooster with a human head, and a bird with human feet. Still others are completely mythological, such as the phoenix, a bird-like creature regarded as an emblem of the south, and the *chilin*, an auspicious being with the body of a deer, the tail of an ox, horse's hooves, and a single horn. Curious and fantastic in appearance, these highly animated creatures are rendered in fine detail with considerable imagination and humor.

Each creature is depicted within a roundel centered on an otherwise exquisitely decorated gold-patterned page, as can be seen in the paintings of an extraordinary tiger endowed with eight heads and a winged, dragon-headed horse-like creature reproduced here. The animals are placed against landscapes that open up asymmetrically to suggest distant space in a manner reminiscent of Chinese landscape paintings of the Southern Sung Dynasty (1127–1279). The landscape elements are executed with bold ink outlines and areas of pale tinted wash which contrast with the detailed treatment of the animals. Despite the artist's seeming zoological interests, the illustrations are decorative and were clearly intended to delight and amuse.

The precise source or model for the text and illustrations of the *Sankai Ibutsu* is unknown, but the work seems to have been greatly influenced by the *San-ts'ai t'u-hui*, a Chinese encyclopedia which was compiled in 1607 by Wang Ch'i (active 1565–1614), with later supplements by his son Wang Ssu-i.[1] Drawing upon many literary sources, the encyclopedia encompassed a wide range of subjects and devoted several sections to descriptions of odd or exotic creatures. It is likely that woodcut illustrations from sections of this Chinese work directly inspired some of the images in the Spencer books. Not all of the creatures represented in the *Sankai Ibutsu* are found in the *San-ts'ai t'u-hui*, however, and it is possible to trace their origins to other, much earlier Chinese textual sources. Many of the animals in the *Sankai Ibutsu*, for example, correspond to those described in an ancient Chinese geographical text entitled the *Shan-hai-ching* (*The Classic of Mountains and Seas*).[2] Containing chapters of unknown authorship which date from as early as the Eastern Chou period (770–256 B.C.) through the Eastern Han (A.D. 25–220), it describes the wilderness beyond the borders of China and its unusual inhabitants.

Regarded as a classic text on exotic lands, the *Shan-hai-ching* was introduced to Japan at an early date; it is recorded in a catalogue of Chinese books in Japanese collections that was edited sometime between 889 and 898.[3]

The fabulous creature with eight heads, legs and tails illustrated here is also included in the *Shan-hai-ching*.[4] The text accompanying the picture describes the animal as follows:

> A spirit called Tengo [T'ien-wu, in Chinese] lives in the Rising Sun Gorge in the east. He is a water spirit. He has a body of a tiger, a human face, eight heads, eight legs, eight tails and is yellow-green in color.

Another odd creature, whose description is found in yet another early Chinese source, the *Hou-han-shu* (*A History of the Later Han*),[5] is depicted in volume II. Called a Kakutan (Chiao-tuan, in Chinese), this dragon-headed "horse" is shown seated beside a small waterfall, beneath the branch of an overhanging tree. Bright red flames shoot from its body. The text on the facing page reads:

> In the land of the Tatars[6] there is a beast called Kakutan. According to the explanation given in the *Han-shu* [*History of Han*],[7] the Kakutan resembles an ox and its horns were used to make bows.

Neither seal nor signature is found in these books; however, since the paintings exhibit unmistakable traits of the Kanō school, the painter must have been trained in it. Landscape elements are clearly outlined in ink; crystalline rocks have sharp pointed edges and large window-like openings; birds, foliage, and small plants are depicted with meticulous care. Large, decorative flowering plants such as peonies create sudden, startling contrasts with the otherwise subdued settings; and gold is applied freely on the ground, sky, clouds, and mist. These features vividly recall the standard artistic vocabulary of a large number of Kanō-school artists who decorated the walls of castles and palaces from the late sixteenth to the early seventeenth century. The paintings in these books, in fact, have the appearance of miniature screens, and should be attributed to a follower of this school active in the early seventeenth century.

NOTES

1. Wang Ch'i and Wang Ssu-i, *San-ts'ai t'u-hui* (Taipei, 1970 reprint of 1609 ed.), 6 vols. A Japanese edition entitled *Wakan Sansai Zue* and edited by Terajima Ryōan was published in 1712 (1906 ed.).
2. *Shan-hai-ching chien-shu* with commentaries by Kuo P'u and Ho I-hsing, originally published in 1809.
3. This catalogue, *Nihonkoku Genzaisho Mokuroku* (*Catalogue of Books in Japanese Collections*), compiled by Fujiwara no Sukeyo (died 898), contains 16,790 titles, the majority of which are Chinese. See Kohase Keikichi, *Nihonkoku Genzaisho Mokuroku Kaisetsu Kō* (Tokyo, 1956).
4. For the original Chinese description, see *Shan-hai-ching*, chüan 9, p. 2.
5. *Hou-han-shu* was edited by Ssu-ma Piao of the Chin Dynasty (265–420) and continued by Fan Yeh of the Sung Dynasty (420–479). For a description of this animal, see chüan 119, p. 268 (reprinted in *Ehr-shih-wu-shih*, Hong Kong, 1959).
6. A non-Chinese tribe which inhabited the land to the north of the Chinese empire.
7. This actually should read *Hou-han-shu*.

31
Teikan Zusetsu (Exemplary Conduct of Ancient Chinese Emperors)

Mid-seventeenth century, Edo period
Twelve books, ink, color and gold on paper
H: 23.5 cm, W: 17.4 cm, each
Spencer no. 66-1

Among the many Chinese literary works introduced to Japan was a Confucian text entitled *Ti-chien t'u-shuo (Exemplary Conduct of Ancient Chinese Emperors)*. Written by Chang Chu-cheng (1525–1582), an important Ming dynasty official who also served as tutor to the Wan-li emperor (reigned 1573–1620), it was published, with illustrations, in 1573.[1] Known as the *Teikan Zusetsu* in Japan, it became one of the most popular of the imported Chinese texts. It details the good conduct of eighty-one emperors and the evil doings of thirty-six emperors who lived from China's legendary times through the Sung Dynasty

(960–1278). The set of twelve volumes in the Spencer Collection contains a Japanese translation of the Chinese original, made in 1650.

The text of the *Teikan Zusetsu* is divided into individual accounts of various emperors' deeds and misdeeds, each accompanied by a colorful miniature painting by an anonymous artist. The images are stylistically consistent in all twelve volumes, and certain compositional elements tend to be repeated: for example, the emperor is frequently depicted seated on a throne directly outside the palace doors. The architecture in each scene is precisely painted, with considerable attention given to decorative detail. Particularly charming are the miniature painted screens which adorn palace interiors. The tiny figures in the screens are meticulously drawn, and the patterns of the clothing are carefully differentiated. In contrast to the rigid geometry of the architecture, landscape elements are freely rendered. Expressively modulated ink outlines define jagged contours of rocks and the trunks of trees, revealing the artist's training in the Kanō school. The ink work contrasts with the bright red of the architecture and the blue-green washes used for the landscape, creating vibrant images of delicacy and elegance. The sumptuous and decorative gold cloud patterns lend an appropriate aura of imperial majesty.

Intended by Chang Chu-cheng as "lessons" for his young protogé, the accounts of the various emperors' activities take on an extremely moralistic tone. An example of a virtuous emperor is depicted in a delightful double-page illustration from volume II, shown here. On the right side of the painting the Shang emperor Wu Ting (reigned 1324–1265 B.C.) is shown asleep at his desk; he is dreaming. According to the text, Wu Ting, for the first three years after he ascended to the throne, did not utter a word because he was mourning the death of his father. He spent his time quietly reflecting on the principles of good government, and broke his silence only after he had a prophetic dream in which he was visited by a wise advisor. (In the painting, the events of the dream take place within a cloud-like formation that emanates from the figure of the sleeping emperor.) Hoping to find this wise man, Wu Ting described the face he had seen in the vision to an artist, and had a portrait painted, copied, and distributed throughout the Shang territory. Finally, at a place called Fu Yen (in modern Shansi province), a man resembling the Heaven-sent advisor of the emperor's dream was found—a common laborer named Fu Yüeh. As is shown in the left half of the picture, he was discovered while building a mud wall. Fu Yüeh then was brought to Wu Ting to serve as his chief advisor. Wu Ting's reign was harmonious ever afterward.[2]

An illustration from volume IX depicts two of the most reprehensible deeds ever committed by a Chinese emperor (see Pl. VII). The first, shown in the lower left-hand portion of the painting, was the book burning ordered in 213 B.C. by Ch'in Shih-huang-ti (reigned 221–210 B.C.), who has become well-known in the West since the 1974 discovery of his tomb and the army of several thousand terra-cotta soldiers buried near it.[3] On the advice of his chief minister, Li Ssu, the emperor ordered that all copies of the *Shih-ching* (*Book of Songs*), the *Shu-ching* (*Book of Documents*) and other philosophical texts be burned.[4] The only books exempted from the emperor's edict were the official Ch'in historical chronologies and utilitarian treatises on divination, agriculture, and medicine.[5] In centralizing the government and standardizing such things as weights and measures, coins, and the writing system, Ch'in Shih-huang-ti's "Legalists" went to extremes in their efforts to achieve a standardization of thought as well. In keeping with this goal, another horrifying act attributed to Ch'in Shih-huang-ti was the execution and mass burial (in a pit grave) of some 460 Confucian scholars accused of refusing to comply with the harsh imperial edicts prohibiting philosophical debate. On the right-hand side of the painting the distraught victims are shown being forced to their deaths, while the emperor, seated on his throne outside the palace, looks on with interest.

The first Japanese copy of the *Teikan Zusetsu* is believed to have been published in 1606, with illustrations which closely followed the original Chinese compositions.[6] The most celebrated renderings of the *Teikan Zusetsu* stories were done shortly thereafter on a pair of six-panelled folding screens by the third-generation leader of the Kanō school, Sanraku (1561–1635).[7]

Stories of the Chinese emperors became indispensable subjects for decorating the interiors of palaces and castles erected by military rulers during the Edo period. These paintings, whether done on large objects, like screens, or in small scrolls and books, faithfully retained original Chinese compositions, as in the Spencer examples.

NOTES

1. Chang produced this book jointly with Lü T'iao-yang. See L. Carrington Goodrich and Chaoying Fan (eds.), *Dictionary of Ming Biography*, vol. 1 (New York, 1976), p. 60.
2. K.C. Wu, *The Chinese Heritage* (New York, 1982), pp. 200–205.
3. Maxwell K. Hearn, "The Terracotta Army of the First Emperor of Qin (221–206 B.C.)," *The Great Bronze Age of China*, ed. Wen Fong (New York, 1980), pp. 351–373.
4. Charles O. Hucker, *China's Imperial Past* (Stanford, 1975), pp. 98–99.
5. Hucker, *China's Imperial Past*, pp. 43–44.
6. Robert Treat Paine and Alexander Soper, *The Art and Architecture of Japan* (Baltimore, 1975), p. 198; and Kawase Kazuma, *Kokatsuji-ban no Kenkyū* (Tokyo, 1937), vol. 1, p. 232. The Spencer Collection also owns a printed set of six volumes of the *Teikan Zusetsu* (no. 274), which is believed to be a slightly later Japanese edition.
7. Doi Tsugu yoshi, *Kanō Sanraku/Sansetsu*, vol. 12 of *Nihon Bijutsu Kaiga Zenshū* (Tokyo, 1976), Pls. 30–32. This pair of screens is currently in the Nishida Collection in Japan.

IV
Heroes and Heroines
of the Stage

Japan today is famous in the West for its remarkable Nō, Kabuki, and Bunraku theatres; it has even been referred to as a theatre historian's delight, as it has assiduously preserved its performance techniques over the centuries.[1] However, these world-famous forms of theatre are all relatively late developments; the ancient performing arts of Japan were sacred magic-dance performances, such as Kagura and Gigaku, intended as offerings to the august gods.

The staging of dramatic texts came into being only in the late fourteenth century, long after the development of poetry and the novel. A close bond soon formed between theatre and narrative prose, since playwrights often found inspiration in works of pure fiction or "historical novels" (see nos. 33 and 36). Occasionally, a play based on a literary work would inspire yet another, "new" novel, such as the story of Umewaka-maru (no. 34).

A similar relationship existed between stage dramas and their illustrations in painting, although this is an area of scholarship which has never been seriously explored. Nō plays were often illustrated in book or scroll format (nos. 32, 33) and stirring performances undoubtedly inspired the illustrators and influenced their paintings' compositions. Paintings illustrating other types of theatre texts, however, such as Kōwaka, were fully creations of the artist's imagination. Although Kōwaka texts include more detailed description of explicit action than do the Nō texts, actual Kōwaka performances were extremely abstract. The painters of Kōwaka texts therefore treated their material in a lively narrative style totally unrelated to what was performed on stage. Works like the *Youchi Soga* and *Taishokkan* handscrolls (nos. 36, 37) were apparently appreciated purely for their literary merit and lively illustrations.

NOTE

1. Peter Arnott, *The Theatres of Japan* (London and New York, 1969), p. 37.

32
Matsukaze Murasame
(*The Brine Maidens, Matsukaze and Murasame*)

Mid-sixteenth century, Muromachi period
One handscroll, ink, color and gold on paper
H: 17.6 cm, L: 670.2 cm
Spencer no. 45

Published: Nara Ehon Kokusai Kenkyū Kaigi (ed.), *Zaigai Nara Ehon* (Tokyo, 1981), no. 11;
Barbara Ruch *et al.* (eds.), *Kaigai Shozō Nara Ehon* (*Nara Ehon from Outstanding Foreign Collections*)
(*Tokyo, 1979*), *p. 43*.

Three handscrolls included in this exhibition (nos. 32, 33, and 34) are closely related
to two of the most popular Nō plays, *Matsukaze* and *Sumidagawa*.

The world-famous Nō plays of Japan originated as ritual dance-dramas performed as part of ceremonies and festivals dedicated to the Shinto gods of Japan's native religion.[1] As various features were adopted from other performing arts, particularly from the *Sarugaku* (literally, "monkey-dance"), a unique dramatic art form evolved during the fourteenth century—what is known today as the Nō, renowned for its elegant, extremely abstract presentation of plot. Nō's masked actors perform on stages graced by a minimum of backdrop details—usually a single pine tree—and props are often nothing more than a fan. Accompanied by the music of a single flute and small drums, and with the utmost economy of movement, the performers are able to suggest the full range of emotions. The elegant, expressive masks and stunning costumes that developed in Nō theatre have also made unique contributions to visual art.[2]

The repertoire and techniques of performance were firmly established sometime between the late sixteenth and early seventeenth century and have been rigorously maintained. Among the libretti of these dramas, about 240 of which are known today, is the text of *Matsukaze*, upon which this scroll in the Spencer Collection is closely based. The play, which continues to be popular, not only on the Nō stage, but as a dance piece, was written by Kan'ami (Kanze Kiyotsugu, 1333–1384), an actor and playwright, and was later reworked by his son Zeami Motokiyo (1363–1443?).

Matsukaze was most likely based on an even older play, which in turn, would have been inspired by the historical fact that the courtier-poet Ariwara no Yukihira (818–893) once spent a brief period in exile at Suma during the reign of Emperor Montoku (reigned 851–858). While there, he is known to have composed the following poem:

> Should anyone,
>   by any chance inquire after me,
> Tell him,
>   I am making salt,
> To while away melancholy days,
>   at the beach of Suma.[3]

The exile of this famous courtier became a celebrated legend; it was embroidered with romantic episodes in later works of literature such as the *Tale of Genji* (see nos. 20–22), in which the fictional protagonist, Prince Genji, is also exiled to the seaside village of Suma, southwest of Kyoto.

The *Matsukaze* story tells of the undying passion of two sisters for the courtier-poet Yukihira, who was exiled to Suma. The sisters, Matsukaze ("wind in the pines") and Murasame ("autumn showers"), brine-gathering maidens at Suma, both fell deeply in love with the exiled poet. When he was pardoned by the court, Yukihira returned to the capital, leaving his cap and gown with the maidens as mementos, along with a promise to send for them in the near future. Shortly after his return home, Yukihira died before he could fulfill his promise. Distraught at the news of his death, the two sisters drowned themselves in the sea.

The play *Matsukaze* is realized as a type of flashback, a common device in Nō theatre. It begins with the arrival at Suma of a travelling monk, who is told by a villager that a large pine tree marks the place where two sisters lived with their lover. Moved by the tale, the priest chants prayers for the souls of the brine maidens. When night falls, the ghosts of Matsukaze and Murasame appear to him, since they are still tied to the world through their passion for Yukihira. Matsukaze, in despair, puts on the robe and cap of her love and encircles and then embraces the pine tree, believing it to be Lord Yukihira. When dawn arrives the sisters disappear, and the priest awakens, not knowing whether or not his vision was a dream.

The handscroll in the Spencer Collection contains nine painted scenes, which were clearly inspired by the stage performance of this drama. Settings for the scenes are sparse, and the figures are depicted as though they are speaking to one another. In each of the painted scenes, the calligrapher actually wrote the character's dialogue around the painted figures, which enhances the impression that the paintings recreate a stage performance.

The text of the scene reproduced here reads:

> (*Matsukaze speaks*)[4]
> Awake or asleep,
> From my pillow, from the foot of my bed,
> Love rushes in upon me.
> Helplessly I sink down,
> Weeping in agony.
> The River of Three Fords[5]
> Has gloomy shallows
> Of never-ending tears;
> I found, even there,
> An abyss of wildest love.
> Oh joy! Look! Over there!
> He calls me by my name, Pine Wind!
> I am coming!
> (*Murasame speaking*)
> For shame! For such [thoughts as these
> You are lost in the sin of passion.][6]

Simple yet charming paintings reveal an expert handling of brush and ink, and a limited palette of red, brown, and green is enhanced by the occasional use of gold leaf on certain details of the maidens' garments.

The Spencer scroll text closely follows the libretto of the play, yet it was not intended to be used as a script, since it omits the notations used in libretti to mark the different roles.[7] The Spencer scroll, in fact, is the earliest known example of an illustrated prose version of the Nō play *Matsukaze*.[8] The tale of the sad fate of the maidens, especially as related in dance performances, later became a popular subject for painting in the Edo period.

Illustrated handscrolls (*emaki*), which developed during the eleventh century, continued to enjoy a great vogue throughout the thirteenth and fourteenth centuries. A much more modest version of the emaki, measuring no more than 15 to 16 centimeters in height, began to appear in the late fifteenth century (see no. 20).[9] Contemporary chronicles of courtiers often affectionately referred to them as *ko-e* (little picture-scrolls).[10] Such ko-e, made from the late fifteenth to the early sixteenth century, represent the last phase in the evolution of emaki; it was during this period that the codex format slowly began to supplant it.

The Spencer scroll was originally made as a book, but later remounted as a handscroll. In its original book form, however, it would have been an early example of the illustrated codex. It is an historical irony that the book should have been remounted as a scroll, the generic ancestor from which it evolved.

Such historical factors, along with the stylistic features of the painting, enable us to date this charming work to the mid-sixteenth century, in the Muromachi period.

NOTES

1. For a historical survey of Nō drama, see Shuichi Kato, *A History of Japanese Literature; The First Thousand Years*, trans. David Chibbett (London, 1979); Donald Keene, *Nō: The Classical Theatre of Japan* (Tokyo and New York, 1966); and P.G. O'Neill, *Early Nō Drama: Its Background, Character and Development 1300–1450* (Westport, Conn., 1958).

2. For Nō masks, see Keene, *Nō: Classical Theatre*, pp. 162ff; Seiroku Noma, *Masks, Arts and Crafts of Japan*, no. 1, English adaptation by Meredith Weatherby (Rutland, Vermont and Tokyo, 1957), and Kyoto National Museum (ed.), *Nomen Sen (Noh Masks)* (Kyoto, 1965). For Nō costumes, see Keene, *Nō: Classical Theatre*, pp. 210ff; and Kongō Iwao, *Nō Ishō* (Kyoto, 1933).

3. This poem is included in the *Kokin Waka Shū*. For another translation, see H.H. Honda, *Kokin Waka shū* (Tokyo, 1970), poem no. 962.

4. Donald Keene (ed.), *Twenty Plays of the Nō Theatre* (New York and London, 1970), pp. 18–34.

5. River of Three Fords is the river of the afterworld.

6. The words in brackets are written on the next section of the scroll.

7. Susan Matisoff identified the source for this narrative text as the version of the libretto used by the group of performers known as the Shimogakari, which includes Komparu, Kongō, and Kita schools of Nō performers. She also believes that the author of this text was an actor of this group. See Nara Ehon Kokusai Kenkyū Kaigi (ed.), *Zaigai Nara Ehon* (Tokyo, 1981), p. 46.

8. For later versions of the tale of Matsukaze and Murasame, see Yokoyama Shigeru (ed.), *Muromachi Jidai Monogatari Shū*, vol. 5 (Tokyo, 1962), pp. 151–169.

9. For other examples of these small emaki, see Okudaira Hideo, *Otogi Zōshi Emaki: Illustrated Narrative Scrolls* (Tokyo, 1982). Some of them are dated, for example, Suzuriwari Sōshi (H: 15 cm, 1494), Kitsune Zōshi (H: 16.2 cm, 1497), and Matsuhime Monogatari (H: 16.2 cm, 1526).

10. For literary references and related problems on ko-e, see Umezu Jirō, "Suzuriwari Emaki sonota: ko-e no mondai (On the Suzuriwari Zōshi Picture-Scroll)," *Kokka* 828 (March 1961), pp. 103–104; and Okudaira, *Otogi Zōshi*, pp. 22–23.

三十六まんゑく

たゑもきけむけれ
るのゆもふせきと
きりめゐておゑき
とこゑゑすゑや

月のうゑやのうゑ
うらゐゆうゑも小

さはすのすすつ
のすゑもまりさゑや

ゑゑゑゑ
らうさはす
ゑ

33
Sumidagawa no Sōshi (The Tale of Sumidagawa)

Dated 1618, Edo period
By Fukuō Jin'emon Moriyoshi
One handscroll, ink and color on paper
H. 26.5 cm, L: 642.1 cm
Spencer no. 54

PUBLISHED: Nara Ehon Kokusai Kenkyū Kaigi (ed.), *Zaigai Nara Ehon* (Tokyo, 1981), Pls. 25–26, 146–149; pp. 47–48, 133–134; Barbara Ruch *et al.* (eds.), *Kaigai Shozō Nara Ehon (Nara Ehon from Outstanding Foreign Collections)* (Tokyo, 1979), Pls. 44–46.

The heart-breaking story of a kidnapped boy and his grief-stricken mother is widely known in Japan through the popular Nō and Kabuki plays *Sumidagawa*, or *The Sumida River*.[1] The tale, one of the most popular in the current Nō repertory, tells of a mother who travels from Kyoto to Edo in search of her young son, Umewaka-maru, who has been kidnapped by a slave trader. Upon reaching the outskirts of Edo, she finds that her boy died near the Sumida River exactly one year before she arrived at the riverbank.

The Nō play *Sumidagawa* was written by Jūrō Motomasa (1394/95–1431/59, the son of the celebrated Nō playwright and critic Zeami Motokiyo (1363–1443?). Motomasa's piece was probably inspired by a famous poem included in the tenth-century literary classic, the *Tales of Ise* (see nos. 18, 19), which expresses a traveler's feelings upon journeying to the Sumida River. The poem, which is woven into the words spoken by Umewaka-maru's mother in the play, reads as follows:

Nanishi owaba	If you are what your name implies,
Iza koto towamu	Let me ask you,
Miyakodori	Capital-bird,
Waga omou hito wa	Does all go well
Ariya nashiya to.	With my beloved?[2]

The half-crazed mother, upon hearing no reply from the birds hovering over the river, realizes that they are not, after all, birds of the capital, Kyoto.

The text of this scroll generally follows the libretto of the *Sumidagawa* Nō play and is interspersed with illustrations—eight in all—which were clearly based on a stage performance. As in the play, the first figure to be introduced is the ferryman, and the next is the mother. Both are dressed as Nō performers, although the mother-figure is maskless. After her long search for the missing Umewaka-maru, the mother has finally arrived at the Sumida River; she has learned of the death of her son, and the kindly villagers are offering Buddhist services in memory of the child. The grieving mother is led to a small tomb mound, marked with a willow tree, where her boy was buried. In the scene reproduced here, she is shown holding a small drum to offer prayers to the departed child's soul. Six villagers form a semi-circle behind her. In the scene that follows, she repeats her prayers to Amida Buddha, and the figure of a small boy suddenly appears from behind the tomb mound. When she reaches for him, however, he vanishes; he is merely an apparition, called up by the prayers to the dead.

The scroll includes notations in the text for the actors, and in places instructions for chanting are marked in red ink. The text itself, however, differs somewhat from that of the standard libretto for the play. All of the figures are clad in Nō costumes, and they hold such stage props as small drums. The movements of the figures, especially the hand gestures and positions of the feet, are strongly reminiscent of the dance poses used in Nō performances. The settings for the painted scenes in the scroll are also as simple as those used on stage. Two of the illustrations, however, are of scenes that do not occur in the play: in the fourth scene (not shown here), the ferryboat is depicted traveling over the water—a scene never performed on the Nō stage—and in the scene reproduced here, villagers are shown seated behind the mother to join in her prayers.

The artist's signature at the end of the scroll can be deciphered as Fukuō Jin'emon Moriyoshi,[3] the second-generation leader of the Fukuō family of supporting actors for the Kanze School of No, who lived from 1560 to 1625. In a postscript, he tells us that he believed he was suffering from a terminal illness while away from home in Edo, and that he made the scroll as a farewell gift to his daughter. The scroll is signed and dated the eighth day of the seventh month of the fourth year in the Gen'na era (1618).

It appears that Fukuō wrote down and illustrated this story in part to record a past performance and its pathos. It is interesting to note that the title written in Fukuō's hand on the frontispiece—which may originally have been the cover of the scroll—reads "Sumidagawa no Sōshi" ("The Tale of Sumidagawa"); the word *sōshi* would not have been used if the work were meant to be used as a libretto.

Although amateurish and naive, the charming illustrations capture the atmosphere of the tale. The text, which seems to have been written in after the paintings were done, has a softness and fluidity in its writing style and certain characteristics of cursive script typical of the calligraphy that was practiced among masters of the Kanze School.[4]

The scroll is the oldest and one of the most rare of the illustrated Nō texts which bear dated inscriptions. The *Sumidagawa* play, whose record of performance can be traced as far back as the early fifteenth century,[5] was so popular a temple known as the Mokuboji was erected on the left bank of the Sumida River to mark the imaginary grave site of the kidnapped child. The *Sumidagawa* story also inspired later artists, who elaborated upon the tale to produce such works as the *Umewaka-maru* scroll (no. 34).

NOTES

1. For the English translation of the play, see Nippon Gakujutsu Shinkōkai, *The Noh Drama: Ten Plays from the Japanese* (Tokyo and Rutland, Vt., 1955), pp. 145–159.
2. Helen C. McCullough (trans.), *The Tales of Ise: Lyrical Episodes from Tenth-Century Japan* (Stanford, 1968), p. 76. Miyakodori is a type of beach plover.
3. The last part of this signature is not easy to decipher, and it has been read in the past as "Morikatsu," but there is no record of a Fukuō family member who used this personal name. See Nara Ehon Kokusai Kenkyū Kaigi (ed.), *Zaigai Nara Ehon* (Tokyo, 1981), p. 47.
4. For calligraphy of Kanze masters, see Itō Toshiko, "Den Kōetsu hitsu Utai-bon to Kanze Kokusetsu (A Book of Utai Generally Ascribed to Kōetsu and Kokusetsu Kanze)," *Kokka* 922, (1970), pp. 5–22.
5. A detailed discussion of how to perform this play is included in a record of Zeami (Kanze) Motokiyo's (1363–1443) personal views on Nō performance, which were written down from memory in 1430 by his son Motoyoshi. The memoire is entitled *Zeshi Rokujū Igo Sarugaku Dangi* (*Zeami's Thoughts on Nō Performance After Age 60*). See Hisamatsu Sen'ichi and Nishio Minoru (eds.), *Nihon Koten Bungaku Taikei*, vol. 65 (Tokyo, 1961), p. 497. It also refers briefly to the Matsukaze and Murasame story (no. 32, and pp. 491 and 495 of this memoir).

34
Umewaka-maru Emaki (The Tale of Umewaka-maru)

First half of the seventeenth century, Edo period
Three handscrolls, ink, light color, gold and silver on paper
H: 27.7 cm, L: 502.4 cm (scroll I); 558.8 cm (scroll II); 525.8 cm (scroll III)
Spencer no. 80

This set of unsigned, unsealed handscrolls illustrates in alternating sections of painting and text the tale of the kidnapped child Umewaka-maru. The small, irregularly shaped "patches" of gold leaf that were applied sporadically both to sections of text and paintings were probably added later since they appear to have been placed over worn or damaged areas of the paper and at times obliterate parts of the text.

The latter half of the Umewaka-maru tale is perhaps best-known through the popular Nō drama *Sumidagawa* (no. 33), by Jūrō Motomasa (1394/95–1431/59). The Nō play deals solely with the activities of the mother of the kidnapped child: her search for her son and encounter with his spirit at the site of his tomb. The story contained within the Spencer scrolls of *Umewaka-maru* is far more detailed; it reproduced, in novel form, the *Sumidagawa* tale as it was popularly known in the Edo period. This *emaki* also incorporates, in its opening section, the plot of another, even earlier Nō play, *Hanjo (Lady Han)*, written by Kanze (Zeami) Motokiyo (1363–1443?), which relates the love story of the parents of Umewaka-maru.[1]

The plot of *The Tale of Umewaka-maru*, which is set in the late twelfth and early thirteenth century, runs as follows. In scroll I a beautiful baby girl, Hanago, is born to a retired archer and his wife. When she is ten years old, her father dies and she is sent to serve in the house of one of the wealthiest men in her mother's home town of Nogami, in Mino. In scroll II, the Emperor Juntoku (reigned 1210–1221) expresses an interest in famous scenic views of distant sites and dispatches a young lieutenant named Yoshida to observe Mt. Fuji during the different seasons of the year. On his way to the mountain, Yoshida stops at the wealthy man's home in Nogami, where he is taken by Hanago's beauty and brings her to his bed. When the lieutenant leaves her to continue on his journey, Hanago is crazed with grief, but after many trials and tribulations she is reunited with her lover. In scroll III Hanago marries Yoshida and gives birth to a son, Umewaka-maru. When her husband dies, she sends the ten-year-old boy to visit his uncle, and the child is kidnapped by an unscrupulous merchant. Once again overcome with grief, the crazed Hanago searches for years for her son, who has fallen ill and died. Upon her arrival at the river, she hears of her son's tragic death; heartbroken, she offers prayers to his soul and lives out the remainder of her life as a nun in a hut close to his tomb.

The painting from scroll I reproduced here depicts the household's activity after Hanago's birth; the mother is shown clad in ritual white for childbirth. Interior sliding screens are decorated with delicately rendered ink paintings, and in the garden a gnarled pine tree by the veranda twists itself into a series of C-shaped bends.

The second scene shown here (scene III from scroll III) recounts the most famous episode from the Umewaka-maru/Sumidagawa story. The grief-stricken mother has been taken by ferry across the Sumida River to the tomb of her son; there she and the villagers utter prayers for his soul. The little ghost of the departed child appears by the willow-crowned tomb-mound, and the mother, with hair and garments fluttering behind her, races with open arms towards his vanishing figure. In its general composition, this painting is very much like one found in a seventeenth-century scroll in the Spencer Collection illustrating the *Sumidagawa* Nō play (no. 33).

The illustrations (fourteen in all) in the *Umewaka-maru Emaki* feature pale, light washes of color, very thinly applied to figures and some areas of landscape, but are dominated by ink. Figures are executed in crisp yet supple ink lines, and though brushlines occasionally begin or terminate with the angular "hooks" drawn from the Chinese-inspired approach to ink painting, landscape elements are rendered in a softer, more free and flowing manner. Ink wash is used liberally in landscape motifs; the outlines of such forms as hills, rounded rocks and trees are often so broad and wet that they create the impression of shading rather than of line. In keeping with the artist's muted approach to color, gold and rare silver washes are only applied to costumes and to miniature paintings-within-paintings in interior scenes. The simplified bands of mist in the upper and lower areas of the scenes are outlined in ink and filled in with pale blue; they serve as decorative borders.

Stylistically, it may be seen that this emaki belongs to an era of eclecticism among painters of narrative handscrolls. Emaki were produced by various schools of artists,

but the examples which bear the closest resemblance to the *Umewaka-maru Emaki* are works attributed to Kaihō Yūsetsu (1598–1677), a second-generation artist of the Kaihō school, which was founded during the Momoyama period by the great master Yūshō (1533–1615).[2] Yūsetsu operated an *eya*, or ready-made picture shop, before attaining the status of a professional painter around 1638; his best-known emaki is a twenty-scroll version of the *Tsurezuregusa* (*Essays in Idleness*) of the fourteenth-century essayist Yoshida Kenkō.[3] Another set of three handscrolls, illustrating the *Genji Monogatari* (*The Tale of Genji*)—unsigned but attributed to Yūsetsu on stylistic grounds—is currently in the Mary and Jackson Burke Collection in New York.[4] Both the *Tsurezuregusa* and the Burke *Genji* feature ink wash, occasionally mixed with color, as in the Spencer scrolls; wet ink/ color washes are often used to delineate ground planes in the absence of strong contour outline. However, the *Umewaka-maru Emaki* appears to have been executed more cursorily than either of the works attributed to Yūsetsu. The Spencer scroll figures are also more slender and attenuated than those commonly found in Yūsetsu's paintings, with small heads and long bodies. Therefore, it may be appropriate to assign the Spencer scrolls to an artist closely influenced by Yūsetsu during his days as an eya proprietor. The first half of the seventeenth century is therefore suggested.

The Umewaka-maru story, like many legends, has its roots in early folklore. After the tale was made famous by the Nō plays *Sumidagawa* and *Hanjo*, there were many recensions, or later variations, of the story. The unknown author of the Spencer text may have been classically educated; poems contained therein were taken from the *Cho-*

kusen Waka Shū—the collective name for the imperially commissioned classical anthologies of native *waka* (thirty-one-syllable verse) poetry.[5] The Umewaka-maru story in its "entirety," as it is represented in the Spencer scrolls, was rarely illustrated; the Spencer scrolls are, in fact, the only known version which can be dated to this time.[6]

The text of the Spencer *Umewaka-maru Emaki* has marked Buddhist overtones; the postscript to the story informs the reader that Hanago, the mother, was a manifestation of the deity Benzaiten, goddess of fortune and music, born as a mortal woman in order to make clear to man the suffering caused by the separation of loved ones. It also identifies Umewaka-maru as a manifestation of the compassionate bodhisattva Kannon. Interestingly, the Umewaka-dera, a temple built on the supposed site of the kidnapped boy's tomb, was renamed the Mokuboji in 1607 by the courtier, senior regent and master calligrapher, Konoe Nobutada (1565–1614).[7] It is conceivable that the renaming of this relatively obscure temple brought it to the attention of the public, and that the tale was recounted in temple ceremonies, which may account for the highly religious nature of the Spencer scrolls' postscript.

NOTES

1. Donald Keene (trans.), "Lady Han (Hanjo)", Wm. Theodore de Bary (ed.), *Twenty Plays of the No Theatre* (New York, 1970), pp. 129–145.

2. For biographical information on Yūsetsu, see Kawai Masatomo, *Yūshō, Tōgan*, vol. 11 of *Nihon Bijutsu kaiga Zenshū* (Tokyo, 1968), p. 137; Takeda Tsuneo, *Shōhekiga*, vol. 13 of *Genshoku Nihon no Bijutsu* (Tokyo, 1967), pp. 194–195; Yamane Yuzo, "Eya," *Bijutsu Shi* 48 (March 1963), 107–117; Miyeko Murase, *Japanese Art: Selections from the Mary and Jackson Burke Collection* (New York, 1975), pp. 193–194.

3. See Miya Tsugio, "Kaihō Yūsetsu hitsu 'Tsurezure-gusa Emaki,' " *Hōjōki, Tsurezure-gusa*, vol. 10 of *Zusetsu Nihon no Koten* (Tokyo, 1980), pp. 165–171.

4. Murase, *Japanese Art*, pp. 190–194.

5. Although the two Nō plays also contain poems from classical anthologies, these are different examples. See Robert H. Brower and Earl Miner, *Japanese Court Poetry* (Stanford, 1961), p. 76.

6. There are other related scrolls, however, notably the three-scroll set, dated to 1679, which is in the collection of Mokuboji, Tokyo. See Keiō Gijuku Daigaku Kokubungaku Kenkyūkai, *Mokuboji zō Umewaka Gongen Engi*, for the reprint of the text (Tokyo, 1984).

7. Nobutada, who was head of the ancient Fujiwara clan, retired from the office of *kampaku* (Regent) in the same year, 1607. He "renamed" the Umewaka-dera by separating the components of the character "ume" (plum) to form the word "mokubo." See Umewaka-zuka Mokuboji, *Mokuboji Bunko*, vol. 4, *Mokuboji Shi* (Tokyo, 1976), pp. 34ff. I am grateful to Abbot Maizumi of Mokuboji, which was rebuilt after World War II, for his generosity in letting me study all the records belonging to the temple.

Tadanori

35
Michimori, "Kōetsu Utai-bon," I

Early seventeenth century, Momoyama period
Paper design by Sōtatsu (died ca. 1641)
One book, 18.2 × 24.2 cm
Ink and mica on colored paper
Spencer no. 271

Tadanori, "Kōetsu Utai-bon," II

Early seventeenth century, Momoyama period
Paper design by Sōtatsu (died ca. 1641)
One book, 18.0 × 24.0 cm
Ink and mica on colored paper
Spencer no. 272

These two elegantly decorated books of *utai* (chants from Nō plays) were published as part of the Saga-bon project (see no. 19), planned and financed by Suminokura Soan (1571–1632) in the early seventeenth century. Their texts were printed on colored paper of blue, green, brown, pink or lilac, bound with silk thread, and decorated with designs of plants, flowers, insects, and other motifs, printed with stamps in silvery-white mica paste.

Nō drama (see nos. 33, 34), which had attained remarkable success during the fifteenth century, continued to attract large groups of staunch supporters in the sixteenth and seventeenth centuries, including warriors of little formal education, such as Hideyoshi and Ieyasu. As knowledge of Nō plays came to be regarded as a mark of sophistication, chanting texts for private entertainment became a popular pastime among devotees, and the demand for books of Nō texts, or *utai-bon*, grew. These books also served as manuals that masters used to instruct their students. The two books included here belonged to this group of books of Nō texts, although those that were published at Saga were luxury editions, the "coffee table" books of their time, not necessarily intended to be used as working instruction books.

The utai volumes which were published at Saga are often called "Kōetsu Utai-bon," implying that models for the type to be used in printing the texts were supplied by Hon'nami Kōetsu (1558–1637), the great tea master, potter, connoisseur of the arts, distinguished calligrapher, and accomplished utai master. Within this group of Nō texts more than one hundred pieces from the standard Nō repertory have so far been identified.[1] Although their texts were printed with movable type, a new technique introduced from Korea at the end of the sixteenth century, two or three letters in the Japanese *kana* script often flow one into the other, giving the impression of a fluid writing style. The kana letters are soft and rounded in form, a feature which is closely associated with the calligraphic idiosyncrasies of Kōetsu.

The stamped decorations in silvery mica paste, another distinctive feature of the Saga-bon utai texts, were designed by Kōetsu's frequent collaborator, Sōtatsu (died ca. 1641), the great designer and painter. The third and final distinguishing characteristic of this group of texts is that they reproduce chants used only by the Kanze school of Nō, which had by this time become the most influential of the Nō schools through the enthusiastic patronage of the Tokugawa shoguns and their vassals.

The two books shown here both reproduce the texts of plays about members of the Taira clan who were killed in a war against the rival Minamoto faction in 1184. One of the volumes reproduced here is for the play *Tadanori* by Zeami Motokiyo (1363–1443?). It was printed on light-brown colored paper with designs of asters, plum blossoms, autumn leaves, pine trees, waves, butterflies, and geometric shapes. The play recounts the sad tale of the warrior-poet Tadanori (1144–1184), a younger brother of the clan leader, Kiyomori.[2] As in many Nō plays, the protagonist first appears in a traveling monk's dream. He begs the monk to help him achieve recognition for a poem included in the imperially commissioned anthology known as the *Senzai Waka Shū* (see no. 17). The woeful story has it that Tadanori made a special visit to the poet Fujiwara no Shunzei (1114–1204) on the eve of battle, and asked him to consider his poems should he ever edit an imperial anthology. When Shunzei compiled the *Senzai Waka Shū* at the order of the retired emperor Goshirakawa in 1187, Tadanori was considered an enemy of the royal house so Shunzei included his poem as an anonymous work.[3]

The second book, for the play *Michimori* (Pl. VIII), by an anonymous author, also concerns a Taira warrior killed in 1184.[4] Again in accordance with the popular pattern used in Nō plays, the ghosts of Michimori and his wife appear in the reverie of a monk praying for the souls of the Taira warriors, and recount their last moments in the fateful battle. Printed on rich cerulean blue paper are designs of bending pines by rolling waves, plum blossoms, autumn grasses, butterflies, and a landscape with a full moon.

The designs in both books were impressed with wooden stamps, which were re-used on many different Saga books in different combinations. The same designs, and even the same stamps, were also used in a number of other works by Sōtatsu. Decorative motifs in all of the Saga utai books are confined to flowers, plants, insects, animals, and occasional landscapes. The models for the designs were familiar flora and fauna: plum trees, ivy, pampas grass, pines; butterflies, bugs, dragonflies, and an occasional nightingale or crane; deer and rabbits, and, in one rare instance, dragons also appear.[5] Not a single human figure can be found in Sōtatsu's designs for the Nō texts. The designs are devoid of symbolism, save seasonal reference, and they have no relationship to the texts. When seen close-up the boldly abstracted designs of nature contain a minimum of detail. As the stamps dripping with mica paste were pressed onto paper that had been heavily sized with colored *gofun* (a substance made from powdered shell), pools of shining silver color appeared, creating rich patterns of sensuous and tactile beauty.

Although Sōtatsu today enjoys great fame as one of Japan's most original painters, he still remains enigmatic.[6] Except for the fact that he was related to Kōetsu through marriage, not much is known about his family or his early training. Even his family name, Nonomura, remains problematic; Tawaraya, the name of the painting shop that he owned and operated, is often substituted for his surname. Most of his earliest known works are paper designs intended as background for calligraphy, such as in these utai books. However, shortly after 1615, Sōtatsu seems to have launched a successful career; some extraordinarily beautiful large screen paintings and small album-sized pictures attributed to him are in major collections in Japan and the United States.

A large number of Sōtatsu's extant works were done on handscrolls and album sheets. The decorative designs of flowers, plants, and other motifs strongly resemble those that grace the utai books. In the past, calligraphy in these works was often attributed indiscriminately to Kōetsu. The utai books have also been so attributed; recent scholarship, however, tends to dispute this assumption.[7] Stylistic differences in calligraphy are recognizable even among the utai books, although texts were all written in the so-called "Kōetsu style" which was extremely popular among early seventeenth-century calligraphers. In recent studies, Kanze Kokusetsu (1566–1626), leader of the Kanze school and a neighbor of Kōetsu's, with whom he is thought to have studied calligraphy, has emerged as a major figure in the production of these books. The possibility that Kokusetsu may have provided the calligraphy models for these books is indeed attractive, since the so-called "Kōetsu-style" calligraphy is not found in utai books used by other schools of Nō performers.

The Kōetsu utai books include various marks for the chanters of Nō text, such as punctuation marks and notes indicating changes in roles; they are either printed or handwritten. Small hook-shaped marks, intended as tone indicators, are supposed to have been instituted by Kokusetsu from about 1604, replacing the inverted V-shaped marks used by earlier masters. Therefore, a possible date of production for these utai books, which include this new type of notation, is the beginning of the seventeenth century.

NOTES

1. All the known pieces published at Saga are reproduced in Ejima Ihei and Omote Akira (eds.), *Zusetsu Kōetsu Utai-bon* (Kyoto, 1970).
2. Tadanori's death is described in the *Heike Monogatari*, the tale about this clan's rise and fall. See Hiroshi Kitagawa and Bruce T. Tsuchida (trans.), *The Tale of the Heike* (Tokyo, 1975), Book 9, Chapter 14, "The Death of Tadanori," pp. 557–558. The Nō play is translated in The Nippon Gakujutsu Shinkōkai (ed.), *Japanese Noh Drama: Ten Plays* (Tokyo, 1959), vol. 2, pp. 17–32.
3. For this poem, see Kubota Jun and Matsuno Yōichi (eds.), *Senzai Waka Shū* (Tokyo, 1969), poem no. 66, p. 74.
4. See Kitagawa and Tsuchida, *The Tale of the Heike*, Book 9, Chapter 18, "Flight," pp. 567–568.
5. Ejima and Omote, *Zusetsu Koetsu*, Pl. 202.
6. For Sōtatsu, see Howard A. Link and Tōru Shimbo, *Exquisite Visions: Rimpa Paintings from Japan* (Honolulu, 1980); Yamane Yūzō (ed.), *Rimpa Kaiga Zenshū: Sotatsu Ha* I, II (Tokyo, 1977–78) and Yamane Yūzō *et al.*, *Kōetsu Sho Sōtatsu Kingindei-e* (Tokyo, 1978).
7. See for example, Itō Toshiko, "Den Kōetsu hitsu Utai-bon to Kanze Kokusetsu (A Book of Utai Generally Ascribed to Kōetsu and Kokusetsu Kanze)," *Kokka* 922 (1970), who states that not a single utai book can be attributed to Kōetsu with certainty, p. 16.

36
Youchi Soga (Night Attack by the Soga Brothers)

Second half of the seventeenth century, Edo period
One handscroll, ink, color and gold on paper
H: 33.5 cm, W: 1949.5 cm
Spencer no. 90

In contrast to the internationally known Nō theatre, the ancient Japanese performing art form Kōwaka had only a brief period of popularity. During its heyday in the age of valour of the late sixteenth century, Kōwaka and Nō seem to have been equally in demand among the warlords. Yet due, perhaps, to the lack of great playwrights such as those who continually refined and rejuvenated Nō theatre, Kōwaka declined in the early seventeenth century and is known today only to a small number of cognoscenti and specialists.

    The true origins of Kōwaka are not known, although it appears to have derived from a number of earlier types of dance performances which were accompanied by text recitation.[1] The name "Kōwaka" began to appear in records only in the mid-fifteenth century, when the Kōwaka family of Echizen (modern Fukui prefecture, northeast of Kyoto) began to claim to be the rightful leaders of this art form.² Needless to say, other families and schools of Kōwaka existed in other areas of Japan; today, however, Kōwaka is performed only in the southern island of Kyushu, where the performers work under governmental protection as Japan's "Intangible National Treasures."³

Kōwaka probably declined in part because of its simple and rustic, if animated, performance techniques, which lack the sophistication and refinement that Nō theatre acquired as it developed. In Kōwaka performances only two principal actors appear: the *tayū* (grand master) and *waki* (supporter). The third player, called the *tsure*, is a minor character. In sharp contrast to the Nō theatre, which has produced a rich visual art tradition, Kōwaka actors wear neither masks nor special costumes. The prose text is recited, rather than sung, punctuated by the beating of a drum and the stamping of feet. Such performances no doubt entertained military encampments waiting for battle; in fact, legend has it that in 1560 the great warlord Oda Nobunaga (1534–1582) performed a Kōwaka dance on the eve of the victorious battle which proved to be decisive in his brief but brilliant military career.

An anthology of the standard Kōwaka repertory compiled in the early seventeenth century contains only thirty-six pieces, although fifty texts are known today.⁴ Of the fifty texts, forty-one are historical war tales, based on military conflicts between the Taira and Minamoto clans, the two leading warrior families who fought for political hegemony in the late twelfth century. The victors were the Minamoto, who established Japan's first shogunal government in 1185. A group of seven stories in the Kōwaka repertory recounts the vendetta of the Soga brothers, carried out in 1193 against the killer of their father during the Taira–Minamoto wars. As battle tales, they extoll the virtues of valorous warriors and glorify honorable death, filial piety, and loyalty to one's masters.

The Spencer Collection is particularly rich in scrolls and books with illustrations of the Kōwaka stories,⁵ some dating from the eighteenth century. They are testimonials to the fact that though Kōwaka (which created these texts as librettos) lost its influence as a performing art, its literary contributions have survived, providing subject matter for illustrated scrolls and books, especially these belonging to the popular genre of narrative illustration now commonly known as *Nara-e*.

The subject of the *Youchi Soga* scroll (*Night Attack by the Soga Brothers*) is one of the most well-known of the tales about the two determined Soga brothers, and was the theme for both Kōwaka and Nō plays.⁶ The tale of the brothers' vendetta is based on an historical novel, the *Soga Monogatari*, written by an anonymous author of the mid-fourteenth century and inspired by an actual event of May 28, 1193.⁷ On that night, amidst the festive atmosphere of a wild-game hunt organized by the shogun Yoritomo, the young Soga brothers Jūrō Sukenari and Gorō Tokimune carried out an eighteen-year-old plot to kill Kudō Suketsune, their father's murderer. The "night attack" episode, as it is depicted in the Spencer scroll, is the climax of the *Soga Monogatari*.

The scroll consists of twelve painted scenes with alternating sections of text. Its opening scene depicts the encampment for the hunt, set in the plains at the foot of Mt. Fuji, where the brothers' long-sought enemy Kudō is also camped (Pl. IX). In this scene, warriors hunt down such wild animals as deer, boar, foxes, and bears; the snow-capped Mt. Fuji looms large in the background. In the fourth scene, Jūrō, the older of the two

162

brothers, manages to sneak into the camp and comes upon a dazzling array of banners bearing family crests of the men who participated in the hunt, set up to provide a temporary enclosure. Jūrō stands in awe in front of the thirty-six banners (only fifteen of which are shown here). The text written around the figure of Jūrō and below the banners describes each design and identifies the owners of the banners. The bold composition, which stretches almost four feet in length, is one of the most dramatic designs to be found in a Kōwaka scroll. Surprisingly, the banners, most of which are painted in white, blue and brown, are decorated with designs that do not reflect their owners' warrior status. Instead, cranes, fans, fish nets, decorative wave patterns, wheels in water, and snow-laden bamboo reveal the poetic predilections of their possessors. Subsequent scenes depict the brothers' encounters with members of the hunt, the near-exposure of their true identities, and, finally, their arrival at Kudō's bedroom, where they "plunged into his breast their swords burning with the enmity of eighteen years . . ." and "cut off his head with the fierce, unfaltering strokes of sons fulfilling a filial duty."[8]

Small flakes of cut gold, sprinkled to suggest mist and cloud in the hunt scene, create a sense of lavishness and an illusion of monumental scale, in spite of the small size of the painting. The anonymous artist of this work differentiated figures of men-at-arms according to their stations in the military organization: high-ranking warriors are idealized, noble-looking gentlemen, while the lower-ranking soldiers are more individualized but somewhat uncouth. Ink outlines of garments are often retraced in gold ink to add lustre and a decorative brilliance, However, the carefully drawn outlines and meticulous rendition of small details give a feeling of constraint and stiffness. These elements place the work in the late seventeenth century.

NOTES

1. For discussions of the possible origin of Kōwaka, see Araki Shigeru, "Kōwaka bukyoku ron note: Kusemai no katari mono to Kōwaka Bukyoku," *Bungaku*, 35 (October 1967), pp. 1064–1072; and Nagazumi Yasuaki, "Kōwaka to sekkyō joron," *ibid*, pp. 1037–1053.

2. The earliest known reference to "Kōwaka" appears in the *Kakitsu Ki (Tales of the War of the Kakitsu Era, 1441–1444)*. See Ōta Tōshirō (ed.), *Gunsho Ruijū, Kassen Bu*, in the entry for the third year of the Chōroku era (1459) (Tokyo, 1929), p. 325.

3. Annual performances of Kōwaka are held at the farming village of Ōe in Fukuoka prefecture, in the northern part of Kyushu Island.

4. For the names and synopses of these pieces, see James T. Araki, *The Ballad-Drama of Medieval Japan* (Berkeley and Los Angeles, 1964).

5. For the other illustrated Kōwaka pieces in the Spencer Collection, see Shigeo Sorimachi, *Catalogue of Japanese Illustrated Books and Manuscripts in the Spencer Collection of the New York Public Library* (Tokyo, 1978).

6. For an English summary of the Youchi Soga story, see Kokusai Bunka Shinkōkai (ed.), *Introduction to Classic Japanese Literature* (Tokyo, 1948), pp. 223–229.

7. This incident is reported in the *Azuma Kagami*, an official record of the Kamakura shogun's government. See the entries for May 8 to May 29 in the fourth year of the Kenkyū era (1193), in Yosano Hiroshi *et al.* (eds.), *Nihon Koten Zenshū*, vol. 3, *Azuma Kagami* (Tokyo, 1927), pp. 158–163.

8. Kokusai Bunka Shinkōkai (ed.), *Introduction to Classic Japanese Literature*, p. 227.

37
Taishokkan (The Great Woven Cap)

First half of the seventeenth century, Edo period
Text by Asakura Shigetaka
Three handscrolls, ink, color and gold on paper
H: 32.1 cm (scroll I and II), 32.4 cm (scroll III)
L: 1545.1 cm (scroll I), 1408.6 cm (scroll II), 1371.3 cm (scroll III)
Signed: "Ichinojō Asakura-shi Shigetaka koreo kaku"
Seal: "Matsuda"
Spencer no. 105

The second work included here which illustrates a piece from the Kōwaka repertory is entitled *Taishokkan* (*The Great Woven Cap*). The "great woven cap" was originally a title accorded to a person who held the highest rank at court, but it became the epithet for

Fujiwara no Kamatari (614–699), one of the greatest statesmen of ancient Japan and the founder of the illustrious noble family of Fujiwara. Woven into the tale are other historical characters of Japan and China, and even an important Buddhist temple, the Kōfukuji in Nara, titulary temple of the Fujiwara clan.

The synopsis of this elaborate, fanciful tale, which is illustrated in three scrolls, runs as follows.[1] In scroll I, Kamatari's daughter, Kōhaku, renowned for her beauty, is summoned by the Chinese emperor, T'ai-tsung (reigned 627–649), to the T'ang court to live as his consort. At the time that her father began the construction of the Kōfukuji in Nara, Kōhaku sent gifts for the decoration of the temple. In scroll II the most precious of the Chinese treasures is stolen by a daughter of the Dragon King of the watery underworld, who coveted it. In scroll III, Kamatari learns of the loss of the precious gem and travels to the coast of Fusazaki, where the jewel was lost. There he meets a woman diver in a fishing village and takes her as his lover. The woman bears him a son, Fusazaki, and is persuaded by Kamatari to dive underwater to recover the stolen gem. Although she manages to retrieve the jewel, she is attacked by a fierce dragon "ten feet long, with large eyes glaring like the setting sun." The scene reproduced here depicts the diver attempting to escape from the fearsome creature, as men aboard the ship try to save her by pulling at the rope attached to her body. In the midst of the agitated courtiers is Kamatari himself, resplendent in a court robe in gold and black, holding a sickle (a gift from a mythical fox) and preparing to jump into the sea to rescue his lover. A monk beside him tries to hold him back from this rash act.

In the story, the dragon lashes at the woman with its claws, but she cuts open her own chest and secrets the gem within. When her lifeless body is washed ashore, the gem is found inside the wound. Kamatari later embedded it securely in the forehead of the Buddha statue at Kōfukuji.

This fanciful tale is also the theme of a Nō play, *Ama* (*Woman Diver*),[2] written by Zeami Motokiyo (1363–1443?). The plots of the *Taishokkan* and *Ama* were both derived from an unusual source—the semi-historical account of the origins of a Buddhist temple, Shidodera, on the Island of Shikoku, across the Inland Sea from Osaka. The temple stands in what was once a Fujiwara enclave and traces its legendary beginnings back to the sixth century. To this temple belongs a set of four large wall hangings dating from the early fourteenth century and illustrating the *engi* (founding and subsequent development of a Buddhist temple or Shinto shrine) of Shidodera.[3] Accompanying the painted hanging scrolls are seven handscrolls of text which describe the engi.[4] According to this account, the major protagonist of the tale was Fujiwara no Fuhito (659–720), the second son of Kamatari, and the Shidodera temple was erected at the site where the diver's dead body was washed ashore.

The legend of the founding of Shidodera differs from the stories told in the *Taishokkan* scrolls in minor respects: the main protagonist in the *Taishokkan* is Kamatari, rather than Fuhito, the actual father of Fusazaki, the baby born to the diver; the Chinese emperor in the tale, T'ai-tsung, is described in the engi as Kao-tsung, T'ai-tsung's successor who reigned from 650 to 683.

The fact that large wall hangings of pictures were accompanied by handscrolls of text clearly suggests that the hanging scrolls were displayed in front of an audience for lecture sessions (*etoki*, or "picture explanation"), while the text was read aloud by a narrator. The *Taishokkan* scrolls, which preserve the Kōwaka libretto, are eloquent proof of the continuing practice of the ancient etoki tradition.[5] On the other hand, traveling narrators of religious texts, who are known to have incorporated local legends and engi of religious establishments into their recitations, are sometimes regarded as having made significant contributions to Kōwaka.[6] This fact might explain the unusual choice of subject matter in the *Taishokkan*, which, along with a small number of pieces in the Kōwaka repertory, was not based on war tales. This group of stories often exhibits strong religious overtones, which sets them fundamentally apart from the tales of bravery and chivalry that make up the rest of the Kōwaka repertory.

The tale of *Taishokkan* is also rich in melodrama and exotic pageantry: the secret marriage of the protagonist—one of the most illustrious statesmen of ancient Japan—to a lower-class woman, which eventually enabled him to make a proper offering to the Buddha, the humble diver's love for her noble husband, and the conflict between her devotion to her husband's cause—for which she must sacrifice her life—and her love for her baby.

The anonymous painter of these scrolls took artistic license in depicting the "imaginary" lands of China and her people, who are shown in fantastic costumes against exotic architectural settings. The battle with undersea monsters also provided him with an opportunity to embroider his work with imaginative details. The vivid scenes in these scrolls are also effectively contrasted with the mundane, genre-like illustrations of the idyllic seaside village where Kamatari meets the diver. Otherwise, the paintings exhibit the artist's eclectic training, which is characteristic of the large group of anonymous painters who produced works such as this as ready-made articles for sale. Standard features include the practice of sprinkling gold flecks within precisely marked areas designating mist and cloud, retracing ink outlines in gold ink, combining brilliant colors with heavy ink outlines on landscape elements, and including the miniature screen paintings-within-paintings, almost always executed in ink monochrome. The paintings in the *Taishokkan* scrolls are lively and fresh, unlike the stiff illustrations in the *Soga* scroll (no. 36), and should be dated to an earlier period in the seventeenth century. Although the text of the *Taishokkan* was signed by a certain Asakura Ichinojō Shigetaka, who may also have impressed the small seal reading "Matsuda" at the end of the third scroll, the identity of the artist remains unknown.

NOTES

1. See James T. Araki, *Ballad-Drama of Medieval Japan* (Los Angeles and Berkeley, 1964), p. 145.
2. Nippon Gakujutsu Shinkōkai (ed.), *Japanese Noh Drama: Ten Plays Selected and Translated from the Japanese*, vol. 3 (Tokyo, 1960), pp. 175–192.
3. Nara National Museum (ed.), *Kokuhō Jūyō Bunkazai, Bukkyō Bijutsu, Shikoku (Tokusima, Kagawa)* (Kyoto, 1973), pp. 114–117; Umezu Jirō, "Shidodera E-engi ni tsuite (On the Pictures of the History of the Shido Temple)" *Kokka* 760 (July 1955), pp. 208–223; and Ichiko Teiji *et al.* (eds.), *Otogi Zōshi*, vol. 13 of *Zusetsu Nihon no Koten* (Tokyo, 1980), pp. 53–54.
4. For the text of the engi, see Nara National Museum, *Kokuhō*, pp. 203–205.
5. For the tradition of etoki, see Barbara Ruch, "Medieval Jongleurs and the Making of a National Literature," in John W. Hall and Toyoda Takeshi (eds.), *Japan in the Muromachi Age* (Berkeley, 1977), pp. 279–309, and Umezu Jirō, "Hen to Henbun: Etoki no kaigashi teki kōsatsu (On Pien and Pien Wen)," *Kokka* 760 (July 1955), pp. 191–207.
6. Araki Shigeru, "Kōwaka bukyoku ron note: Kusemai no katari mono to Kōwaka bukyoku," *Bungaku* 35 (October 1967), pp. 1064–1072, and Nagazumi Yasuaki, "Kōwaka to sekkyō joron," *ibid*, pp. 1037–1053.

V
Men and Women of the Real World

THE imperial court's move, in 794, from the old capital city of Nara to a new city (known today as Kyoto), had far-reaching effects upon Japanese society and culture. In this new city, named Heian-kyō ("Capital of Peace and Tranquility"), a truly indigenous culture developed during the relative peace and stability of the Heian period.

Surrounded by extraordinarily beautiful hills and mountains on three sides, visible from all parts of the city, the citizens of Kyoto could not help but be acutely aware of the changing seasons, and court ceremonies became intimately connected with seasonal celebrations. Today, most national holidays in Japan are associated with celebration of the four seasons; viewing autumn maple leaves or spring cherry-blossoms are traditional national pastimes. Even labor negotiations and strikes are planned with regard to the rhythm of the changing seasons.

Early paintings depicting festivities of the different seasons have not survived, but a series of *waka* (thirty-one-syllable poems; see section II) preserves the response of ancient poets to lost paintings of such sights.[1] The earliest dated poem of this type was composed by the priest Sosei sometime between 869 and 876; he was challenged to write a poem about a screen painting that depicted maple leaves floating down the Tatsuta River, in an area famous for its autumn foliage.[2] Other poems about seasonal sights reveal the significant fact that the lost paintings often included men and women enjoying the scenery. These works, then, were not merely landscape paintings; they were genre paintings, depicting moments from day-to-day existence. Pictures of outings to the suburbs of Kyoto and festivals of various sorts at different times of the year were referred to as *shiki-e* (pictures of the four seasons), or *tsukinami-e* (pictures of monthly activities).

Certain scenic views and locations were singled out for their beauty during particular seasons; maple viewings were conducted at one designated spot, cherry-blossom viewings at another, and snow viewings at yet another place. Thus, another genre of painting, known as *meisho-e* (pictures of famous scenic spots), developed contemporaneously with the genre of seasonal painting to which it was closely tied. Along with narrative illustration, paintings of beautiful sites in different seasons constituted a major category of *yamato-e*, the indigenous painting style of Japan. Yamato-e, which was clearly distinct from the older, Chinese-inspired type of painting known as *kara-e*, reached its maturity during the late Heian period.

Unfortunately, very few examples of seasonal painting from the Heian period have been preserved. However, as the tradition of yamato-e was perpetuated through the succeeding centuries, it laid the foundations for genre painting of the sixteenth century, in the late Muromachi period. Genre painting achieved ever-increasing importance during the Momoyama and Edo periods, as it documented the lives of all segments of the population. Two scrolls included here (nos. 38 and 39), in particular, provide a glimpse of what the lost Heian genre scene paintings may have been like.

Genre paintings, in turn, laid the foundation for the development of the *Ukiyo-e* woodblock prints of the Edo period, prints that depicted both the ordinary and extraordinary moments in the lives of the plebian population of the city of Edo (see section VII).

NOTES

1. For these poems, for example, see Saheki Umetomo (ed.), *Kokin Waka Shū*, vol. 8 of *Nihon Koten Bungaku Taikei* (Tokyo, 1959), poem nos. 293, 305, 310, 351, 357, and 932. Also see H. H. Honda, *The Kokin Waka-shū* (Tokyo, 1970), for translation of the poems, although not all of the prose prefaces that explain the paintings are translated.
2. Saheki, *Kokin Waka Shu*, no. 293. Also see Kenji Toda, "Japanese Screen Paintings of the Ninth & Tenth Centuries," *Ars Orientalis*, 3 (1959), pp. 153–163.

38
Shiki no Sōshi (Story of the Four Seasons)

Second half of the seventeenth century, Edo period
One handscroll, ink, gold, silver and color on paper
H: 32.8 cm, L: 1031.4 cm
Spencer no. 113

The *Shiki no Sōshi (Story of Four Seasons)* scroll consists of eight sections of text and eight illustrations, with the four seasons represented by two sections each of text and painting. The first two sections of text explain the nature of the activities that take place on New Year's Day and in early spring. One of the accompanying paintings depicts a bustling street. The second represents the national pastime of early spring—viewing the cherry blossoms.

The following two sections of text describe late spring and early summer, which are illustrated by pictures of rice-planting, shown here, and people relaxing by a cool river on a summer evening. The third section represents late summer and early autumn and shows an autumn evening moon-and-maple-viewing picnic. The seventh and eighth pictures represent late autumn, the time for making offerings to the gods and praying to them for success in business enterprises. The flurry of year-end activities, such as stocking up food, beating *tatami* mats (as a part of heavy housecleaning) and making household repairs are shown.

Drawn to the scenic topography of their region and the unfailing beauty and subtlety of seasonal change, the citizens of the ancient capital of Kyoto came to order their lives according to them. Their festivals and ceremonies were organized around the celebrations of new seasons, which became popular subjects for secular painting. During the Heian period, in the ninth and tenth centuries, seasonal festivities and activities associated with each month of the year became the most important subjects of the secular paintings which adorned imperial palaces and aristocratic mansions.[1] Termed *shiki-e* (pictures of the four seasons) or *tsukinami-e* (pictures of the twelve months), they came to symbolize the indigenous Japanese painting. This seasonal approach to secular painting was considered characteristic of *yamato-e* ("Japanese-style" pictures), distinguishing it from *kara-e* ("Chinese-style" painting).

Unfortunately, these Heian paintings, many of which were on sliding panels of paper, were installed in buildings of wood and paper and had little chance of survival. Except for an insignificant number of extant works which were executed on small objects like folding fans,[2] the only glimpse we have of what the paintings must have been like are poetic descriptions of lost works. It was fashionable for the Japanese aristocracy of the Heian period to express their thoughts and emotions in the form of short thirty-one-syllable poems (*waka*), which often included reactions to and appreciations of scroll or screen paintings of the shiki-e or tsukinami-e type.[3]

As far as can be determined from such scanty material, pictures of the four seasons or the twelve months usually depicted court nobles' festivities and outings. The oldest essay to bear a related title, the *Shiki no Monogatari* (*The Tale of Four Seasons*), attributed to an early thirteenth-century Buddhist monk named Kamo no Chōmei, describes what were, for the most part, court functions and ceremonies associated with different seasons.[4] During the late Muromachi period, however, in the early sixteenth century, when the commercial segment of the population gained influence and stature, a profound change occurred within the traditional structure of society; the genre paintings that have survived from this period reveal that the focus of the arts was now plebian society. Our scroll reflects that shift, which took place more than one hundred years before it was painted.

The text of this scroll may have been inspired by earlier literary forms like the thirteenth-century essay by Chōmei, but it strictly confines itself nevertheless to describing the celebrations of the anonymous author's plebian contemporaries which were observed throughout Japan. The text poetically describes the changing seasons and climate of different times of day, month and year. It occasionally refers to places, but they are common names that do not help to pinpoint specific locations. The text does not give detailed explanations of the people's activities, yet the painter clearly elaborated upon them.

The anonymous painter of the Spencer scroll took great care in depicting the clothing of men and women, often tracing over the ink outlines with gold. Gold "outlines" even appear on the kimonos of women farmers working in the field. The large, bold designs on the kimonos use stylized forms of maple leaves, chrysanthemum, wisteria, grape vines, and waterwheels, often filled in with tie-dye patterns. These designs, and the women's narrow sashes (*obi*) and hairstyles, reflect the type of fashion depicted in many of the so-called "Kambun Beauties" paintings—portrayals of single figures of beautifully clad women—which were believed to have been produced solely during the Kambun era (1661–1672); actually they continued to be produced a few years longer.[5] The faces in this painting are inexpressive and painted powder-white. Unlike the equally stereotyped doll-like figures of popular tales like the *Bunshō Sōshi* (no. 24), however, figures in this scroll are more mature in appearance, and their eyes are not mere slits or dots, but are clearly drawn. Although the painter was undoubtedly one of the untold number of unknown artists who produced ready-made pictures for mass consumption, his interest in his actual surroundings reflects a training and specialization that distinguishes him from the painters of narrative scrolls and books who illustrated fictitious tales.

NOTES

1. Kenji Toda, "Japanese Screen Painting of the Ninth and Tenth Centuries," *Ars Orientalis* 3 (1959), pp. 153–166, and Ienaga Saburō, *Jōdai Yamato-e Nempyō*, rev. ed. (Tokyo, 1966).
2. For examples of these painted fans, see Asano Nagatake, *Itsukushima*, in *Hihō*, vol. 10 (Tokyo, 1967), Pls. 182–187.
3. Toda, "Japanese Screen," and Ienaga, *Jodai Yamato-e*.
4. This is also true of the mid-twelfth-century scrolls of annual court functions and ceremonies, the *Nenjū Gyōji Emaki* (only seventeenth-century copies remain). These scrolls include some figures of commoners, but they are marginal elements. See Fukuyama Toshio (ed.), *Nenjū Gyōji Emaki*, vol. 24 of the *Shinshū Nihon Emaki-mono Zenshū*, ed. Tanaka Ichimatsu (Tokyo, 1978). For a reprint of Chōmei's essay, see Motoori Toyokai (ed.), *Kokubun Taikan*, vol. 7 (Tokyo, 1903), pp. 555–590.
5. For examples of the "Kambun Beauties," see Donald Jenkins, *Ukiyo-e Prints and Paintings: the Primitive Period, 1680–1745* (Chicago, 1971).

39
Hachiman Shrine Festival

First half of the seventeenth century, Edo period
Two handscrolls, ink, color, gold and silver on paper
H: 37.6 cm (scroll I), 37.6 cm (scroll II), L: 1804.6 cm (scroll I), 1988.7 cm (scroll II)
Spencer no. 56

This set of two long handscrolls depicts a procession of the Hachiman Shrine Festival, an event which took place in what is now the city of Tsu, south of Kyoto.

Annual festivals are important to the Shinto religion, as they are a means of reinforcing the protective role of the deity and strengthening communal ties. Hachiman was and is one of the most popular gods of Shinto, and his cult has been associated with various activities throughout the ages.[1] At one time, he was regarded as the guardian of clans that lived in the copper-mining region, at another as a deity who protected man against epidemics; his veneration was also incorporated into the Shingon sect of Buddhism. In the course of time, Hachiman came to be generally known and revered as the god of war; in this role, he was adopted as a tutelary deity by many clans, cities and communities, and many shrines were dedicated to him.

On the morning of the Hachiman Festival, a symbolic embodiment of the deity is brought out of the shrine by the chief priest and transferred to a *mikoshi*, a portable shrine. A procession then escorts the mikoshi through the city and returns it to the shrine at the end of the festivities. In this work, the jubilant procession of celebrants, dressed in an astonishing array of costumes and ornaments, covers the entire length of the two handscrolls (close to 40 meters). In a reversal of the traditional direction of movement associated with handscrolls, the figures move across the picture plane from left to right; viewers thus encounter the marchers head-on, a device intended to increase visual tension. The vanguard of the parade may be seen at the beginning of the first scroll, where it has reached the city gate, the end of the procession. The main body of the parade marches slowly through the city streets, which are lined with empty houses and shops. The empty buildings and the absence of spectators along the parade route indicate that virtually everyone has joined in the procession. Curtains hanging in the doorways are richly designed: family crests and shop signs depict fans, hats and thread, identifying the crafts to be found within. The rear guard of the parade, led by the headman of the Tsu district, is depicted at the end of the second scroll.

Each group of celebrants appears to represent a district, or a trade (as the small labels occasionally affixed to the paper above the figures suggest). There are cormorant fishermen, falconers, bird-catchers, dog trainers and brine-gathering maidens. Some figures are dressed as Europeans (known as *Namban*, or "Southern Barbarians"); others seem to move in dancing steps. Some, like the hatchet-bearers shown here, are almost completely hidden beneath their elaborate headgear. The decorations featured in this group consist of a bonsai plant, flowers in a vase, and bamboo and peony plants, which suggest that the participants' trade is gardening. This group's concern with the weather is apparent— one of its members carries a fanciful statuette of the thunder god, surrounded by drums and menacing rays of lightning and thunder that issue from his body. Another marcher carries a dragon—a symbol of rain.

Some of the most dramatic decorations are carried by a group of men who obviously serve as attendants to warriors (Pl. X). On their backs they carry enormous inflated bags which, in battle protected soldiers from enemy arrows.[2] The oversized ornaments they hold above their heads are most amusing; among them we find a monkey with long arms, holding a silver moon, an enormous conch-shell, and a gigantic brush. It is possible that they were intended to represent the family crests of samurai.

The artist of these scrolls was able to record the jubilant excitement of the festival's participants, as well as their bold imagination and inventiveness in creating their fabulous costumes and decorations. This artist apparently was one of a large group of painters who specialized in ready-made pictures and who incorporated the techniques of a variety of schools into their work.

One of the most popular themes chosen by these artists was *Rakuchū-Rakugai* (Inside and Outside the Capital). Paintings of this genre depicted famous sites in Kyoto and its suburbs, and often included scenes of festivals such as the one included here.[3] The artist of these scrolls also appears to have been influenced by a technique of figure painting, popular during the first half of the seventeenth century, which Iwasa Matabei (1578–1650) is thought to have originated.[4] Some of the figures in these scrolls, particularly the male and female spectators shown at the end of scroll II (the only non-participants in the event), have large, oblong heads with long chins and elongated bodies, which are distinguishing characteristics of the so-called "Matabei figure type." The hair-styles and bold kimono designs depicted here were fashionable in the first half of the seventeenth century.

The labels attached to the outside covers of the scrolls read, "Hachiman Shrine Festival of Isashi County in Ise Province." Isashi County, which is south of Tsu City, was incorporated into the territory of the Tsu fief in 1608.[5] In that same year, Tōdō Takatora became the lord of the area (now the modern city of Tsu) and restored its castle. In 1632, the second-generation leader of the Tōdō family, Takatsugu, built a Hachiman shrine in Tsu City proper. On August 15, 1635, a festival dedicated to the god Hachiman was held there for the first time; it was held annually thereafter. The singular importance attached to this festival and its enormous popularity were attested to in a report included in the local gazetteer, the *Seiyō Zakki* of 1656, which stated that a total number of 1,750 people from the surrounding areas had participated in the annual seven-day festival.[6] The two scrolls in the Spencer Collection may have been commissioned to record the auspicious beginnings of an event that became a time-honored tradition.

NOTES

1. For Hachiman worship, see Haruki Kageyama, *The Arts of Shinto* (New York, 1973), and Haruki Kageyama and Christine Guth Kanda, *Shinto Arts: Nature, Gods, and Man in Japan* (New York, 1976).
2. H. R. Robinson, *A Short History of Japanese Armour* (London, 1965).
3. For examples of such screens, see Kyoto National Museum (ed.), *Rakuchū Rakugai Zu* (Tokyo, 1966); and Miyeko Murase, *Japanese Art: Selections from the Mary and Jackson Burke Collection* (New York, 1975), no. 45.
4. For Matabei's works, see Tsuji Nobuo (ed.), *Iwasa Matabei*, vol. 13 of *Nihon Bijutsu Kaiga Zenshū*, ed. Tanaka Ichimatsu *et al.* (Tokyo, 1980).
5. Shimonaka Kunihiko (ed.), *Nihon Rekishi Chimei Taikei* (Tokyo, 1983), vol. 24, pp. 357–382 for Tsu City and pp. 421–477 for Isashi County.
6. It was edited by Yamanaka Tametsuna.

40
Portraits of Six Ladies of the Pleasure Quarters

Second half of the seventeenth century, Edo period
One handscroll, ink, gold and color on paper
H: 26.2 cm, L: 91.7 cm
Spencer no. 82

Portraiture of famous courtesans developed as an offshoot of the genre painting that came into vogue during the late sixteenth and early seventeenth century. The genre paintings depicted, on large screens, street scenes or events in the entertainment districts of Kyoto. In the early seventeenth century, artists gradually shifted their attention to indoor settings, and they began to focus on individual figures, costumes, and hairstyles. Indeed, these paintings often remind us of modern fashion photographs, reflecting the changing modes of the time. Two particularly popular subjects for this type of figure painting were courtesans and theatrical performers. Termed Early *Ukiyo-e* (Pictures of the Floating World), such paintings anticipated the mass-produced woodcuts on similar subjects, many of which are included in this exhibition (see section VII).

Portraits of courtesans were purchased as souvenirs of the pleasure quarters, and purportedly represented actual individuals. More often they were stereotyped, delicate-faced, interchangeable women. The six depicted in this scroll have fragile bodies and powder-white faces punctuated with tiny red mouths. They are indistinguishable from one another, and from the small male attendant who is identified as a male only by his hairstyle and short-sleeved kimono. The first five of the ladies are identified by the names written beside them (Pl. XI); they are, from right to left, Washū, Kaoru, Samon, Karyū, and Wakamatsu. Also included are seals, either their own or those of the houses to which they belonged. With the exception of the two reading "Kaoru" and "Karyū," these seals were carved with flowers, fans, and swirling patterns, designs which were also incorporated into their kimono patterns as clues to the ladies' identities (no doubt included for the benefit of the cognoscenti). A single calligrapher, who also inscribed the verses, apparently "signed" the names of four of the ladies; the signature of "Karyū" is an exception, and the final courtesan has a seal but no signature.

Although there is no documentary proof, the six women are identified here as courtesans of Shimabara,[1] the red-light district in Kyoto, which was licensed to operate in 1640. The Shimabara enjoyed only a brief period of prosperity and popularity, however, since Kyoto began a slow decline shortly thereafter.[2] A late seventeenth-century essay by an anonymous author, entitled the *Shokoku Yūri Kōshoku Yurai Zoroi* (*Amorous Adventures at the Pleasure Quarters of the Country*),[3] refers to a certain courtesan by the name of Kaoru, citing her as having been one of the greatest and most talented beauties of the Shimabara, shortly after the area opened for business. However, the identification of the second figure in the painting as this Kaoru cannot be verified.

As in so many portraits of courtesans, a classical theme is superimposed on a contemporary scene; in this case, the painting could almost be interpreted as a variation on the theme of paintings of the immortal poets (see no. 12). The *waka* (thirty-one-syllable poems) written around the figures of the women are, with the exception of the second example, quoted from classical anthologies of the Heian and Kamakura periods. Also, as in the paintings of poetry contests (see nos. 13, 15), figures in the scroll are paired. The first two ladies face each other, while the next three form an intimate trio; the last courtesan sits alone, gazing off into space, a fact which suggests that this scroll was once longer.

Although the poems are transcriptions of Heian and Kamakura works, several contain a number of errors, or willful changes, which in some cases slightly change the meaning. The first poem was composed by Ki no Tomonori (late ninth century), one of the Thirty-six Immortal Poets. Tomonori became an official late in his life, in 897. In 905, he helped his cousin Tsurayuki compile the *Kokin Waka Shū* (*The Collection of Poems of Ancient and Modern Times*). Tomonori's poem appears in the chapter on summer themes from this anthology:

<blockquote>

Yo ya kuraki	Is the night so dark, and have
Michi ya madoeru	you lost your way on high,
Hototogisu	O Cuckoo, who stays so long
Waga yado o shimo	above my house and cries?[4]
Sugigate ni suru.	

</blockquote>

The second poem, written around the figure of Kaoru, has not been found among the classical works. Although it seems unlikely, it could have been an original contribution by the lady herself:

<table>
<tr><td>Kazunaranu</td><td>Me, the one who does not count,</td></tr>
<tr><td>Waga omokage o</td><td>Do you lift</td></tr>
<tr><td> oku ka mata</td><td> the brush again,</td></tr>
<tr><td>Fude tori some te</td><td>To set down that image?</td></tr>
<tr><td>E ni utsuhi ken.</td><td></td></tr>
</table>

Kaoru sits in a relaxed pose, holding a long-stemmed smoking pipe, with a smoking stand at her right side. Ladies of the pleasure quarters were often portrayed with pipe in hand, a practice they took up when smoking was introduced to Japan in the early seventeenth century.

The third lady, Samon, reclines gracefully, looking pensively off to the left. The fan design on her stunning crimson kimono is in the shape of her seal. Above her figure is a poem by the monk Kenshō (ca. 1130 to ca. 1209), which is included in the *Shūgyoku Shū* (compiled in 1328), an anthology characterized by poems with strong Buddhist overtones. Kenshō, the adopted son of Fujiwara no Akisuke, was a major literary figure of the early Kamakura period. His poem reads:

<table>
<tr><td>Ikani sen</td><td>What am I to do?</td></tr>
<tr><td>E ni kaku imo ni</td><td>She may not be worth a painting,</td></tr>
<tr><td>Arane domo</td><td>But, so little truth is in</td></tr>
<tr><td>Makoto sukunaki</td><td> one's heart.[5]</td></tr>
<tr><td>Hitogokoro kana.</td><td></td></tr>
</table>

The portrait of Samon forms a triad with two other ladies, with Karyū in the center and Wakamatsu at the far left. The first part of Karyū's name is "signed," and is combined with the character "ryū" imbedded within the rectangular seal. Karyū lifts her left hand to her face languidly and tucks her right hand within her short kimono sleeve. Her verse was composed by Fujiwara no Teika (1162–1241), who is regarded as one of Japan's greatest poets. Teika participated in many poetry matches and in 1205 helped compile the *Shin Kokin Waka Shū* (*New Collection of Poems of Ancient and Modern Times*). The waka here is from the *Shūi Gusō*, a collection of verse by Teika.

<table>
<tr><td>Nushi ya tare</td><td>Whose face is it?</td></tr>
<tr><td>Minu yo no iro o</td><td>While I try to set down</td></tr>
<tr><td>Utsushi <u>oku</u></td><td> the beauty of the unknown world,</td></tr>
<tr><td>Fude no susabi ni</td><td>It flickers between the</td></tr>
<tr><td><u>Ukabu</u> omokage.</td><td> movements of my brush.[6]</td></tr>
</table>

Two words in the poem (underlined above) were changed in this scroll to read "nuto" and "Kayou," without significantly altering the meaning of the poem.

The fifth woman, Wakamatsu, wears an elaborately tie-dyed kimono decorated with large medallions enclosing orange-blossom motifs similar to the orange blossom designs in the seal below her "signature." The verse written around her was composed by an unknown poet, and is included in the summer chapter of the *Kokin Waka Shū*. The poem is meant as an obvious reference to the orange blossom designs:

<table>
<tr><td>Satsuki matsu</td><td>When I smell the flower of the orange</td></tr>
<tr><td>Hana tachibana no</td><td> whose buds unfold</td></tr>
<tr><td>Ka o kageba</td><td>in May I call to mind the girl</td></tr>
<tr><td>Mukashi no hito no</td><td> I loved in days of old.[7]</td></tr>
<tr><td>Sode no kazo suru.</td><td></td></tr>
</table>

The final courtesan depicted in this scroll has affixed her diamond-shaped seal to the left of her portrait, and has avoided "signing" her name. Her identity thus remains uncertain. She plucks at a *samisen* (a three-stringed instrument), which was introduced to Japan in the early seventeenth century, and gazes out beyond the edge of the painting. Above her figure is a waka, also from the *Kokin Waka Shū*, that was composed by the famous poetess Ise (late ninth to early tenth century).

Satsuki koba	When May comes e'en your voice
Naki mo furinamu	will lose its new charm,
Hototogisu	Cuckoo-bird.
Mada shikihodo no	Pray, come flying now,
Koe o kikaba ya.	and let your fresh sweet
	song be heard.[8]

The two different types of hairstyle that appear in this handscroll—a pony tail and a topknot—also appear in paintings of the so-called "Beauties of the Kambun Era" (1661–1672). These Kambun Beauties were also depicted clad in sumptuous kimonos decorated with tie-dyed designs. It is believed that the extensive use of this dyeing technique was banned by the anti-luxury law of 1683. The painting in the Spencer Collection may be dated to shortly before that year.[9]

NOTES

1. Shigeo Sorimachi, *Catalogue of Japanese Illustrated Books and Manuscripts in the Spencer Collection of the New York Public Library* (Tokyo, 1978), no. 82.
2. Moriya Katsuhisa and Hayashiya Tatsusaburō (eds.), *Kyoto I*, in Akai Tatsurō et al. (eds.), *Edo Jidai Zushi*, vol. I (Tokyo, 1975), pp. 138–140.
3. This anonymous essay was edited in the Genroku era (1688–1704). See Hayakawa Junzaburō (ed.), *Kinsei Bungei Sōshi*, vol. 10 (Tokyo, 1911), p. 1.
4. A few words were changed in this poem, as follows:

Yo ya tsuraki	Is the life so hard,
Michi ya madoeru	And have you lost your
Hototogisu	way on high,
Wagaya mo towaji	O cuckoo,
Sugigate ni naku	Who stays away from my house,
	Cries in passing.

For the original poem, see, H. H. Honda (trans.), *The Kokin Waka-shū* (Tokyo, 1970), p. 55.
5. Taga Munehaya (ed.), *Kōbon Shūgyoku Shū* (Tokyo, 1971), p. 180.
6. Sasaki Nobutsuna (ed.), *Fujiwara no Teika Kashū* (Tokyo, 1949), p. 72.
7. Honda, *The Kokin*, no. 139.
8. *Ibid.*, no. 138.
9. Narazaki Muneshige (ed.), *Zaigai Hihō: Japanese Paintings in Western Collections* (Tokyo, 1969), vol. III (text), p. 26.

41
Ladies' Pastimes in Spring and Autumn

First half of the eighteenth century, Edo period
Attributed to Tamura Suiō (active late seventeenth to early eighteenth century)
One handscroll, ink and color on paper
H: 31.5 cm, L: 243.8 cm
Spencer no. 166

This relatively short handscroll depicts groups of sumptuously dressed women—most likely courtesans—enjoying their leisure hours. Some stroll in a garden, others are engaged in the scholarly pursuits of ancient China, the "Four Accomplishments" (painting, calligraphy, music, and backgammon); some appear to be simply enjoying the cool breeze out of doors. The scroll consists of two clearly unconnected compositions of about equal size. The first, a spring scene, is set close by a large blossoming cherry tree; the second scene is graced by the delicate flowers of an autumn garden.

In the first scene (Pl. XII) we see several women seated on green mats: two play a game of backgammon, one tries her hand at painting, while another reads a book. Minute as the writing on this book may be, it is legible enough to identify it as a genealogy of characters from the *Tale of Genji* (see nos. 20–22), the most popular of the literary classics of Japan. The names and brief identifications of several of the most important characters are mentioned: Prince Genji, the central figure of the novel; his favorite lady, Murasaki; his grandson Niou; his wife the Third Princess; her ill-fated lover Kashiwagi; and the child of their illicit union, Kaoru. Two women in this scene, one playing a *samisen* (a three-stringed, lute-like instrument), and another reading from a handscroll, are seated on carpets which are probably Chinese, judging from the key-fret and chrysanthemum borders with the stylized cloud patterns which were popular motifs in traditional Chinese ceramics and textiles.

The pleasant activities popularly known as the Four Accomplishments were originally regarded as gentlemen's pastimes and were common subjects in ink monochrome paintings of the Muromachi and Momoyama periods. Gradually, women began to be included as participants in the same pursuits. Artists of *ukiyo-e* (Pictures of the Floating World), who often preferred to portray groups rather than single figures, used the theme of the Four Accomplishments as a pretext for depicting an array of beautifully dressed ladies.

The second scene in the scroll shown here is the antithesis of the first. The season is autumn. Unlike the static first scene, this composition "flows" from right to left, as the women clearly gaze towards the left, where a companion is about to pluck a bunch of chrysanthemum flowers growing by a stream. One woman raises a bamboo blind to gain a better view of the garden; a gentle breeze sways the tassels of another, rolled-up blind. A note of cultural refinement is also suggested: the mature, voluptuous woman in a black kimono, sprawled in the middle of the room, holds a book of the "Thirty-six Immortal Poets" in her hands (see no. 12). Two poets and their poems can be identified in the miniature writing. The first poem is by Minamoto no Kintada (889–948):

Yuki yamite	I stay on in the mountain
Yamaji kurashitsu	pass,
Hototogisu	Unwilling to leave it
Ima hitokoe no	Before I hear the cuckoo's
Kikama hoshisa ni	cry once more.[1]

The second is by Fujiwara no Takamitsu (died 994):

Kaku bakari	In such a world that is so
Hegataku miyuru	hard to deal with,
Yononaka ni	The enviable moon shines bright
Urayamashiku mo	and clear.[2]
Sumeru tsuki kana	

The stately, elegant women with full, sensuous bodies and plump, oval faces reveal no emotion. Enveloped in sumptuous kimonos, they are idealized women—sophisticated, graceful and mature. Just as important as the women's beauty is the magnificent array of brightly colored kimonos in a rich variety of designs, treated as though the wearers were fashion models. Fabric patterns include large, bold designs of cherry blossoms, gingko leaves, morning glories, paulownia, fans, waterwheels, waves, and phoenixes. Stylized tripartite hollyhock leaf designs, similar to those used by the Tokugawa shogun's clan as its family crests, enjoyed a great vogue among women of all classes before their use by commoners was banned in 1723.[3] The bold, dramatic designs and the tie-dyed patterns of the kimonos were fashionable in the early eighteenth century.[4]

Although this scroll is unsigned, the sensuous figures and the kimono designs closely resemble those found in works by the ukiyo-e painter Tamura Suiō, who was active in Kyoto from the late seventeenth to the early eighteenth century. A number of his signed paintings repeat figures almost identical to those found in the Spencer scroll.[5] Other features in this scroll, such as the elegant autumn grasses swaying delicately in the garden, and the meandering gentle stream, delineated in light washes of ink and blue, are also characteristic of works by Suiō.

NOTES

1. This poem is included in the *Shūi Waka Shū*, which was edited either by the Emperor Kazan (968–1008) or by Fujiwara no Kintō (966–1041). See Tsukamoto Tetsuzō (ed.), *Shūi Waka Shū* (Tokyo, 1926), p. 19.
2. This poem is also included in the *Shūi Waka Shū*. See Tsukamoto, *Shūi Waka Shū*, p. 82.
3. Numata Yorisuke, *Nihon Monshō Gaku* (Tokyo, 1926), 2 vols., p. 180.
4. For examples of textile designs from this period, see Amanda Stinchecum *et al.*, *Kosode: 16th–19th Century Textiles from the Nomura Collection* (New York, 1984), and Seiroku Noma, *Japanese Costume and Textile Arts*, trans. Armins Nikovskis (New York, 1974).
5. For Suiō's works, see "Tamura Suiō hitsu Bijin Zu (A Beautiful Woman)," (no author), *Kokka* 729 (December 1952), p. 383; "Tamura Suiō hitsu Saishi hō Kajin Zu kai (A Beau Visiting a Lady)," (no author), *Kokka* 435 (February 1927), pp. 50–55; and Muneshige Narazaki, *Masterworks of Ukiyo-e: Early Paintings*, trans. and adapted by Charles A. Pomeroy (Tokyo, 1968), Pl. 55.

春弘連城港
閣閘坐日移

42
Jōkyōshū (Happy Improvisations on a Boating Journey)

Dated 1767, Edo period
Itō Jakuchū (1716–1800)
One handscroll, woodblock printed
H: 28.1 cm, L: 1157.4 cm
Signatures: "Jakuchū ga"; "Taishin"
Seals: "Tōjokin In", "Keiwa", "Jinjō no In", "Shōchū", "Jōten"
Spencer no. 425

The handscroll opens with three bold characters which read "Jōkyōshū" ("Happy Improvisations on a Boating Journey").[1] The scroll, which consists of ten long sheets of paper printed with a scene of misty landscapes in contrasting blacks, greys and white, records sites along the Yodo River, the major link between Kyoto and Osaka until modern times. About a half-day's journey downstream from Kyoto by boat, the return trip took about one full day, going upriver. The artist, Itō Jakuchū, sketched the scenery during a trip that he made in the spring of 1767 with his mentor, the Zen monk Taiten (1719–1801) of Shōkokuji, in Kyoto. Taiten, who was regarded as the greatest poet among the Zen monks of his day, composed twenty-two Chinese-style couplets, and both his calligraphy and Jakuchū's designs were rendered into a series of woodblock prints for a handscroll. Although mistakenly identified in the past as stone rubbings, these prints were definitely executed using the woodcut technique; a small fragment of an original block, in cherry wood, was identified in 1926.[2] The woodcut technique

employed here, however, was somewhat different from that used regularly by *ukiyo-e* printmakers, in which outlines were printed in ink or colors. Jakuchū's prints seem to have been produced by gouging out the outlines, thus creating white "negative" lines against darkened background areas in the finished prints.[3]

Shortly after leaving Fushimi, of Kyoto, the boat carrying Jakuchū and Taiten moves down the river, which flows through mountains, hills, and small villages. Riverbanks with clusters of houses are printed in light greys, while the narrow ribbon of the river and the looming mountains in the distance are left in white. The boat passes such famous monuments as Yodo Castle (completed in 1625 but destroyed in 1874),[4] the Iwashimizu Hachiman Shrine, and the outpost villages that today form a ring of bustling suburbs: Hashimoto, Takahama, Hirakata, and Torikai. As the boat approaches its destination in Osaka, flat plains take over, and the artist's viewpoint shifts to a higher point over-looking the graded riverbanks. The black sky merges with the flat land at this point without causing a noticeable break in composition; the trees and houses are thereby silhouetted against the broad, slow-moving river. Throughout the scroll, light grey areas—the river, houses, hills, foliage and other objects—show finely grained misty spots of ink, which are believed to have been produced by the method of blowing ink onto the blocks.[5] The artist kept details to a minimum; even so, small figures of travellers in straw raincoats, a scholar-angler dangling his fishing rod, or a worker with an ox, are sketched with a telling accuracy and charm.

Although the views that unfold before us are mainly those of the western banks, the hills and towns on the eastern bank are also occasionally shown. In doing this, Jakuchū maintains the same viewpoint, giving the impression that he was standing at a distance when he first drew the scene—on land, and not on the river. This is in marked contrast to a slightly earlier rendition of the same subject by another Kyoto artist, Maruyama Ōkyo (1733–1795), who painted a long river view scroll in color in 1765.[6] Deeply concerned with the portrayal of every detail of reality, Ōkyo depicted the eastern bank of the river upside-down, as though he were actually facing that direction, turning his back to the western shore. This difference in approach notwithstanding, Jakuchū's rendition was probably inspired by Ōkyo's earlier work.

Itō Jakuchū is especially well known to Western audiences for his dramatic ink paintings of proud roosters, which he executed in a magnificent "expressionistic" manner, with dynamic brush lines. He is equally famous for his brilliantly chromatic works depicting exotic birds and flowers, in which he juxtaposed realistic details against two-dimensional, highly decorative patterns.

Jakuchū was the oldest son of a wholesale grocer of the Nishiki-kōji in Kyoto, the bustling section of the old city where vegetables and fish markets still operate. Much of what is known about his life is found in the *Tō Keiwa Gaki* (*Notes on Paintings by Tō Keiwa*)[7]—Tō Keiwa being the name that Jakuchū often used. The essay was written by the priest Taiten, who notes that, as a young man, Jakuchū disliked study and did not have any particular vocational or avocational interests. In accordance with the Japanese custom of primogeniture, Jakuchū inherited the family trade and continued the business for more than fifteen years after the death of his father, in 1738. During this period he seems to have developed an interest in Buddhism, becoming a disciple and friend of Taiten, whose circle of acquaintances included many important painters of the time. His best-known name, Jakuchū ("like emptiness"), reflects his religious interests.

It is not known how and when Jakuchū began to paint, but some believe he studied first with a minor master of the Kanō school, Ōoka Shunboku (1674–1757). In 1754, Jakuchū persuaded his younger brother to take over the family business so that he could devote himself to painting. His close friendship with the priest Taiten at Shōkokuji may have contributed to his development as an artist, since the temple possessed a sizeable collection of Chinese and Japanese paintings.

Early in his painting career, Jakuchū focused his attention on the life around him. He painted humble birds, wildflowers and shellfish, which had never been respectable themes for a serious painter. No doubt his youth, spent in a market teeming with life, influenced his early art. We know, too, that during Jakuchū's lifetime Japanese scholars became interested in natural science, inspired by Chinese and European books on botany, zoology and mineralogy. In such an atmosphere, Jakuchū was encouraged to pursue his observation of things around him and to represent nature as he saw it. Although he seldom chose landscape as subjects, this scroll of the river journey is an eloquent expression of his interest in naturalistic painting.

Around 1755, Jakuchū conceived an ambitious project which involved painting a set of thirty large hanging scrolls—twenty-seven of flowers, birds, and fishes, and three on Buddhist themes. The paintings were completed in 1761 and donated to Shōkokuji, which, in 1889, presented all but the triad of Buddhist paintings to the imperial family. Few of Jakuchū's works date to the years immediately following this project; it is almost as if the massive undertaking had exhausted his desire to paint. Rather, the small number of woodblock prints that he made date to this short period from 1767 to 1771. In addition to the scroll in the exhibition, Jakuchū produced, in 1768, a collection of forty-eight printed pictures of flowers and birds, entitled *Gempo Yōka* (no. 43–II), and another series, the *Soken Sekisutsu*, which consists of thirty-six pictures (no. 43–I). Both books include reproductions of Taiten's calligraphy, transcribing his own poems. In 1771, Jakuchū again produced a small collection of prints done in brilliant colors.[8]

Such an involvement with printmaking was quite unusual for a major painter of Jakuchū's day. No doubt Jakuchū was influenced by the Chinese books, with printed illustrations, which were being imported to Japan in large numbers at that time. He must also have been inspired by some significant developments made by ukiyo-e print-makers working in Edo—particularly the perfection, in 1765, of the technique of producing multicolored prints, *nishiki-e* (brocade pictures), a feat which is generally attributed to Suzuki Harunobu (1725–1770). Such developments in Edo even caught the attention of Kyoto Zen monks like Taiten, who noted in his collection of essays, the *Shōun Seikō* (dated from 1759 to 1773),[9] that the ukiyo-e prints of Edo were becoming very colorful. The increasing popular demand for good reproductions of paintings might also have interested Jakuchū in printmaking methods.

The twenty-two couplets by Taiten which are interspersed throughout the scroll of the Yodo journey describe the passing scenery, pointing out the monuments, changes in time of day, weather and people. The last two poems, which are reproduced here, read in translation as follows:

> The spring water leads to the Osaka harbor.
> One after another, the scenes slowly pass by
>   in front of me.
>
> A 300-foot long bridge crosses the water like a rainbow.
> Many travelling boats come and are moored to it.

At the end of the scroll, Jakuchū signed his name and impressed two seals which read "Tōjokin In" and "Keiwa." An inscription by Taiten follows:

> In the spring of 1767, Keiwa and I took a boat trip to Osaka. As Jakuchū did drawings of the sites along the way, I added short poems. The poems are not complex at all, they are nothing but a happy improvisation of the journey.

His signature reads "Taishin" and the three seals, "Jōten," "Jinjō no In," and "Shō-chū."

NOTES

1. Another version of this scroll is reproduced in its entirety in Tokuriki Tomikichirō *et al.*, *Jakuchū no Takuhanga* (Tokyo, 1981), pp. 125–148.
2. Akiyama Teruo, "Jakuchū kenkyū josetsu: shiryō shūi (An Introduction to the Study of Jakuchū)," *Museum* 245 (August 1971), p. 6.
3. Kobayashi Tadashi, "Itō Jakuchū no hanga (Wood-block Prints by Itō Jakuchū)," *Museum* 377 (August 1982), p. 20.
4. Ōta Tamesaburō (ed.), *Teikoku Chimei Jiten* (Tokyo, 1974), and Tsubai Kiyotari and Kodama Kōta (eds.), *Nihon Jōkaku Taikei* (Tokyo, 1980), vol. 11, pp. 61–62.
5. Kobayashi, "Itō Jakuchū", p. 27.
6. This painting is reproduced in Sasaki Jōhei, *Ōkyo and the Maruyama-Shijō School of Japanese Painting* (St. Louis, 1980), no. 10. The painting is in the collection of the Arc-en-ciel Art Foundation in Tokyo.
7. This essay is reproduced in Tsuji Nobuo, *Jakuchū* (Tokyo, 1974), p. 241.
8. Kobayashi, "Itō Jakuchū," Figs. 14–19.
9. *Ibid.*, note 11.

43

I. Peach Blossoms from the *Soken Sekisatsu* (*The Book to Embellish Nature*)

Dated Winter, 1767
By Itō Jakuchū (1716–1800)
Book of printed pictures and calligraphy, 24 pages
Ink on paper
H: 28.8 cm, W: 18.4 cm
Seals: "Jinjō no In"; "Schōchū"; "Jakuchū"
Spencer no. 426

II. Flowers and Plants from the *Gempo Yōka* (*Exquisite Flowers from the Abode of Hermits*)

Dated Third Month, 1768
By Itō Jakuchū (1716–1800)
Book of printed pictures, 50 pages
Ink on paper
H: 28.2 cm, W: 17.8 cm
Seals: "Tobei"; "Tōjokin"; "Jakuchū Koji"; "Chikujō no ln"; "Shūchū"
Ex coll.: Tomioka Tessai
Mitchell Collection

Creating the black and white images of his journey along the Yodo River, in the spring of 1767 (*Jōkyōshū*, no. 42), must have stimulated Jakuchū to continue working in this particular medium of woodblock rubbing. In the two books included here, Jakuchū moved away from landscape and returned to his favorite genre, flowers and birds. He did, however, continue to use the same rubbing technique, a method which was commonly employed to reproduce calligraphic works, but had never been used by painters to reproduce paintings. No doubt Jakuchū was fascinated by the great artistic potential of the technique for creating images of startling beauty in black and white.

After the *Jōkyōshū*, Jakuchū's next project was the *Soken Jō* (*Embellishments of Nature*)[1] a small book of thirty-six pictures of plants and flowers—among them the peach blossoms reproduced here—which was printed in the winter of 1767. Only a few months later, in March of 1768, Jakuchū again produced a small book, containing forty-eight pictures of plants, insects, and other small creatures, entitled the *Gempo Yōka* (*Exquisite Flowers from the Abode of Hermits*).[2] In both projects, Jakuchū's spiritual mentor, the monk–poet Taiten (1719–1801), contributed the poems and calligraphy.

Each picture in the *Soken Jō* is accompanied by a three-line poem by Taiten, written in the bold and supple style that was the hallmark of this monk's calligraphy. The poem accompanying the peach blossoms reads,

> I shall not envy the peaches,
> known to grace the Temple Hsuan-tu.[3]
> Nor am I able to visit the legendary
> Peach Blossom Spring Valley.[4]
> The lone tree in my garden bears flowers,
> Young and playful in the sunlight of spring day.

Following the poem are two seals of Taiten which read "Chikujō no In" and "Shōchū."

The blossoms which have sprouted from the old tree are full of life and energy; the branches that shoot diagonally across the small page seem to defy the confines of a small format. The square seal reading "Jakuchū" looks like a minature bird perched on the old tree.

The book in the Spencer Collection is not complete: it retains only twelve of the thirty-six pictures that Jakuchū created for it. However, it preserves a preface by Taiten, in which he names the book *Soken Sekisatsu*, and a postscript which gives the carver's name as Se Keisen, and identifies the owner of the plate as the Kyoto temple of Junshōji. The date, corresponding to winter, 1767, is also given.

Jakuchū's third project, the *Gempo Yōka*, was printed in the spring of the following year. He seems to have perfected the use of his woodblock rubbing technique in this work, as well as his dramatic treatment of large pictorial forms. Dramatic views of nature in extreme close-up, flat decorative patterns, bizarre black circles for wormholes, and strangely still forms of insects create a surrealistic world of large white forms silhouetted against a coal-black background. As in many other works by this extraordinary artist, the choice of plants, which are generally arranged according to their season, is striking and unique. Rather than the staples of Far Eastern flower-and-bird painting—plums, orchids, and bamboo—Jakuchū preferred common weeds, such as spiderwort, or vegetables like turnips, pumpkins, squash, and beans. He also depicted plants like sunflowers and maize, which had been introduced from the New World only a century earlier.[5] Many of the pictures include such mundane creatures as centipedes, salaman-

绛帻报晓

出江濯涟

玉粒熟

189

ders, snails, grasshoppers, praying mantis, and ants. Some, like the tiny frog perched on a spiderwort leaf, are cleverly concealed.

Jakuchū's forms became bolder in the *Gempo Yōka*, and his dependency on Taiten's poetic colophons has been noticeably reduced in the later work. About a third of the pictures have no inscriptions, while others include only brief phrases by Taiten, of three or four characters each, which resemble prefaces to poems. The examples reproduced here are, for the picture of a water lily, "Coming out of mud, Bathing in ripples"; for the picture of cockscomb, "Scarlet combs announce dawn"; and for the picture of maize, "Corn has ripened like precious beads."

Jakuchū's upbringing in the greengrocer family business undoubtedly made him attentive to artistic possibilities to be found in ordinary plant life—subject matter alien to Eastern flower-and-bird painting, a genre whose subjects were generally imbued with symbolism. At this time, too, Japanese artists were becoming increasingly interested in the natural world, inspired by the introduction of Western scientific knowledge. A younger contemporary of Jakuchū, Sakai Hōitsu (1761–1828), the last great master to work in the decorative tradition of the Rimpa school, was also keenly aware of the diverse artistic styles of his day. At some time early in the nineteenth century, Hōitsu copied ten compositions from Jakuchū's *Gempo Yōka*, adding colors and other more naturalistic details.[6]

Although they have been lost from the Spencer book, the *Gempo Yōka* originally included a postscript by Taiten and another by a scholar named Takatsuji Tanenaga (died 1803). The latter signed his name as Sugawara Sechō and dated his colophon to 1768.

NOTES

1. For the entire reproduction of another version of this book, see Tokuriki Tomikichirō *et al.*, *Jakuchū no Takuhanga* (Tokyo, 1981), pp. 52–123.
2. For the reproduction of another version of this book, see *ibid.*, pp. 1–50. Gempo is an abode of hermits at the top of Mt. Koulkun, Tibet.
3. This temple was in the T'ang capital of Ch'ang-an.
4. See no. 204.
5. Tokuriki, *Jakuchu*, p. 21.
6. These are in an album, now in the Seikadō Bunko Foundation, Tokyo. See Yamane Yūzō (ed.). *Rimpa Kaiga Zenshū: Hōitsu Ha* (Tokyo, 1978), Pls. 61–66, item no. 111. Some of these copies from Jakuchū compositions bear Hōitsu's seal, reading "Uka," the name which he is believed to have adopted around 1809.

VI
Keeping Traditions Alive

THE sketches and drawings in this group were made as records of various types—historical, scientific and artistic. Records were made to document such unusual historical events as a Korean delegation's state visit to Japan in the seventeenth century (no. 44), and to preserve and perpetuate the secrets of plant and herbal medicine, like many scientific manuscripts of the ancient Middle East and medieval Europe (no. 45). For most monks of the Mikkyō (Esoteric) sect of Buddhism, the ability to draw was an essential prerequisite to their training. The Spencer Collection's drawings of Buddhist deities include some of the earliest extant examples of sketches made for the purpose of study, instruction, and the preservation of tradition (see nos. 5–9).

Copying older works of art formed the foundation of training for Far Eastern painters of pre-modern times. Not only did these artists value tradition dearly, they also considered the act of copying to be the best method of gaining technical experience. Three sets of sketches included here (nos. 47–49) represent the efforts of different generations of Kanō School masters during the Edo period. As official guardians of the painting tradition during that era, Kanō artists placed a premium upon this particular practice.

Unlike finished works made on commission, these sketches and drawings not only reveal the artists' strong determination to keep traditions alive, they also give us a glimpse into private moments in the lives of the practitioners of the various arts and activities depicted.

44

Chōsenjin Zu (*Picture of the Koreans*)

Dated 1682, Edo period
By Kanō Eikei (1662–1702)
One handscroll, ink and light color on paper
H: 30.4 cm, L: 612.9 cm
Signed: "Eikei zu"; "Tenrō Dōsai sho"
Seals: "Izai Hissen"; "Ginpūrō In", "Hirano shi", "Dōsai no In", "Hirano Shō"; "Kaigyoku chinzō"
Spencer no. 75

This handscroll depicts a procession of the Korean envoys who arrived in Japan in 1682. In unusual fashion, the scroll starts at the left, with a title, *Chōsenjin Zu* (*Picture of the Koreans*), followed by the procession scene. The illustration, in turn, is followed by a copy of the letter sent by the Korean Director of the Board of Rites, Yun Ka-chung, to the lord of the Sō clan of Tsushima Island, near the southern tip of Korea. Toward the end of the scroll is a long list of the names and titles of the envoys.

Diplomatic relations between Japan and Korea, which came to an end after Hideyoshi's campaign against Korea in 1592, were revived at the beginning of the Edo period through the efforts of the lord of the Sō clan. Tsushima's economy largely depended on trade with its neighbor and it desired to renew commercial relations. In 1607, Tokugawa Ieyasu released some of the Korean prisoners captured during Hideyoshi's invasion, and Korea sent—for the first time since the war—envoys on a "return courtesy" mission. Thereafter, until 1811, Korean envoys were sent to Japan on twelve occasions (including the first visit in 1607).[1] In most instances, the visits were to congratulate newly installed shoguns; Korea was notified of each shogun's succession by the Sō clan. However, the Koreans also took the opportunity to watch the movements of the Japanese, whom they regarded as "untrustworthy" neighbors. Throughout these diplomatic exchanges, the Sō clan played an intermediary role, and Tsushima was the first place the envoys landed. From there, accompanied by Sō clan members, the envoys proceeded to Edo where they were greeted by the shogun. The missions were composed of from 300 to 500 people and each visit usually took three months. Lodging and feeding the entire Korean diplomatic crew for three months was a financial burden on the Japanese government, but since the missions offered a chance to show off the wealth and power of the shogunate, both domestically and to a foreign audience, it sponsored them on a grand scale.

Along the route from Tsushima to Edo, the Korean missions drew the attention of feudal lords as well as townspeople; the curious would visit the Koreans in their lodging and inquire about affairs of the world outside of Japan. There was also a great deal of cultural exchange in literature and the arts. Taking this into consideration, the Korean government carefully selected its envoys; each mission consisted of high-level civil officials with a chief envoy of the "third degree" (the top third level in a nine-degree official system). Envoys brought gifts, mainly silk and ginseng, and occasionally musical instruments requested by the Japanese. In return, the Japanese presented them with silver and cotton.

These diplomatic events were recorded pictorially as well as in literature. The Tokugawa government may have commissioned artists of the official Kanō school to paint such works in large numbers to be given to the Korean kings, Japanese emperors, and various feudal lords as souvenirs. They were often painted on handscrolls and screens and were also reproduced in woodblock prints.[2] Most of the extant handscrolls—including the Spencer work, which is the earliest known among the dated examples[3]—depict the procession of envoys against an empty background with labels identifying each figure; unlike the screens executed with decorative backgrounds, these scrolls have great historical-documentary importance.

The Spencer scroll depicts the seventh mission, carried out in 1682 to congratulate Tokugawa Tsunayoshi on his installation, in 1680, as the fifth Tokugawa shogun. The chief envoy was Yun Chi-wan (1635–1718); he held two provincial governorships before his mission to Japan and was appointed Minister of Board of Rites after his return to Korea. The scroll seems to represent the arrival in Tsushima, since the attached letter, copied here by the calligrapher, Hirano Dōsai, is addressed to the Tsushima lord. In this letter, the Korean court congratulates the lord on the accession of a new shogun and expresses hopes for improved relations between the two countries.

The procession is headed by several Japanese on foot carrying small and large drums, probably gifts from the Koreans. The minor military officials from Korea who head the procession of envoys are followed by a musical band on horseback. The highest-ranking envoys, civilian officials, appear toward the end of the procession. Three chief envoys, and two envoys who are next in rank, ride a palanquin carried by Japanese. Illustrated here is the opening section of the procession. The labels indicate a large drum, halberds, different types of flags, and the titles of the envoys. Low-ranking military officials whose role was to accompany provincial governors or visiting Chinese officials are on horseback, carrying bows and arrows. The numbers recorded in the labels do not match the number of figures actually depicted ; the artist probably did not bother to paint the exact number of individuals. The facial characteristics and movements of the figures are precisely rendered. Executed mainly in ink outline, forms were quickly touched up with light colors in green, blue, and earth tones. The artist has accurately depicted the envoys' manners and costumes, probably after observing the Korean procession first-hand. Although the background is not depicted, the figures are skillfully grouped across the surface to create a feeling of life and action.

Kanō Eikei (1662–1702), the son of Kanō Einō (1631–1697) and grandson of Kanō Sansetsu (1589–1651), succeeded to the position of fourth-generation head of the Kyoto Kanō school. His surviving works are rare; however, it is obvious from this scroll, done when he was twenty, that he was thoroughly trained in the Kanō tradition. Quick and sketchy outlines depict foreshortened horses galloping and turning. The dragons that decorate the flags are drawn with few but vigorous brushstrokes. The title and the remainder of the calligraphy in the scroll are the work of Hirano Dōsai, an otherwise unknown calligrapher.

NOTES

1. For the history of Japan–Korea exchanges, see Nakamura Hidetaka, *Nissen Kankei no Kenkyū*, vol. 3 (Tokyo, 1970), pp. 300–312; and Chin Dan-hakoe (ed.), *Hanguksa*, vol. 4 (Seoul, 1965), pp. 73–81.
2. Yoshida Hiroshi, "Paintings of the Korean Envoy," in *Choson T'ongshinsa*, by Nakamura Hidetaka *et al.*, trans. Kim Yong-son (Seoul 1982), pp. 161–197.
3. Two early eighteenth-century works, a woodblock print by Okumura Masanobu, dated 1711, and a three-scroll set of emaki, dated 1719, have been published. See Donald Jenkins, *Ukiyo-e Prints and Paintings: The Primitive Period, 1680–1745* (Chicago, 1971), no. 131; and the Asahi Shimbun article of September 2, 1984. The New York Public Library also owns the Masanobu print.

45

Bai Sōshi (Handscroll of Horse Doctors), I and II

I. Mid-nineteenth century, Edo period
One handscroll, ink and light colors on paper
H: 31.0 cm, L: 377.4 cm
Spencer no. 229

II. Mid-fourteenth century, Nambokuchō period
One handscroll, ink and colors on paper
H: 21.4 cm, L: 282.7 cm
Ex coll.: Frank Horley (?)
Spencer no. 29

The scenes reproduced here, depicting a Buddhist monk, a horse and a groom, and two plants, are chosen from two seperate scrolls which bear the same title: *Bai Sōshi* (*Handscroll of Horse Doctors*). The plants are from the shorter, incomplete scroll, a medical handbook dating from the mid-fourteenth century, which resembles a medieval herbal.

The plants in this scroll, however, are intended not only as horse medicine but for humans as well. For example, a common shrub such as *ōbako* (right-hand side) is edible, and is known to prevent coughing and vomiting, to lower temperatures, and to sooth stomach ailments.[1] Tubers (left-hand side), called *fukuryō* (also identified here by their family name, *mokusō-ten*; in Latin, *Poria Cocos Wolf*),[2] grow underground in pine groves and are believed to have been used for urinary ailments. Other plants, such as *umenohoya*, are nutritional food for horses and cattle; *kusanō* is reported to have been used as a substitute for opium as a painkiller. Still others were used as disinfectants and to stop bleeding. Every plant is depicted carefully, with the salient characteristics faithfully reproduced. The plants and herbs closely resemble those found in modern *materia medica* and botanical handbooks.

This scroll of herbal medicine was originally twice as long. The lost parts, its beginning and end sections, are reproduced in an almost identical but much later work, which dates from the mid-nineteenth century. The first section of the nineteenth-century work is almost complete, save for the partially damaged opening scene. The figure of the doctor is missing, but his name is given in a cartouche as Po Lo (Hakuraku, in Japanese). The rest of this section contains a series of imaginary portraits of eight Chinese and two Japanese horse doctors, assembled as if to suggest that they are of a lineage dating back to legendary times. Cartouches at the upper left of each figure identify the ten doctors as Po Lo, I-wang Fa-yao (illustrated here), Lai Kung, Tung Chün, T'ien, Ōnamuchi (Japanese), Wang Liang, Fan Kai, Shen Nung, and Echigo no Tansuke (Japanese). In most cases, the doctors are depicted as high-ranking Chinese officials. All of the figures are executed in fine ink outline and pale colors, and the compositions are uncluttered. The cartouches also contain the doctors' death dates, the names of the horses for whose cures they became famous, and the names of grooms. Invocations of Buddhist deities, made in the form of mantras (sacred chants) which are transliterations from Sanskrit, reveal that early veterinary medicine relied on faith in the buddha as well as a knowledge of herbal treatments.

The figure shown here, I-wang Fa-yao (no. 2), is the only doctor to be represented as a Buddhist monk: the first part of his name, I-wang (King of Doctors), is sometimes used to refer to the Buddha of Healing, Yakushi. I-wang Fa-yao died on the day of the snake; the name of the black horse tied to the stable is Kuchimu; and the groom, Aizen Hōshi. The small figure of a seated buddha enclosed within the circle above his head is shown as if he is holding a medicine jar in his left hand (although the jar is missing). This was a standard gesture of Yakushi, suggesting that the monk–doctor is, in fact, an incarnation of this deity.

Probably the best-known of the Chinese doctors included in the scroll is Shen Nung (no. 9). According to ancient legend, he was one of the earliest Chinese emperors, believed to have reigned between 2737 and 2697 B.C. Along with the discovery of plants' medicinal properties, his many achievements are supposed to include the introduction of settled agriculture and the development of a barter system.[3] The only females represented in the scroll are the Japanese doctor Ōnamuchi (no. 5) and her youthful attendant Kotori ("Little Bird").

The herbal section of the nineteenth-century scroll is almost identical to that found in the earlier work. It is followed by a series of copies of old inscriptions, which help us trace the prototype of both scrolls to a much earlier period. The inscriptions also enhance the importance of the nineteenth-century work, since they were lost from the earlier scroll in the Spencer Collection. One of the inscriptions states that the scroll— i.e., an earlier prototype—had been transmitted to a man, presumably a horse doctor, named Shichirōbei-no-jō Tadayasu, and that it was copied by a certain Saia in 1267. A second inscription suggests that the model was, in turn, based on a Chinese painting bearing a T'ang dynasty (618–906) date corresponding to the year 742.[4]

Another comment recorded near the end of the Edo-period scroll sheds light on why such works as the *Bai Sōshi* were painted: "The transmission of this art is a restricted matter. If there is no one to transmit these secrets to, this manuscript should be returned [to me]. The safety of this manuscript must be insured after my father Saia's death." Clearly, the *Bai Sōshi* scrolls were originally made to preserve the secrets of the art of horse doctoring for a select few.

The two *Bai Sōshi* scrolls in the Spencer Collection stem from a painting tradition

which appears to have been at its height in Japan during the Kamakura period. A *Bai Sōshi* handscroll (in the Tokyo National Museum) and a number of fragments, all dating from the Kamakura period, have been preserved in Japanese collections.[5] The warrior class had become dominant in Japanese society, and horses—and horse doctors—were in great demand because of the strategic military advantage they provided.

The two versions offered here resemble one another extraordinarily closely, which testifies to the copyists' almost religious respect and care in following their models. The knowledge and administering of medicine were indeed sacred arts. Manuals such as the *Bai Sōshi* must have been preserved and transmitted from generation to generation within the families of veterinarians as tightly guarded secrets of their trade.

NOTES

1. Shibusawa Keizō, *Emakimono ni yoru Nihon Jōmin Seikatsu Ebiki*, vol. 3 (Tokyo, 1966), p. 81.
2. *Ibid.*
3. Herbert Giles, *A Chinese Biographical Dictionary* (London, 1898), p. 646.
4. A discrepancy in the cyclical date here, which refers to the year 730 or 790, is also found in other versions.
5. For these versions, see Mombushō Bunkachō (ed.), *Jūyō Bunkazai*, vol. 9 (Tokyo, 1974), figs. 174 and 175 for the two fragments, and fig. 176 for the scroll belonging to the Tokyo National Museum. A different section from this scroll is also reproduced in "Scroll Painting of Veterinary Surgery," (no author) *Kokka* 270 (November 1912), pp. 108–109. Another fragment from the third version is reproduced in Narazaki Muneshige, "Bai Zōshi Zanketsu (Portion of a Picture-scroll Entitled the Bai-zōshi)," *Kokka* 797 (August 1958).

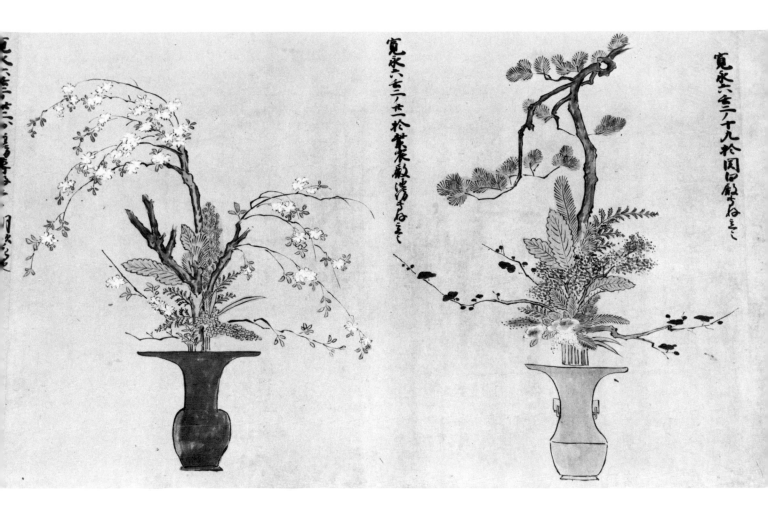

46
Records of Flower Arrangements Made by Ikenobō Senkō II

Dated January 6, 1629 to March 5, 1635, Edo period
One handscroll, ink and light colors on paper
H: 35.4 cm, L: 17.9 m
Spencer no. 62

This long handscroll records sixty-one flower arrangements created by Ikenobō Senkō II over a period of six years. The first example is dated 6 January 1629 and the last, 5 March 1635.

From its religious and court-centered origins, flower arranging developed into an art form that inspired several different schools.[1] This scroll documents the work of a famed practitioner of the art, Ikenobō Senkō II, who served in the imperial court and taught several members of the imperial family the technique of flower arranging.

Familiar in the west as *ikebana* (literally, "let live flowers"), a word that came into use in Japan only in the late seventeenth century, arranging flowers as an art form had its origins in the floral offerings which were placed before altars in Buddhist temples. Strongly influenced by the native Shinto belief that all elements of nature are endowed with a divine spirit, the ancient Japanese regarded Buddhist altars as natural environments for floral arrangements. Known as *rikka* (or *tatebana*, "let flowers stand"), floral arrangements were not appreciated merely for their beauty. The temporary introduction of nature into architectural interiors, where flowers could be brought together and arranged as they were not seen in nature, was given various symbolic meanings. For example, the transitory nature of life was suggested by the blooming and fading of seasonal flowers; conversely, the eternity of life was brought to mind by the temporal lives of cut flowers. Each blossom and branch of a plant was symbolic, and correctly arranged flowers came to be regarded as suggestive of the universe—the worlds of heaven, earth, and human beings—and the interrelationships between its realms.

As small chapels were built within noblemen's residences during the Late Heian period, architectural distinctions between sacred and secular structures within a palace compound became blurred, and floral offerings to buddhas came to be accepted as interior decoration. The development of the *shoin* (literally, "study") style of residential architecture in the late fifteenth century gave an added impetus to the use of flower arrangements in secular settings, since the shoin's focal point, the recessed alcove (*tokonoma*), provided an ideal showcase for them. In such settings, some of the arrangements, which could be several feet high, possessed a specific relationship to architecture. Flower arrangements were also viewed together with other forms of art, such as hanging scrolls or other valuable objects.

At about the same time, during the late fifteenth century, the Ikenobō school, the most influential of all the schools of flower arranging in pre-modern Japan, was founded by Senkei. The school's typical style of arrangement was then still dominated by religious influence, characterized as it was by a prominent central motif regarded as a link to the gods. The thirteenth-generation master of this school, Senkō I (died ca. 1622), was active during the Momoyama period and fundamentally changed the style of flower arranging, freeing it from its religious associations and enlarging the repertory of arrangements to suit the large, opulent interiors of palaces and castles of Momoyama warlords. His radical departure from the earlier technique is illustrated by a well-known story. For the occasion of Hideyoshi's visit to the residence of one of his vassals, Maeda Toshiie, Senkō was commissioned to create an arrangement for the alcove, where four large hanging scrolls depicting twenty monkeys were displayed. Senkō placed a huge pine tree in a large basin (six by three feet and nine inches deep), so that the twenty painted monkeys appeared to be perched on its widely spreading branches. The arrangement gained instant fame as the greatest masterpiece by Ikenobō"[2]

Senkō II, the creator of the arrangements recorded in the Spencer scroll, perfected the school's technique by inventing even more impressive and expansive arrangements. His domination of the field was complete, particularly after 1624, when he began to work for Gomizunō (1596–1680), then the reigning emperor. Gomizunō was an enthusiastic patron and disciple; his commitment and enthusiasm were such that he held free flower arranging contests at his palace, admitting not only courtiers and gentlemen merchants but also commoners—as long as they had the skill to compete. Senkō II served as judge and referee at such official occasions. A number of courtiers' chronicles from this time record the vogue that flower arranging enjoyed at the emperor's court.[3] Many of their diaries also record the instructions and advice that they received from Senkō II, who had strict injunctions governing the materials to be used, the proper placement of branches and the relationships between them, as well as specifications on the types of vessels to be used as containers. With the popularization of the tea ceremony during the Edo period, however, the Ikenobō style of rikka gradually fell from favor among the general public, and was replaced in the late seventeenth century by ikebana, a simpler type of arrangement more suitable to small tea rooms.

More than one hundred of Senkō II's arrangements are recorded in pictures, (not counting duplicates);[4] that so many were preserved is truly extraordinary. These pictorial records include manual-like sketches, such as those found in the Spencer scroll, and also "finished" paintings, among them screens in the Tokyo National Museum and the Yōmei Bunko in Tokyo.[5] Before books of instruction became available, the only way to learn Senkō's techniques was to study with him personally, or to imitate those of his arrangements which were recorded in pictures. Gomizunō himself hired a painter to record the works that Senkō II created for him and for other courtiers.[6] It seems that from time to time such records were borrowed to be copied.[7] The Spencer scroll appears to be one of these copies, rather than an on-site record of arrangements made at different places. The fact that the drawing technique and the calligraphy style for notations on places and dates are consistent throughout the work supports this hypothesis.

The sixty-one arrangements in the Spencer scroll were made for places such as the audience and ceremonial halls of the imperial palace and Gomizunō's personal quarters. Also included are arrangements made at the homes of the prime minister and other noblemen, and those created at Senkō II's own residence. The year 1629 was a busy one for Senkō II; close to half of the sixty-one arrangements recorded here were made then.

The author of this scroll labelled almost all of the arrangements depicted with year, month, day and location reference. In the first dozen or so arrangements, a smaller script, close to the painting, identifies the type of foliage used. In a few places the colors have been applied in graded washes to suggest the modeling of a leaf. Other artistic devices includes sprinklings of dots to demarcate the areas in which flower blossoms are to be sketched in with color washes.

Senkō II's arrangements are consistently placed in Chinese-style vessels, and the same type of container is often used for more than one arrangement. The vessels are tall vases with a thin neck and wider mouth—like the example reproduced here—often decorated with flanges, or with rings and handles that echo ancient Chinese bronze vessel designs.

The right-hand example in the pair of arrangements illustrated here is dated Kan'ei 6 (1629), leap-February 19th, and it was made for the palace of the Prime Minister Konoe Nobuhiro (1599–1649); the other, dated the twenty-first day of the same month, was created for the Shishinden (ceremonial hall) of the imperial palace. Both have the tall central stem signifying Heaven (pine in the arrangement at the right, and a flowering cherry in the work at the left), with additional branches clustered lower to represent the "stems" of man and earth. Careful observation of the arrangement of wide vertical leaves and clusters of flowers at the right, and the bare branch stub and feathery ferns at the left reveals a rhythm of flowers and leaves, bare and foliated branches, exposure and concealment, depth and surface, documenting the richness of Senkō II's three-dimensional art, carefully recorded in this handscroll for posterity.

A handscroll in the Yōmei Bunko in Tokyo contains ninety-three arrangements by Senkō II, ranging in date from 1628 to 19 March 1635; it also includes a postscript with a date corresponding to 2 July 1635.[8] The Spencer scroll, which duplicates many works in this version, may be dated to roughly the same time.

Scrolls such as this one are extraordinary because of the insight they give into the aesthetic activities of the seventeenth-century Japanese court. They are also valuable as artistic and historical documents, as they can be compared to and matched against written records in the courtiers' diaries.

NOTES

1. For the history of early Japanese flower arranging, see Harold P. Stern, *Birds, Beasts, Blossoms and Bugs: The Nature of Japan* (New York, 1976), no. 40; Hiroshi Ohchi, *Ikebana* (Teufen, 1956); Kubota Shigeru and Segawa Ken'ichirō, *Nihon Kadō Shi* (Tokyo, 1971); and Itō Teiji and Donald Richie, *Nihon no Dentō*, vol. I, *Ikebana* (Tokyo, 1967).

2. This episode is recorded in the *Maeda Tei Onari Ki* (*The Record of His Majesty's Visit to the Palace of Lord Maeda*), in the entry for the third year of the Bunroku era (1594). See Kubota, *Nihon Kado*, pp. 175–176.

3. For the entries in courtiers' diaries, see Kubota, *ibid.*, pp. 174–177, since almost none of these chronicles have been published.

4. Yamane Yūzō, "Kan'ei jidai no Senkō no Rikka Zu ni tsuite (On Flower Arrangement of the Kan'ei Era, 1624–1643)"; *Yamato Bunka* 48 (February 1968), p. 16.

5. For a list of other paintings of flower arrangements, see Yamane, "Kan'ei jidai," pp. 16–17.

6. *Ibid.*, p. 16.

7. See, for example, the entry for 4 November, seventeenth year of the Kan'ei era (1640), in Akamatsu Toshihide (ed.), *Kakumei Ki* (a chronicle of the monk Hōrin Shōshō of Rokuonji, also known as Kinkakuji), vol. I (Kyoto, 1958), p. 264.

8. For the scroll in this collection, see Yamane, "Kan'ei jidai," Pls. 26 and 27; figs. 1 and 2.

47
Scenes from the *Tan'yū Shukuzu* (*Small Sketches by Kanō Tan'yū*)

Edo period
By Kanō Tan'yū (1602–1674)
One handscroll, ink, gold, and light colors on paper
H: 12.8 cm, L: 749.5 cm
Seals: "Seimei"; "Ko"; "Gei" (?)
Spencer no. 721

Kanō Tan'yū (1602–1674) has long been recognized as one of the most important artists of the Edo period.[1] Born into one of the pre-eminent families of Japanese painters, Tan'yū's artistic talents were encouraged at an early age. He first studied painting with his father, Kanō Takanobu (1571–1618), and later with Kanō Kōi (died 1636). As a result of an aggressive campaign waged by his father, the remarkably precocious eleven-year-old Tan'yū was given audience, in 1612, by the founder of the Tokugawa shogunate, Ieyasu. Two years later, the second shogun dubbed him the Reincarnation of Eitoku (1543–1590), Tan'yū's grandfather and the major master of the Momoyama period. In 1621, young Tan'yū was granted a large tract of land at Kajibashi in Edo by the shogun. There he established the prestigious Kajibashi Kanō branch of the family, the most influential group of Kanō artists, who served the shogunate as "official" painters.

Tan'yū set the tone for the official taste of his era, creating a style that appealed to the shoguns and their vassals; he thus ensured the school's survival throughout the lengthy reign of the Tokugawa family, which lasted until the mid-nineteenth century. The great number of his works which survive display exceptional inventiveness in composition and superior mastery of brush and ink. As the extraordinary range of subject and style in his paintings testifies, Tan'yū was a restless genius, constantly seeking inspiration from ancient masterworks and other artists. Thousands of his rough sketches have also been preserved.[2] With unflagging curiosity and diligence, he copied many masterworks of China and Japan, paintings to which he had privileged access because of his exalted position. Some sketches were made as records of paintings brought to him because of his connoisseurship: as official painter to the shoguns one of his duties was to pass judgment on the authenticity and attributions of paintings. On such occasions, he made copies of the works as records, just as artwork is photographed today.

The production of these records and copies—called *shukuzu* (reduced pictures)—must have provided Tan'yū with an ideal opportunity for study, as the need to grasp and quickly capture the essential character of original works sharpened his perception and expressive powers. Apparently, shukuzu also were used as tools to train pupils. After the family's model books—important tools of instruction for young painters at the time— were destroyed by a fire at Edo Castle in 1657, the number of shukuzu Tan'yū produced increased dramatically.[3]

Some of the originals Tan'yū copied can be identified among extant paintings; the shukuzu often include notations on the condition of the original works, their artists, dimensions, dates of execution, provenance, seals, signatures and colophons. Tan'yū's own comments on their quality, attribution, or price, were also included.

Although not all of the sketches in the Spencer scroll were executed at the same time,

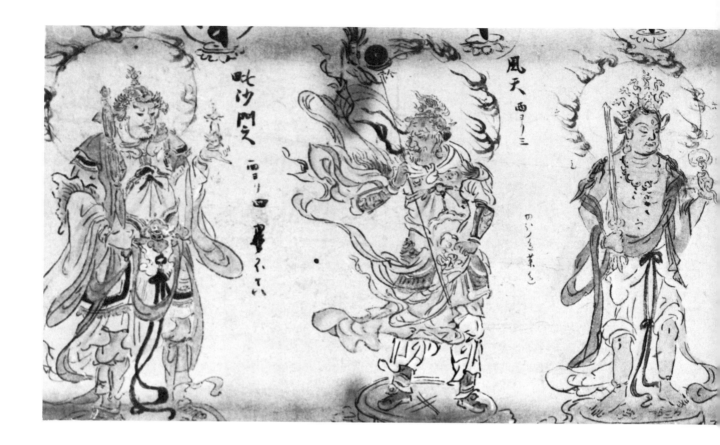

an inscription found on one of the drawings refers to the year 1672, two years before Tan'yū's death. Although diminutive in height, the scroll is quite long and contains sketches of seven or eight different works, many of them impressed, at the beginning and the end, with one or two of the seals reading "Seimei," "Ko," or "Gei(?)." The sketches vary considerably in style and subject matter. While some appear to be based on Chinese models, others are clearly copies of Japanese works depicting both religious and secular subjects. The sketches originally must have differed considerably in size; most now bear evidence of trimming at both top and bottom. All were executed on paper in ink, light colors, and some gold pigment, and record in rough, summary brushstrokes the compositions of paintings which Tan'yū must have had before him. Although they were rapidly executed, Tan'yū's eye for detail stands out in the careful rendering of small details and the notations that appear throughout the scroll, designating the colors and other characteristics of the original pieces.

The Spencer scroll opens with a segment most likely based on a Chinese work by a Ming dynasty (1368–1644) academic painter. The six Buddhist deities reproduced here are chosen from the second section of the scroll, which depicts the Jūniten, or twelve Devas. Indian in origin, these heavenly beings were assimilated into Esoteric Buddhism as symbols of the major forces controlling the physical world; their functions include the protection of the four cardinal directions and their midpoints.[4] The six deities are (from right to left): Katen (Agni in Sanskrit), the god of fire, standing amidst burning

flames; Ishanaten (Iśāna), a plump god of wealth who holds a bowl in his right hand; the golden-bodied Taishakuten (Indra, here mislabeled as Rasetsuten), the god of rain and justice and the leader of heavenly guardians, so identified because of his courtly attire and the vajra held in his right hand; Suiten (Varuṇa), the green-bodied god of water, holding a snake (a water spirit), while six serpents rise from his head; Fūten (Vāyu), the god of wind, whose skirts and scarves billow in the breeze; and Bishamonten (Vaiśravaṇa), the guardian of the north and god of wealth, identified by the miniature stupa (symbol of the Buddha's Law, a rare treasure granted to him by the buddha himself) in his left hand. The other six deities, not shown here, are Gatten (Candra), the moon god; Bonten (Brahma), counterpart to Taishakuten; Nitten (Sūrya), the sun god; Emmaten (Yama), god of the nether world; Rasetsuten (Rākṣasa, mislabeled here as Taishakuten), the leader of evil spirits; and Jiten (Pṛthivī), god of the earth.

Some of the devas are represented as benign-looking bodhisattvas with delicate, almost feminine features, while others are shown as fierce guardians. Flaming haloes encircle all of the devas' heads, with Sanskrit letters written above them (which in most cases were trimmed off in the mounting process). Throughout this section of the scroll, notations are scribbled in Japanese, recording the colors in the original works. For example, a notation referring to the necklace worn by Ishanaten (the second figure from the right) reads "white color," while another note states that his face is painted a "green color."

Numerous sets of paintings of the Jūniten survive from the Late Heian and Kamakura periods. Although the precise models for Tan'yū's devas are not known, certain stylistic features, such as the two half-circles framing the eyes of Suiten (third from the left),[5] lively facial expressions, poses in which the figures often turn to face one another, and the powerfully rendered musculature of several of the guardian figures suggest that Tan'yū's models probably dated from the Kamakura period.

Following this group of Buddhist deities are several scenes on Chinese historical subjects, a landscape reminiscent of the bold, expressive ink style of the Muromachi-period master Sesshū (1420–1506), and a scene of dancers performing the ancient courtly dance known as Bugaku.

Another scene reproduced here, depicting the procession of a large army of soldiers, belongs to the final section of the scroll. As is the case for many of the sketches that precede it, the specific model is difficult to identify. It is most likely a copy of a Chinese painting depicting the entry of the first emperor of the Han dynasty (206 B.C. to A.D. 221) into the city of Kuan-chung, a popular subject for historical painting in both China and Japan.[6] Among those who rebelled against the cruel administration of the Ch'in (221–195 B.C.) emperors was a man of humble origins named Liu Pang (247–195 B.C.), who later founded the Han dynasty and was known posthumously as Emperor Kao-tsu. In 207 B.C., Liu Pang, leading an army from the state of Ch'u, attacked Kuan-chung, the Ch'in stronghold, the first in a series of events that led to the fall of the Ch'in imperial house five years later.

NOTES

1. For the life and works of this artist, see Takeda Tsuneo, *Nihon Bijutsu Kaiga Zenshū*, vol. 15, *Kanō Tan'yū* (Tokyo, 1978); Kōno Motoaki, *Kanō Tan'yū*, no. 194 of *Nihon no Bijutsu*, ed. Staff of the National Museums of Tokyo, Kyoto, and Nara (Tokyo, 1982); and John M. Rosenfield, Fumiko E. Cranston, and Edwin A. Cranston, *The Courtly Tradition in Japanese Art and Literature* (Cambridge, Mass., 1973), p. 304.
2. The largest collection of Tan'yū's sketches is in the Kyoto National Museum. See Kyoto National Museum (ed.), *Tan'yū Shukuzu*, 2 vols. (Kyoto, 1980).
3. It is also believed that Tan'yū began making sketches of paintings as a young man, and they could have been destroyed in the same fire. See Kyoto National Musuem catalogue (English summary), vol. 2, p. 315.
4. For other representations of these deities, see John M. Rosenfield and Elizabeth ten Grotenhuis, *Journey of the Three Jewels: Japanese Buddhist Paintings from Western Collections* (New York, 1979), p. 95.
5. I am grateful to Taka Yanagisawa of the Institute for Art History Research, Tokyo, for her expertise.
6. For an example of Chinese works on this subject, see Kojiro Tomita, *Portfolio of Chinese Paintings in the Museum (Han to Sung Periods)*: Museum of Fine Arts, Boston (Cambridge, Mass., 1933), Pls. 66–69.

48

Chin Kao and Shang Yuan Fu-jen from the *Scroll of Chinese Immortals*

Early nineteenth century, Edo period
By Kanō Naganobu (1775–1828)
One handscroll, ink and color on paper
H: 39.7 cm, L: 758.5 cm
Signed: "Isen-in Hōin mo"
Seal: "Fujiwara Naganobu"
Spencer no. 204

This scroll of Chinese immortals consists of ten imaginative, brightly colored scenes representing episodes from legends of celebrated Chinese Taoist figures. With no textual interruption, the ten separate episodes run one into the next, set against a landscape which gives the scenes the appearance of one continuous composition. Since the legendary immortals were believed to have lived in widely disparate regions and eras, shifts in time and space are subtly suggested by tall cliffs, deep gorges, turbulent ocean water, a cave, and a natural stone bridge.

Long a favorite theme in Chinese literature and art, the immortals also became popular subjects in Japanese art, following the introduction of Chinese-style monochrome ink painting during the Muromachi period. As the two components of the Chinese word for immortal, *hsien* ("man" and "mountain") indicate, the original term evidently referred to someone who withdrew from society to live as a mountain hermit. Gradually, however, legends surrounding the "immortals" evolved, and their ranks were expanded to include mythical, fairy-like spirits believed to inhabit the celestial realms, as well as historical figures revered for their great wisdom or supernatural powers. The quest for immortality was a consuming preoccupation for many in China, beginning in the Han dynasty (206 B.C. to A.D. 221), and the lives of beings who were thought to have attained it became a source of great fascination.

An early source of biographical information about numerous "immortals" was a book entitled the *Lieh-hsien-chüan* (*Biographies of the Immortals*), attributed to the Taoist scholar Liu Hsiang (77–6 B.C.),[1] which describes the fantastic events that occurred in the lives of human beings upon attaining immortality. Stories included in the *Lieh-hsien-chüan*, and in the enormous number of similar works which followed in later centuries, stirred the imaginations of many artists.

Particularly helpful in identifying the immortals depicted in this scroll is a book which was compiled during the Ming dynasty (1368–1644) by Wang Shih-chen (1526–1590), the *Lieh-hsien-ch'üan-chüan* (*Complete Biographies of the Immortals*).[2] It contains the biographies of a large number of immortals and includes charming woodcut illustrations which seem to have influenced many later painters.

The nine episodes in the Spencer scroll were derived from these so-called "biographies." The opening scene of the scroll, however, differs somewhat from these works, as it illustrates one of the most well-loved poems of Far Eastern literature. Composed by the famous Six Dynasties recluse, T'ao Yüan-ming (365–427), the poem, entitled "Peach Blossom Spring,"[3] became one of the most enduring subjects for painting in

both China and Japan.⁴ It tells the story of a fisherman who, while paddling his boat along a stream through a grove of blossoming peach trees, encountered a seemingly utopian society whose inhabitants had lost all contact with the outside world.

In some of the scenes in the Spencer scroll, actual historical figures are shown performing miraculous feats. The fifth episode, shown here, for example, depicts one of the most popular "immortals" in Japanese painting, Chin Kao (Kinkō in Japanese), rising from the sea on the back of a giant carp during his voyage to the Fish Kingdom.⁵ Chin Kao is supposed to have lived during the fourth century B.C., and to have come from the state of Chao in northern China. One of the three female members of the group is depicted in the eighth scene (Pl. XIII). She is Shang Yuan Fu-jen, shown riding on a *lin*, an animal sometimes called a female unicorn in China.[6] The scroll includes other figures riding on fabulous mythical animals.

Other scenes are more down-to-earth images of hermits such as Lao-tzu (sixth century B.C.?), whose teachings earned him the appellation "Founder of Taoism."[7]

At the very end of the scroll are the artist's signature, reading "Isen-in Hōin mo" ("Isen-in, holding the title of Hōin, copied this"), and a square seal reading "Fujiwara Naganobu." Naganobu, who used the august family name of Fujiwara in this seal, was actually born a member of the Kanō family, the prestigious school of painters which served the shoguns of the Edo period. He is reported to have studied painting with his father Kanō Yōsen-in Korenobu, whom he later succeeded as the seventh generation head of the Kobikichō branch of the Kanō family—the influential and prestigious branch of this powerful school—located in Edo. Serving as official painter to the Tokugawa shogunate, he was awarded the rank of *Hōgen* in 1802 and the rank of *Hōin* in 1816, at which time he took the name of Isen-in.[8]

Naganobu painted in a variety of styles, including a colorful, meticulously detailed decorative style, and a monochrome ink style of bold, sweeping brushstrokes, revealing the artist's interest in earlier Muromachi period painting techniques.[9] This scroll of Chinese immortals, which dates to the last period of his life, has the vivid freshness and immediacy of a brushwork that moves briskly with staccato rhythm, and a relatively light use of color. Clouds and mist are painted in yellows, pinks, and greens, suggesting that different hues of gold pigment were used in the model which Naganobu copied. As voluminous examples left by Kanō Tan'yū (1602–1674) testify, copying old masterpieces was a necessary part of the training of Kanō school artists (see no. 47 for Tan'yū's copies). Naganobu's model, not yet identified, might have been a work by one of his illustrious ancestors, such as Kanō Motonobu (1476–1559), or one of Motonobu's close associates. Particularly informative with regard to this question is a passage in the Spencer scroll which illustrates a fantastic-looking bridge of natural stone, a structure which probably represents the well-known natural geographic formation at Mt. T'ien-t'ai, Chekaing privince, in China (a mountain sacred to the T'ien-t'ai Buddhist sect, known as Tendai in Japan). An almost identical scene is found in a handscroll by Motonobu, the *Shakadō Engi*, [10] which illustrates the history of the Kyoto temple of Shakadō and the well-known legend of the journey of its main icon, the Udāyana Buddha, from India, through China, to Japan.

NOTES

1. Liu Hsiang, *Lieh-hsien-chüan*, in *Ku-chin-i-shih*, chüan 49 (Shanghai, 1937).
2. Wang Shih-chen, *Lieh-hsien-ch'üan-chüan*, in *Chung-kuo ku-tai pan-hua tsung-k'an*, originally printed in 1601, 1961 reprint.
3. Translated into English by James Robert Hightower in *The Poetry of T'ao Ch'ien* (Oxford, 1976), pp. 254–258.
4. For examples of paintings which illustrate this subject, see Richard Barnhart, *Peach Blossom Spring* (New York, 1983).
5. *Lieh-hsien-ch'üan-chüan*, chüan 1, biography, p. 4a; illustration, p. 22a.
6. *Ibid.*, chüan 1, biography, p. 1b; illustration, p. 8b.

7. His teaching is recorded in the *Tao-te-ching*, *Ibid.*, chüan 1, biography, p. 1a; illustration, p. 6a.

8. Laurence P. Roberts, *A Dictionary of Japanese Artists: Painting, Sculpture, Ceramics, Prints, Lacquer* (Tokyo and New York, 1976), pp. 55–56.

9. For examples of his work, see Tokyo National Museum (ed.), *Kanō-ha no Kaiga* (Tokyo, 1979), Pls. 171–173; also Saitō Ken and Yoshiura Yūji (eds.), *Kanō-ha Taikan* (Tokyo, 1912), Pls. 76–79.

10. Miyeko Murase, *Emaki: Narrative Scrolls from Japan* (New York, 1983), pp. 169–173.

49
Wakan Hissha Chūrui
(*Insects by Japanese and Chinese Artists*)

Early nineteenth century, Edo period
By Kanō Kagenobu
One handscroll, ink and color on silk
H: 35.7 cm, L: 1.97 m
Signature: "Munemasu Fujiwara Kagenobu utsusu"
Seal: "Kanō"
Spencer no. 159

This scroll is a compendium of sketches by Kanō Kagenobu in the styles of Japanese and Chinese artists ranging from Chao Ch'ang (died 960) to Kanō Isen-in Naganobu (1775–1828). With its painted insects, frogs, bats, crabs, and flowers, this short handscroll serves not only as a source of stylistic references (extending from Sung dynasty Chinese naturalism to Japanese decorative Rimpa), but as a natural history reference.

The scroll illustrates the variety of styles available to the Kanō artists of the early nineteenth century, and by including both Chinese and Japanese masters verifies the artist's serious interest in art history.

In a seemingly random array of groups of insects and other creatures, Kagenobu depicted his subjects in the manner of various past masters; however, he also included several realistic vignettes taken from life. There is also a rough logic to the overall composition, with winged creatures occupying the upper register of the scroll and crawling ones in the lower register.

Of the seventeen artists whose names appear in the section illustrated here, three are Chinese masters from the Northern Sung (960–1127) and Southern Sung (1128–1279) dynasties. The grasshopper on the leafy twig at the extreme right is labeled as a work by Hui-tsung (1082–1135), a Chinese Sung emperor who specialized in delicate bird and flower paintings. The brushwork on the wings is fine and delicately drawn, faintly echoing the technique of the Sung emperor's paintings. At top center, a cricket, bug, and dragonfly hover above a large hibiscus leaf and blossom; a group of six butterflies and moths, slightly to the left, display different wing patterns and a variety of poses, seen from different angles. These two groups are attributed to Chao Ch'ang, who was acclaimed for his paintings of flowers and birds. The last of the Chinese artists represented here is Ma Lin of the Southern Sung dynasty (active in the first half of the thirteenth century), whose small bee is placed next to Hui-tsung's grasshopper.

The Japanese works copied here are for the most part by Kanō masters, among them Motonobu (1476–1559), one of the giants of the school, who was affectionately referred to as "Ko Hōgen" during the Edo period. He is represented by a pair of insects, a cricket and a praying mantis, at top right. Kanō Tan'yū (1602–1674, see no. 47) is represented by a dragonfly at the upper left, and a bat at the top left. Other great figures from Japan's artistic past include Sesshū (1420–1506), whose name appears by the large black scowling frog at the bottom. Among the Chinese and Kanō-school luminaries we also find Sōtatsu (died ca. 1641), the founder of the decorative Rimpa tradition (see no. 35), whose name is attached to a grasshopper perched on a pink blossom near the center. The "Sōtatsu" drawing is slightly freer in execution; the flower is painted in the "boneless" style, using no outline, with only color washes to define volume. Other models for objects and creatures in this scroll were derived from paintings by obscure artists—for example, the large bee's nest on the left, identified as the work of a certain Chikuō.

Like the *shukuzu* (miniature copies of old paintings) which Kanō Tan'yū made throughout his career (see no. 47), this scroll of creatures and insects by Kagenobu is evidence of the training particularly favored by Kanō artists; mastery of the painting techniques found in old works was considered a prerequisite to being trained in the Kanō school style. The Japanese artists Kagenobu studied covered a wide range of periods from the Late Heian era to his own time, while the Chinese artists date from the Northern Sung to the eighteenth century in the Ch'ing dynasty. Understandably, in this scroll Kagenobu most frequently copied works by earlier Kanō masters, as he himself was a member of that august school. Yet he also paid homage to such outsiders as Sotatsu, and even Kusumi Morikage (active in the late seventeenth century) and Hanabusa Itchō (1652–1724), both of whom were considered black sheep of the Kanō school.

Although Kagenobu mixed different painting techniques—ink monochrome with polychrome, or soft wash with precisely drawn outlines—his creatures lack immediately recognizable characteristics to distinguish one model artist from another. It is likely that he copied his motifs from an "intermediary" work, such as a painting manual once or twice removed from the originals, rather than a series of unrelated, original works by the different masters. It is also likely that this scroll was a relatively youthful work. The names of the artists, written throughout the scroll, the title of the scroll, and Kagenobu's own signature—"Munemasu Fujiwara Kagenobu"—at the end of the work, are written stiffly rather than fluidly and confidently.

Although no biographical information on this artist is available, a nineteenth-century catalogue of old paintings, the *Koga Bikō*,[1] records an album of paintings by a Kanō artist who used the name "Munemasu Kagenobu." Since the latest artist whose work was copied in this scroll, Kanō Naganobu (see nos. 28, 48), is identified in one sketch by the pseudonym "Isen-in," which he adopted in 1802, this study should be dated to the early nineteenth century.

NOTES

1. Asaoka Okisada, *Zōtei Koga Bikō*, vol. 2 (Tokyo, 1912), p. 1297.
2. For the Kanō School, see Hosono Masanobu, *Edo Kanō to Hōgai*, vol. 52 of *Book of Books, Nihon no Bijutsu* (Tokyo, 1978) and Tokyo National Museum (ed.) *Kanō-ha no Kaiga* (Tokyo, 1979).

VII
Scenes From the Floating World

Although woodblock printing was used in Japan as early as the eighth century, it remained largely a tool for text reproduction, seldom applied to the reproduction of painting. From the eighth through the sixteenth century, printing projects were primarily confined to copying scriptures for Buddhist temples; only occasionally were images of buddhas produced for a large audience.[1] Therefore, the *Saga-bon* project (see nos. 19, 35) of the early seventeenth century was truly innovative in several ways; it employed the newly introduced movable type technique to reproduce text, and created renditions of such secular literary works as the *Genji Monogatari* and *Ise Monogatari*, complete with printed illustrations (see no. 19). It was also the first Japanese printing project planned and financed by a private citizen. The increasing affluence of the merchant middle class during the Edo period was the impetus for the flowering of this art form in the eighteenth century.

It must not be forgotten that woodblock prints, whose beauty and technical display we commonly attribute to the efforts of such known artists as Harunobu (1725–1770), Kiyonaga (1752–1815), and Utamaro (1753–1806), were the products of close cooperation among many skilled artists and artisans. With their astonishing skill and their ability to carve hair-thin lines into wood, woodblock engravers in particular played a key role in establishing the superb quality of these prints. Equally important were the colorists and printers, without whom the fine designs executed by famous artists could not have been realized so magnificently.

The gradual evolution of the art of woodblock printing can be traced from the seventeenth through the early years of the eighteenth century. From simple woodcuts in black ink, prints developed into rather crudely hand-colored works; after various experimental stages in which one or two colors were printed together, the so-called *nishiki-e* (brocade picture) technique, which could reproduce many colors, was perfected around 1765.[2]

What we know today as *ukiyo-e* (pictures of the floating world) were also known during the Edo period as *Edo-e* (Edo pictures), which indicated that they were exclusive products of this city. The city of Edo (renamed Tokyo in 1868), was a tiny fishing village before Ieyasu, who became the first Tokugawa shogun in 1603, established the seat of his government there, in his former fief. The city soon attracted an army of immigrants from rural areas, lured by the promise of better jobs, and it claimed the enormous population of one million by the end of the seventeenth century.

The near-miraculous general economic growth of the country at around the same time gave rise to a series of changes in Japanese social structure, one of the most significant being the rise of the merchant class. In accordance with Confucian codes of ethics and government, the social system divided the population outside of the nobility into four classes: warriors, farmers, craftsmen, and merchants. As the growth of the economy spread nationwide, the warriors and farmers found themselves in severe financial straits, while the merchant class began to enjoy unprecedented well-being. Because of the ancient tax system, which was based on rice production, farmers suffered from increasingly harsh taxation, and warriors, whose income was paid in rice, suffered even more from unabating inflation. The merchants' cash wealth, on the other hand, was left untouched by this badly balanced system. By the beginning of the eighteenth century, merchants asserted their social and cultural independence for the first time in the nation's history. Edo merchants were extravagant and spend-thrift; they allegedly never considered holding on to any money "upon which the sun had set." Happiness came to them in the form of the luxurious pleasures promised them at the licensed red-light districts and Kabuki theatres, where they were able to enjoy temporary freedom and release from strict social codes as long as their money held out.

Life in such a city as Edo was called *ukiyo*, or "the floating current of life." The original connotation of the word was somewhat bleak; in Buddhist usage it referred to the belief that life on this earth (*yo*) was full of suffering and was something of which to be weary (*uki*). By the mid-seventeenth century, however, rather than suggesting renunciation, the word, written with a different Chinese character, denoted the injunction to enjoy this floating current of life while it lasted. The word ukiyo then became synonymous with the two worlds of entertainment, the theatres and the brothels.

For this reason, the two most important subjects of ukiyo-e—both in woodcut and hand-painted picture form—were the pleasure quarters and the stage, with their courtesans and actors. This is not to say that print designers ignored pure genre scenes or narrative subject matter. Two of the greatest print designers, Hokusai (1760–1849) and Hiroshige (1797–1858), are known for their genre scenes, landscapes, and flower-and-bird compositions. Other artists, like Harunobu and Utamaro, also depicted men and women engaged in daily chores or mundane routines. Yet the principal subjects for ukiyo-e prints remained the brothels of Edo, with their famous courtesans, and the Kabuki theatres, with their most popular actors in their most famous roles. Portraits of courtesans and prints depicting the pleasure quarters were sold as mementos of good times. "Actor prints" included portraits of favorite performers, program notes, and advertisements.

The largest and most important of the licensed quarters in Edo was called the Yoshiwara (literally, "reed field"). It was set up in the middle of the city in 1618 as part of the government's attempt to regulate the city's mushrooming prostitution business. A devastating fire in 1657 destroyed much of the city, and the Yoshiwara was moved to new and more spacious quarters, in eastern Edo, which covered more than 1,500 acres of land.[3] The unofficial census of 1716 reported that more than 3,000 courtesans were then living in this sequestered city-within-a-city. The heyday of the Yoshiwara district, which was closed officially in 1956, lasted through the eighteenth century, but in the later 1700s other less expensive brothel districts grew up in different parts of the city. A number of Utamaro's prints (see no. 8, for example) portray women of these new quarters. The use of *geisha* as subjects of prints was a practice which arose at around this time (ca. 1770), adding a new sub-genre to the print repertory. Geishas (literally, "talented people") were originally the male and female dancers and musicians who enlivened drinking parties with their talents (nos. 1, 26). It was officially forbidden for geishas to practice prostitution, but like many laws, this stipulation was often ignored.

The Kabuki theatre, which is now world-famous for its female impersonators, was actually begun by a group of female dancer-actresses. A woman named Okuni is thought to have been the first to capture public attention in Kyoto's entertainment district with her troupe of actresses in the early seventeenth century. The women soon became a focus of government scrutiny as they became enormously successful, both on- and off-stage. The rapid transformation of an all-female Kabuki theatre into an all-male art form, as a result of the government's concern for the morality of its people, has been historically documented. Female Kabuki was banned in 1629 and replaced by a theatre of young male performers. When these youths began to attract the attention of older male patrons, they too were banished from the stage in 1652, and the present system, in which older men play the leading roles, was instituted. During the late seventeenth century, great actors inspired powerful dramatists like Chikamatsu (1653–1724); the theatrical boom encouraged such geniuses as Sharaku (active 1794–1795) to produce masterful actor prints.

The Kabuki theatre also served as a safety-valve for the near-explosive energies of the populace, as it often offered thinly disguised criticism of the military regime. For example, violent action on stage (*aragoto*, "rough stuff") showed dramatically made-up warriors conquering evil forces symbolic of the military government. The theatrical makeup of these performers, and their exaggerated facial expressions, became the focus for designers of actor prints. Prints which show only the upper torsos of actors, and depictions of beautiful courtesans (influenced by them), were among the best works of Sharaku and Utamaro. The works of these two artists represent a pinnacle for the two most important and popular subjects of ukiyo-e prints through the eighteenth century.

The third subject for woodblock prints, a latecomer to the ukiyo-e repertory, was landscape, in which man's environment played the most important role. This was a late development, which occurred only after all the possibilities of theatre and courtesan prints had been exhausted. Even Hokusai, who was the first artist to design landscape prints, did not begin working in this sub-genre until late in his life; his famous *Thirty-six Views of Fuji* was completed around 1831, when he was over 70 years old. An improved system of roads, which facilitated both official travel and tourism, also stimulated the development of landscape prints, as travelogues and guidebooks often included pictures of famous sites and picturesque views. Other influences were Chinese and Western prints, which inspired print designers to create new types of composition incorporating elements of Western-style perspective.

The art of the woodblock print continued to be practiced after the midnineteenth century. However, when Japan opened its doors to the Western world and its influences, the demise of ukiyo-e was made certain as the social conditions which had nurtured it underwent drastic change.

NOTES

1. For an historical survey of early prints, see David Chibbett, *The History of Japanese Printing and Book Illustration* (Tokyo, New York and San Francisco, 1977) and Mosaku Ishida, with English adaptation by Charles S. Terry, *Japanese Buddhist Prints* (New York, 1964).
2. There are many good books on woodblock prints available in English. For the subjects portrayed in Ukiyo-e prints, see Basil Stewart, *A Guide to Japanese Prints and Their Subject Matter* (New York, 1979); for such technical problems as seals of publishers, see Richard Lane, *Images from the Floating World: The Japanese Print, Including an Illustrated Dictionary of Ukiyo-e* (New York, 1978). For good reproductions of works in the representative public collections, see *Ukiyo-e Shūka* (Tokyo, 1978–1985), 18 vols.
3. J. E. De Becker, *The Nightless City: or the History of the Yoshiwara Yūkwaku*, rev. ed. (Tokyo and Rutland, Vt., 1971).

Utamaro as a Portraitist of Women

Although Utamaro (1753–1806) designed beautiful prints of subjects other than women,[1] he was decidedly fascinated with feminine beauty. With an insatiable appetite for work and remarkable concentration, he portrayed hundreds of women from both high and low social classes, among them professional women—high-class courtesans at the pinnacle of their careers—and such lowly laborers as shellfish divers, as well as housewives and young maidens. Women were immortalized in his prints, which depicted them in different moods, at work or at rest; although some showed his subjects fully made up, as though for "official" portraits, others caught them at their toilet or in intimate, unguarded moments. The rich variety Utamaro achieved in pursuing one subject is astonishing, particularly considering that many of his better works exclude background settings, concentrating instead on faces and upper bodies in simple compositions. Utamaro's singular achievement has earned him the well-deserved accolade "Artist of Women."

Only a bare outline of his life is available; the dates of his birth and death are thought to be 1753 and 1806, although some uncertainty still remains. Most likely born in Edo, Utamaro is known to have studied painting with Toriyama Sekien (1712–1788), an artist trained in the orthodox Kanō school who also worked as an illustrator of books. Although Sekien never designed single-sheet prints, his two most famous pupils, Utamaro and Chōki (active in the late eighteenth century) made their names in this genre. Until 1779, Utamaro primarily illustrated books, although during this time he also produced a number of "actor prints."

Around 1780, he became acquainted with Tsutaya Jūzaburō (1750–1797), the son of a brothel-keeper in the Yoshiwara and a man of astute business sense and artistic insight. Tsutaya has to his patronage credit many highly successful prints designed by Utamaro, Sharaku, and others; he was also a staunch supporter of popular writers. Thus began a long, fruitful relationship between two gifted men, whose collaboration resulted in unprecedented achievements in the art of the ukiyo-e print.

The final decade of the eighteenth century is often referred to as the "Golden Age" of ukiyo-e printmaking, when both technical and aesthetic peaks were attained. Among the masters of that era were Utagawa Toyokuni (1769–1825) and Tōshūsai Sharaku (active 1794–1795), both of whom produced actor prints; in addition to Utamaro, artists specializing in the "beauties" genre included Utagawa Toyoharu (1735–1814), Torii Kiyonaga (1752–1815), and Kitao Shigemasa (1739–1820). Utamaro's breathtakingly beautiful works would not have been possible, however, without the notable technical accomplishments of his collaborators, particularly his engravers, who recreated the most minute details with negative and positive lines in the woodblocks—cut excruciatingly fine for such features as hairlines and transparent materials. Printers also contributed to these tours-de-force, with infinite patience repeating the process of applying colors as many as fifteen times for each print.

As the traditional arts of Japan, prior to modern times, neither represented the nude figure nor, for the most part, realistically depicted individual physiognomies, the methods of conveying individual expression available to Utamaro were rather limited; variety and a sense of "truthfulness" were achieved through poses, clothing and background settings. Designers of actor prints enjoyed a unique degree of freedom of expression in this regard, as their primary role was to recreate dramatic actions performed by real actors. Even if the faces of the actors in their works are still somewhat stereotyped by our standards, the vivid designs of their makeup provide sufficient clues to their theatre roles. This was especially true of prints produced by artists of the Katsukawa school during Utamaro's time. Most likely used for advertising purposes, large prints depicting heads and torsos of actors, with easily recognizable makeup designs, were made and distributed among the patrons of the Kabuki theatre. In 1791, under the probable inspiration of these ōkubi-e (literally, "large-neck pictures"), Utamaro began to produce bold compositions featuring women's heads and upper bodies, with a clear focus on the faces; thus he was able to capture his subjects' individual personalities and particular moods. Among the first of his series in this ōkubi genre were the *Seven Beauties at Their Toilet* (no. 3) and the *Ten Studies of Female Physiognomy* (no. 7). Within the short period of time before Tsutaya's death in 1797, he and Utamaro together produced an astonishingly rich assortment of prints of unrivaled beauty.

Even though ōkubi-e enabled Utamaro to scrutinize his subjects close-up, methods of actually delineating their features were still largely dictated by tradition. These did not include using shading on the faces to achieve three-dimensional effects or depicting truly unique physical characteristics of his subjects. The identity of the female subject is thus often indicated, if not in a cartouche, by means of a family crest on the kimono (no. 2), or by objects held in the hands (see no. 6). Physical differences were limited to such minor details as the shapes of noses (no. 2).

Again caught within the confines of tradition, Utamaro was obliged to evoke sensuality and eroticism without nudity. However, at the slightest excuse, he boldly bared his women's breasts (nos. 7, 8, 25, or 45). In order to overcome traditional restrictions, he resorted to various technical devices; for example, for the illusion of three-dimensionality, he often used the so-called *karazuri* (gauffrage printing without outlines) for facial contours or the inner details of the ear (nos. 13, 16), or for the entire background (no. 12). To suggest soft flesh, he used vermilion instead of black ink on the facial outlines.

Utamaro was also able to capture and recreate, or subtly hint at, the moods, feelings and personalities of his subjects. He relied on certain obvious devices, such as a downcast posture of the head to indicate a pensive mood (no. 20), or gestures meant to indicate a rift between lovers (nos. 28–34). Other more subtle hints, as in the "Flirt" print (no. 7), include the figure's hairstyle, the shape and angles of the eyes, and the parted lips baring the teeth. The dead-seriousness of the business of the female toilet is brilliantly expressed by the concentration seen in the eyes of women seated before their mirrors (nos. 3, 14, 15). Utamaro repeated his favorite device of showing the women's faces reflected in the mirror, while the beauty of their napes (considered as important as the beauty of their faces) is exposed to the viewer from the rear (nos. 3, 14).

Tsutaya's death is often cited as having caused a decline in Utamaro's art. The final blow to him as an artist was his brief imprisonment (for three days) and handcuffing (for fifty days) as punishment for publishing prints which depicted scenes from the *Taikō Ki*, a book about a former enemy of the Edo regime, Hideyoshi. Various governmental laws aimed at "social reform," such as the repression of works by popular writers, the bans on cartouches used in prints to identify courtesans by name (1796), and regulations against the production of ōkubi prints (1800), exerted undeniable restrictions upon Utamaro as well. The choice of subject matter in some of his prints, among them the series on women at work (nos. 36–46), must be viewed as his (and his publisher's) attempts to circumvent the laws.

It is not easy to date Utamaro's prints precisely or to follow his stylistic development year by year; it is most probable that different types of compositions were produced concurrently, not following any single line of development.[2] Internal or external evidence only occasionally supplies a hint at a date; for example, the series *Tōji Zensei Bijin Zoroe* (*The Greatest Beauties of Our Time*, see nos. 9–11), can be dated to 1794 because of a combination of factors, the most important of which is that the prints identify the most popular courtesans and their attendants by name. Yet works like these are rare exceptions. What amounts to only a rough outline of Utamaro's stylistic development has been formulated by recent scholarship; it is generally agreed, for instance, that before Utamaro began working on his ōkubi series in 1791, his female figures were tall and statuesque, revealing the strong influence of the works of Kiyonaga, whose prints dominated the "beauties" genre. However, Utamaro seems to have veered back and forth between different figure types during his career, utilizing relatively naturalistic forms during the early 1790s; extremely slender, elongated figures in the mid-1790s; and returning to the more naturalistic approach during the last phase of his artistic production.[3]

NOTES

1. For an example of such work, see his 1788 book of insects; Yasuko Betchaku and Joan B. Mirviss, *Songs of the Garden* (New York, 1984). For books on Utamaro, see Kobayashi Tadashi, *Utamaro* (Tokyo, San Francisco and New York, 1982), trans. Mark A. Harbison; J. Hillier, *Utamaro Colour Prints and Paintings* (New York, 1979); Money Hickman, "Utamaro no Ukiyo-e hanga," in *Ukiyo-e Shūka: Museum of Fine Arts, Boston, III* (Tokyo, 1978), pp. 202–206; Kikuchi Sadao, "Kansei-ki no bijin-ga kai," *Ukiyo-e Taikei*, ed. Takahashi Seiichirō *et al.*, vol. 6 (Tokyo, 1976), pp. 73–88; Narazaki Muneshige and Kikuchi Sadao, *Masterworks of Ukiyo-e: Utamaro*, trans. John Bester (Tokyo, 1968); James A. Michener and Richard Lane, *Japanese Prints: From the Early Masters to the Modern* (Tokyo and Rutland, Vt., 1959); and Louis V. Ledoux, *Japanese Prints: Bunchō to Utamaro in the Collection of Louis V. Ledoux* (New York, 1948).
2. Hickman, "Utamaro no", p. 203.
3. *Ibid.*, p. 205.

UTAMARO

All the prints included here are of *ōban* size, which measures on the average approximately 25 cm × 37 cm.

1.

"Seirō Niwaka Onna Geisha no Bu, Tōjin, Shishi, Sumō" ("Geisha Masquerading in a Niwaka Festival of August in Yoshiwara; a Chinese at left, a lion in the center, and a Sumō wrestler at right")
(*See* Color Pl. XIV)

Signed: "Utamaro ga"
Publisher: Tsuruya Kiemon
Censor's seal: "Kiwame"
NYPL no. 16

3.

Okita of the Naniwaya Teahouse, from the series *Sugatami Shichinin Keshō (Seven Beauties at Their Toilet)*

Signed: "Utamaro ga"
Publisher: Tsutaya Jūzaburō
Censor's seal: "Kiwame"
NYPL no. 19

2. (*opposite page*)

Three Beauties: Tomimoto Toyohina (a Yoshiwara courtesan) in the center, Naniwaya Okita (a teahouse girl) at the right, and Takashima Ohisa (a daughter of a famous rice cracker maker).

Signed: "Utamaro hitsu"
Publisher: Tsutaya Jūzaburō
Censor's seal: "Kiwame"
NYPL no. 15

222

223

5.

Takashima Ohisa, Daughter of a Rice Cracker Maker

Signed: "Utamaro hitsu"
Publisher: Tsutaya Jūzaburō
Censor's seal: "Kiwame"
NYPL no. 22

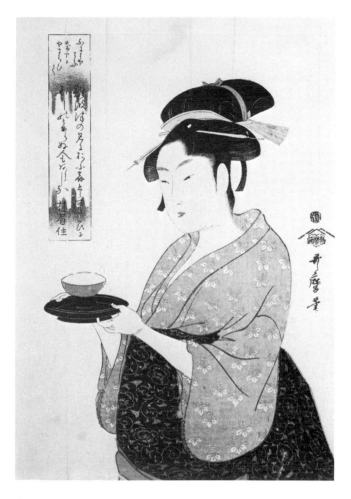

6.

"Meibutsu Osembei" ("A Bag of Famous Rice Crackers"), probably depicting Takashima Ohisa, the daughter of the rice cracker maker

NYPL no. 36

4.

Okita of the Naniwaya Teahouse

The poem in the cartouche, composed by Katsura Mayuzumi (died 1833), is entitled "Naniwaya chō chaya ni yasurai te" ("While resting at the teahouse called Naniwaya"):

Naniwazu no	Like the port of Naniwa,
Nani ou mono wa	Ceaseless the wayfarers,
Yukikai ni	And, there is no one
Ashi no tomara nu	who does not stop by.
Hito mo araji na	

Signed: "Utamaro hitsu"
Publisher: Tsutaya Jūzaburō
Censor's seal: "Kiwame"
NYPL no. 21

8.
"Minami-eki Ha-jirushi" ("A Courtesan of Shinagawa")
(*See* Color Pl. XVI)

Signed: "Utamaro hitsu"
Publisher: Tsuruya Kiemon
Seal of the Blondeau Collection
NYPL no. 109

7.
"Uwaki no Sō" ("The Flirt"), from the series *Fujin Sōgaku Jittai (Ten Studies of Female Physiognomy)*

Signed: "Sōmi Utamaro ga"
Publisher: Tsutaya Jūzaburō
Censor's seal: "Kiwame"
NYPL no. 20

10.
"Tamaya uchi Hanamurasaki; Sekiya, Teriha" ("Courtesan Hanamurasaki of Tamaya; Her Attendants are Sekiya and Teriha"), from the series *Tōji Zensei Bijin Zoroe* (*The Greatest Beauties of Our Time*) (See Color Pl. XV)

Signed: "Utamaro hitsu"
Publisher: Wakasaya Yoichi
NYPL no. 25

9.
"Tamaya uchi Komurasaki; Kochō, Harue" ("Courtesan Komurasaki of Tamaya; Her Attendants are Kochō and Harue"), from the series *Tōji Zensei Bijin Zoroe* (*The Greatest Beauties of Our Time*)

Signed: "Utamaro hitsu"
Publisher: Wakasaya Yoichi
NYPL no. 24

11.

"Matsubaya uchi Somenosuke; Wakagi, Wakaba" ("Courtesan Somenosuke of Matsubaya; Her Attendants are Wakagi and Wakaba"), from the series *Tōji Zensei Bijin Zoroe (The Greatest Beauties of Our Time)*

Signed: "Utamaro hitsu"
Publisher: Wakasaya Yoichi
NYPL no. 26

12.

Noda no Tamagawa, from the series *Mu Tamagawa (Six Rivers Named Tamagawa)*

   The poem in the cartouche, composed by Jingidō Michimori (died 1835), reads as follows:

Tamagawa no ause ni   Come, the waves of Tamagawa,
Shikeyo namimakura   Come and line the bed of
Kamuro chidori ni   our meeting.
Tachi asobu ran   Young companions of courtesans
                               play with beach plovers.

Signed: "Utamaro hitsu"
Publisher: Matsumura Yahei
NYPL no. 35

13.

A Courtesan, from the series *Nishiki-ori Utamaro-gata Shin Moyō (Utamaro's New Brocade Patterns)*
(*See* Color Pl. XVII)

The gist of this self-praising inscription is that, with simple strokes and only ink, he creates an image of unsurpassed beauty. Therefore his fee is as high as his nose. Publishers who buy cheap must take the consequences; their proud noses will be crushed.[1]

Signed: "Utamaro hitsu"
NYPL no. 74

14.

Two Women at Their Toilet

Signed: "Utamaro hitsu"
Publisher: Uemura Yohei
NYPL no. 59

15.

A Woman at Her Toilet

Signed: "Utamaro hitsu"
Publisher: Uemura Yohei
NYPL no. 60

16.

"Uma no Koku" ("The Hour of the Horse, Noon"), from the series *Musume Hidokei (A Sundial of Maidens)*

"In ancient times, women's bathing pictures such as this were for the hour of the monkey (4 p.m.)"

Signed: "Utamaro hitsu"
Publisher: Murataya Jirōbei
Censor's seal: "Kiwame"
NYPL no. 108

17.

Two Women with Gold Fishes

Signed: "Utamaro hitsu"
Publisher: Uemura Yohei
NYPL no. 57

18.

Mother and Boy

Signed: "Utamaro hitsu"
Publisher: Uemura Yohei
NYPL no. 58

19.

Courtesan Hana Ōgi of Ōgiya
"Toshi" ("Age") "Seishi no Go-en'nichi" ("The Feast of Seishi")

Signed: "Utamaro hitsu"
Publisher: Matsumura Yahei
NYPL no. 81

20.

A Woman at a Brazier *(above left)*

Signed: "Utamaro hitsu"
Publisher: Matsumura Yahei
NYPL no. 82

21.

A Maid of the Chiyozuru *(above right)*

Signed: "Utamaro hitsu"
Publisher: Yamaguchiya Chūsuke
NYPL no. 72

22.

A Maid of the Fukuju

Signed: "Utamaro hitsu"
Publisher: Yamaguchiya Chūsuke
NYPL no. 73

23.
"Tori no Koku" ("The Hour of the Cock, 5 to 7 p.m."),
from the series *Seirō Jūniji Tsuzuki (Twelve Hours at the Pleasure Quarters, Continued)*

Signed: "Utamaro hitsu"
Publisher: Tsutaya Jūzaburō
Censor's seal: "Kiwame"
NYPL no. 77

24.

"Chūbon no Zu" ("Picture of Middle Class"), from the series *Fūzoku Sandan Musume* (*Young Women of the Three Grades of Refinement*)

Signed: "Utamaro hitsu"
Publisher: Wakasaya Yoichi
NYPL no. 79

25.

"Gebon no Zu" ("Picture of Lower Class"), from the series *Fūzoku Sandan Musume* (*Young Women of the Three Grades of Refinement*)

Signed: "Utamaro hitsu"
Publisher: Wakasaya Yoichi
NYPL no. 80

26.
A Geisha and a Male Attendant in Snow

Signed: "Utamaro hitsu"
Publisher: Tsutaya Jūzaburō
Censor's seal: "Kiwame"
NYPL no. 13

27.
A Couple Under an Umbrella

Signed: "Utamaro hitsu"
Publisher: Tsuruya Kiemon
NYPL no. 30

28.

From the series *Tōsei Koika Hakkei (Eight Vows of Modern Love)*[2]

Wasuraru ru	It does not matter
Mi oba omowazu	That I am now forgotten,
Chikai teshi	But making an oath
Hito no inochi no	Is the most precious moment
Oshiku mo aru kana	In the whole life of a man.

Poem no. 38

Signed: "Utamaro hitsu"
Publisher: Sensa
NYPL no. 63

29.

From the series *Tōsei Koika Hakkei (Eight Vows of Modern Love)*

Au koto no	Now, if making love
Taete shi naku ba	Were just an extinct custom,
Naka naka ni	Neither to oneself
Hito omo mi omo	Nor to the lady would come
Urami zarama shi	these heavy hours of regret.

Poem no. 44

Signed: "Utamaro hitsu"
Publisher: Sensa
NYPL no. 69

30.

From the series *Tōsei Koika Hakkei (Eight Vows of Modern Love)*

Kimi ga tame	Now because of you,
Oshikara zari shi	After feeling that my life
Inochi sae	Was but tiresome time,
Nagakumo gana to	I begin at last to wish
Omoi keru kana	That it may be very long.

Poem no. 50

Signed: "Utamaro hitsu"
NYPL no. 68

31.

From the series *Tōsei Koika Hakkei (Eight Vows of Modern Love)*

Wasureji no	Not to desert me
Yukusue made wa	Even to the very end,
Katakere ba	As you have told me—
Kyō o kagiri no	Should that wish prove difficult,
Inochi tomo gana	Rather let life end today.

Poem no. 54

Signed: "Utamaro hitsu"
Publisher: Sensa
NYPL no. 65

32.

From the series *Tōsei Koika Hakkei (Eight Vows of Modern Love)*

Urami wabi	When love turns to spite,
Hosa nu sode dani	Sleeves are dampened in anguish;
Aru mono o	Yet one thing still is
Koi ni kuchi nan	Worse than wilting, forgotten:
Na koso oshikere	That is, being talked about.

Poem no. 65

Signed: "Utamaro hitsu"
NYPL no. 67

33.

From the series *Tōsei Koika Hakkei (Eight Vows of Modern Love)*

Se o hayami	Because the river
Iwa ni sekaru ru	Swiftly pours over these rocks,
Takigawa no	It divides in two;
Warete mo sue ni	Yet in the end these fragments
Awan to zo omou	Will rush to meet each other.

Poem no. 77

Signed: "Utamaro hitsu"
Publisher: Sensa
NYPL no. 66

34.

From the series *Tōsei Koika Hakkei (Eight Vows of Modern Love)*

Naniwae no	Because of one night,
Ashi no karine no	A lovers' nap on those reeds
Hitoyo yue	Of Naniwa Bay,
Mi o tsukushi te ya	Ought I, giving my body,
Koi wataru beki	Love you always, do you think?

Poem no. 88

Signed: "Utamaro hitsu"
NYPL no. 64

35.
"Fujin Tomari-kyaku no Zu, Sammai Tsuzuki" ("Triptych of Women Guests at an Inn")

Signed on all three: "Utamaro hitsu"
Publisher: Tsuruya Kiemon
NYPL no. 121

36.
Spinning, from the series *Fujin Tewaza Ayatsuri Kagami*
(*A Mirror of Feminine Handicrafts*)

Signed: "Utamaro hitsu"
Publisher: Yamahide
Censor's seal: "Kiwame"
NYPL no. 54

37.
Weaving, from the series *Fujin Tewaza Ayatsuri Kagami*
(*A Mirror of Feminine Handicrafts*)

Signed: "Utamaro hitsu"
Publisher: Yamahide
Censor's seal: "Kiwame"
NYPL no. 55

38.

Sewing, from the series *Fujin Tewaza Ayatsuri Kagami* (*A Mirror of Feminine Handicrafts*)

Signed: "Utamaro hitsu'
Publisher: Yamahide
Censor's seal: "Kiwame"
NYPL no. 56

39.

Women Preparing Bean Curd at a Gion Restaurant, from the series *Fujin Tewaza Jūnikō* (*Twelve Feminine Handicrafts*)

Signed: "Utamaro hitsu"
Publisher: Wakasaya Yoichi
NYPL no. 38

40.
Preparing Silk Floss, from the series *Fujin Tewaza Jūnikō* *(Twelve Feminine Handicrafts)*

Signed: "Utamaro hitsu"
Publisher: Wakasaya Yoichi
NYPL no. 39

41.
A Painter, from the series *Fujin Tewaza Jūnikō (Twelve Feminine Handicrafts)*

Signed: "Utamaro hitsu"
Publisher: Wakasaya Yoichi
NYPL no. 40

244

42.
A Hairdresser, from the series *Fujin Tewaza Jūnikō (Twelve Feminine Handicrafts)*

Signed: "Utamaro hitsu"
Publisher: Wakasaya Yoichi
NYPL no. 41

43.
Laundresses, from the series *Fujin Tewaza Jūnikō (Twelve Feminine Handicrafts)*

Signed: "Utamaro hitsu"
Publisher: Wakasaya Yoichi
NYPL no. 42

44.
Drying Cloth
Triptych

Signed: "Utamaro hitsu" on all three
Publisher: Yamadaya Sanshirō
NYPL no. 120

45.
Women at Sewing
Triptych

Signed: "Utamaro hitsu" on all three
Publisher: Uemura Yohei
NYPL no. 274

46.
The Kitchen Scene
Diptych

Signed: "Utamaro hitsu" on both
Publisher: Uemura Yohei
NYPL no. 116

NOTES

1. For the full translation of this inscription, see J. Hillier, *Utamaro Colour Prints and Paintings* (New York, 1979), p. 109.

2. Poems included in these prints were quoted from the *Ogura Hyakunin Isshu (The Little Treasury of One Hundred People, One Poem Each)*, edited by Fujiwara no Sadaie (1162–1241). For the translation of the poems, see Tom Galt (trans.), *The Little Treasury of One Hundred People, One Poem Each* (Princeton, 1982).

Hiroshige and His *Fifty-three Stations of the Tōkaidō*

Enormously popular during his own lifetime, Hiroshige (1797–1858) is one of the few Japanese artists known to Westerners who are not familiar with Japanese art.[1] His surname is generally given either as Andō, his family name, or as Utagawa, the name of the school of printmakers in which he was trained. Born to a family of low-echelon samurai—his father was a fireman in Edo—he is known to have entered the studio of a popular printmaker, Utagawa Toyohiro (1773–1828), when he was fourteen years old. Following the path taken by many print designers of his day, Hiroshige began his career as an illustrator of books and designer of prints depicting actors and beautiful women. However, it was his evocative landscape prints that won him recognition, particularly scenes along the Tōkaidō, the famed road between Kyoto and Edo.

Hiroshige's artistic genius had few equals, but the huge success of his *Tōkaidō* series may also be attributed to the changes occurring at the time.[2] The most significant of these were the daring innovations of his older contemporary Katsushika Hokusai (1760–1849), who treated landscape as a bona fide subject for *ukiyo-e* prints, thus freeing this genre from the claustrophobic world of brothels and theatres. During the eighteenth century, virtually all of the print designers had evidenced an interest in landscapes, especially in compositions suggesting perspective in the Western manner. Yet landscapes remained a background element in prints by such great masters as Torii Kiyonaga (1752–1815) and Kitagawa Utamaro (1753–1806), whose primary concerns were portraying the beauty of women and fashionable clothing. Even Hokusai, who is best known today for his magnificent depictions of Mt. Fuji in the series *Thirty-six Views of Fuji*, produced only a small number of landscape prints during his long career. The young Hiroshige was deeply indebted to Hokusai's *Fuji* series, which was completed in 1831—the year that he published the first of his landscape series, *Tōto Meisho (Famous Views of Edo)*.

Social conditions also contributed to the success of the *Tōkaidō* series. Roads had been improved considerably, and the Tōkaidō—which had inspired maplike paintings on screens and handscrolls by many artists of different schools long before Hiroshige's time—began to inspire travel. Travel was becoming a national passion, in fact, fanned by the publication, from 1802 to 1809, of an extremely popular series of ribald tales by Juppensha Ikku (1765–1831), the *Tōkaidōchū Hizakurige*.[3] Many similar works of fiction and factual travelogues about the highway were written during this time. Prints of Tōkaidō scenery by Toyohiro, Hiroshige's teacher, reflected the great travel vogue, and Hokusai also designed prints on this increasingly popular subject, starting in 1818.

In July of 1832 Hiroshige was offered the opportunity to join a "travel group" accompanying, it is thought, officials whose duty it was to transport gift horses from the shogun to the imperial family. The occasion was the *komahiki* (selection of horses for imperial use) to be held in Kyoto on the first day of August, as the scene at Fujikawa (thirty eighth station, no. 62), depicting officials and travelers prostrate on the road and two horses bedecked with Shinto purification tablets standing in the background, suggests.[4]

The Tōkaidō route, which is followed today by the Bullet Train, runs along the southern coast of Honshū Island until it turns inland near Yokkaichi (Forty-fourth station, no. 63). It covers a distance of over three hundred miles, and in Hiroshige's time took more than two weeks to cover on foot. The set of *Fifty-three Stations*, which seems to have been completed between 1833 and 1834, actually includes fifty-five prints, as it depicts the beginning of the journey at the Nihonbashi (Japan Bridge) in the center of Edo, the "cross-roads of Japan," and concludes with a scene of the Sanjō Ōhashi (The Great Sanjō Bridge) in the hub of Kyoto.

As in Hokusai's *Fuji* series, Hiroshige's depictions of stopping-places along the Tōkaidō are not pure landscapes. Certain scenes, like those of Hakone and Yui (the eleventh and seventeenth stations, respectively, nos. 52, 55), look deceptively "pure": figures of travelers are virtually crushed between the towering mountains, or appear as small dots perched on mountain tops. Most of the scenes focus on travelers' experiences—becoming acquainted on a ferryboat at Kawasaki (third station, no. 48) or being accosted by prostitutes at the small village of Goyu (thirty-sixth station, no. 61). Many scenes also record the hardships travelers encountered—a gust of wind at Yokkaichi (forty-fourth station, no. 63), a sudden shower at Shōno (forty-sixth station, no. 64), deep snow at Kambara (sixteenth station, no. 54), or the wide rivers to cross at Shimada and Kanaya (twenty-fourth and twenty-fifth stations, nos. 57, 58). The weariness that overcomes travelers is suggested by the scenes of morning mist at Mishima (twelfth station, no. 53) and the dawn departure at Seki (forty-eighth station, no. 65). Hiroshige was truly an "artist of rain and snow": his landscapes record the changing mood of the natural surroundings during different times of the day, different seasons, in different kinds of weather. The atmosphere evoked in these scenes must have stirred memories in the hearts of those who had traveled the same route, and aroused wanderlust in those who had not.

Hiroshige's compositions consistently deploy a low horizon line, which indicates his familiarity with Western-style perspective. His use of strong diagonal lines to delineate contours of hills and roads, or the gradually staggered rows of houses, followed a device which was also adopted from Western art and was popular among print designers. Unlike Hokusai's often exaggerated views of nature, Hiroshige's pictures are calm and serene, only occasionally interrupted by such a humorous note as a kite soaring beyond the actual frame of a picture (Kakegawa, twenty-seventh station, no. 59). It is understandable that the public, who had enthusiastically applauded Hokusai's dramatic views of Fuji only a few years earlier, shifted its allegiance to the younger artist.

Although Hiroshige drew on his own experience in designing these prints, he took artistic license: the view of snowy Kambara (sixteenth station, no. 54), one of the most popular works in the series, is probably the most blatant example. It is believed that Hiroshige left Edo sometime in July, in time for the presentation of the horses in August, and returned home early in autumn, far too early for the heavy snowfall depicted.[5]

The *Tōkaidō* series proved so popular that Hiroshige produced at least sixteen different versions of the same subject. The present series, however, distinguished from the others as the "Hoeidō Version" after the publisher's name, was the most popular.[6] Later editions are known to number more than 10,000,[7] and include some variant plates; for example, the Nihonbashi scene (first station, no. 47) contains more travelers; the Totsuka scene (sixth station, no. 49) depicts a traveler mounting a horse, and the Kawasaki scene (third station, Pl. XVIII) is rendered without Mt. Fuji in the background.[8] The reasons for some of the changes are not clear.

Twenty-two of the scenes have been chosen to represent the series here.

NOTES

1. For general books on Hiroshige, see Edward F. Strange, *Hiroshige's Woodblock Prints: A Guide* (New York, 1983); Yamaguchi Keizaburō, *Hiroshige*, vol. 11 of *Ukiyo-e*, ed. Takahashi Seiichirō *et al.* (Tokyo, 1975); R. W. Robinson, *Hiroshige* (New York, 1963); and Edward F. Strange, *The Colour-Prints of Hiroshige* (London, New York, Toronto, and Melbourne, 1925).
2. The full reproduction of this series is in Yamaguchi, *Hiroshige*; Tomikichirō Tokuriki (trans.), Thomas I. Elliot, *Tōkaidō: Hiroshige* (Osaka, 1963).
3. For an English translation of this book, see Thomas Satchell (trans.), *Shank's Mare* (Tokyo and Rutland, Vt., 1960).
4. Yamaguchi, *Hiroshige*, p. 80.
5. *Ibid.*
6. His real name was Takenouchi Magohachi (1781–1854).
7. Narazaki Muneshige, *Hiroshige*, no. 104 of *Nihon no Bijutsu*, ed. Staff of the National Museums of Tokyo, Kyoto, and Nara (Tokyo, 1975), p. 45.
8. Yamaguchi, *Hiroshige*, p. 81.

HIROSHIGE

All the prints are of *ōban* size; they bear the cartouche, "Tōkaidō Gojūsantsugi no Uchi" ("From the Fifty-three Stations of the Tōkaidō"), Hiroshige's signature, "Hiroshige ga," and the censor's seal, "Kiwame." The name of each station, a description of the view, which is given in red seal, and the publisher's seal also appear in each print, as they are translated below.

47.
First Station
Nihon-bashi
Asa no Kei (Morning View)

Seal: "Takemago Tsuruki"

48.
Third Station (*See* Color Pl. XVIII)
Kawasaki
Rokugō Watashi-bune (Ferry at Rokugō)

Seal: "Senkakudō Hoeidō"

49.
Sixth Station
Totsuka
Motomachi Betsudō (Motomachi Detour)

Seal: "Tsuruki Takemago"

50. Eighth Station / Hiratsuka / Nawate Michi (Nawate Road) / Seal: "Hoeidō Senkakudō"

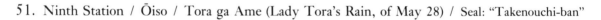

51. Ninth Station / Ōiso / Tora ga Ame (Lady Tora's Rain, of May 28) / Seal: "Takenouchi-ban"

52. Eleventh Station / Hakone / Kosui Zu (The Lake) / Seals: "Hoei"; "Dō"

53. Twelfth Station / Mishima / Asagiri (Morning Mist) / Seal: "Hoeidō"

54. Sixteenth Station / Kambara / Yoru no Yuki (Night Snow) / Seal: "Takenouchi"

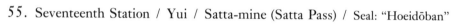

55. Seventeenth Station / Yui / Satta-mine (Satta Pass) / Seal: "Hoeidōban"

56. Twenty-second Station / Okabe / Utsu no Yama (Utsu Mountain) / Seal: "Senkakudō"

57. Twenty-fourth Station / Shimada / Ōigawa Sungan (Suruga Bank of the Ōi River) / Seal: "Hoeidō"

58. Twenty-fifth Station / Kanaya / Ōigawa Engan (Distant Bank of the Ōi River)
    Seal: "Takenouchi"

59. Twenty-seventh Station / Kakegawa / Akibayama Embō (Distant View of Akiba Mountain)
    Seal: "Hoeidō"

60.
Thirty-fourth Station (*See* Color Pl. XIX)
Futakawa
Saruga Baba (Monkey Plateau)

Seal: "Hoeidō"

61.
Thirty-sixth Station (*See* Color Pl. XX)
Goyu
Tabibito Tome-onna (Women Soliciting Travelers)
Inside the teahouse are the names of the engraver, Jirōbei;
the printer Heibei; and Hiroshige's acronym, Ichiryūsai;
and Takenouchi-ban.

Seal: "Takenouchi"

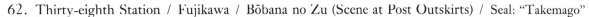

62. Thirty-eighth Station / Fujikawa / Bōbana no Zu (Scene at Post Outskirts) / Seal: "Takemago"

63. Forty-fourth Station / Yokkaichi / Miegawa (Mie River) / Seal: "Hoeidō"

64. Forty-sixth Station / Shōno / Haku'u (Driving Rain) / Seal: "Hoeidō-ban"

65. Forty-eighth Station / Seki / Honjin Hayadachi (Early Departure of Daimyō) / Seal: "Hoeidō"

66. Forty-ninth Station / Saka no Shita / Fudesute-mine (Fudesute Mountain) / Seal: "Hoeidō-ban"

67. Fiftieth Station / Tsuchiyama / Haru no Ame (Spring Rain) / Seal: "Hoeidō"

68. Fifty-fifth Station / Keishi / Sanjō Ōhashi (Great Sanjō Bridge) / Seal: "Hoeidō"

Index